MW01170394

The Revelation of Power

Reverend James M. Lamb
CADC, CCS

INFINITY
PUBLISHING

ISBN 0-7414-5999-X

Printed in the United States of America

Published October 2010

INFINITY PUBLISHING
1094 New DeHaven Street, Suite 100
West Conshohocken, PA 19428-2713
Toll-free (877) BUY BOOK
Local Phone (610) 941-9999
Fax (610) 941-9959
Info@buybooksontheweb.com
www.buybooksontheweb.com

Acknowledgments

I would like to express my eternal gratitude to my Mother Florence M. Lamb who went home to be with the Lord (2008). She prayed me through all my failures and did live to witness the results of her prayers.

I am grateful to Bishop William Philpot, Pastor of Christ Chapel and former Pastor of Community Baptist Church in New Haven Connecticut and the Christ Chapel members who played such an important role in my life and prayed me through a self-created hell.

I cannot write any book about recovery without a special thank you to Dr. Mimi Silbert Ph D., and her staff at the Delancey Street Foundation. They took my devastated life and trained me how to live. Those four years and ten months in Delancey Street were some of the best preparation years of my life.

To all my friends and fellow counselors within the Arkansas Department of Correction, thanks for all your critical insights, suggestions and your support that challenged me to continue writing.

I want to especially thank my loving and patient wife Lashauna for her undying support. Many a night as I studied, researched and wrote, she prayed and encouraged me to press on. She is a rare and special gift from God.

Most importantly, to my son James M. Lamb II, I owe you a debt that I cannot fully repay. It is you who motivates me to continue the quest of bettering myself. It is your hope, faith and prayers, my son, which lifted me. It is the look in your eyes that took many years to earn. It is the look of love and pride I see in your eyes that continues to inspire me and move me forward.

Dedication

This book is dedicated to my Lord and Savior Jesus Christ

The Revelation of Power
was edited prayerfully and professionally by
Sheila M. Clark

Table of Contents

Table of Contents

Table of Contents

Table of Contents

Table of Contents

Prologue

Somewhere near Tong Binh province, Republic of Vietnam. In the pitch black of night, just before dawn the blast shook the hours of darkness. KARAABOOMMMMOOOM!!!! It was followed immediately by an endless staccato of machine gun and AK-47 fire. That steady noise was punctuated by the KRRUMMMPP of 40MM shoulder launched rockets that flashed in explosions all around. The flashes briefly pushed back the blackness of night. Then, just as quickly, the light was extinguished by the suddenly returning, suffocating blanket of night. In one swift stroke, two companies of North Vietnamese soldiers overran our outposts, fire control center, communications center and one gun parapet. We could not see but we heard death approaching.

At the moment of the first deafening explosion, there was the sound of a man screaming. The sound was ghastly and inhuman. It sounded like a dog that had been hit by a car. The howling of that man could be heard, singled out by the shrill sound of him caught in the agony of death's grip, distinct and different from the steady screams of horror on the battle field that night. The shrill howling of that one man, caught in the agony of death's grip was distinct from the steady screams on the battlefield that night.

Later, after the attack, we found him. He was shot once in the side, a small entry wound and a large exit wound. It was the mark of a tumbling M16 round spinning through the body. There was also a large hole in his head, provided by the first sergeant who emptied a full clip of M16 rounds on full automatic. The muzzle tip pressed into the eye of the still-moaning victim. The same first sergeant turned to me,

1

smiled, and said, "Lamb, next time we catch one alive, I'll show you how to castrate 'em." The brutality of war is seldom talked about, but it has been witnessed by many of us and we are forever changed because of it.

I believe this was the man who was screaming, howling and who could be heard above the haunting sounds of war and death. He must have been the victim of a grenade exploding right under his feet or a Claymore antipersonnel mine.

I have already described his wounds down to his waist. But, from his waist to just above the knees showed his major muscles contorted and protruding as if he had the worst cramps you could imagine. Every muscle could be seen bulging from his skin. The reason was that, from just above his ankles to where his legs should have been, was what looked like ground hamburger with pieces of bone sticking out. There was no form at all. You could not tell that those masses of meat were once someone's legs. Also, placed neatly between the two masses of meat was the bottom of one of his feet. It was just like someone had sliced the bottom of his foot off with surgical precision and placed it upside-down between his legs. What a horrible way to die.

The first blast that night snapped me out of my sleep. I heard the blast, the machine gun fire and the screams just as if someone had dropped the starting flag at a drag race. I peered over the sandbags to find out if I could see anything. But I saw nothing. While I was looking into the darkness, the soldier next to me, my friend, Pvt. Starcher begged me to get down. We couldn't see anything.

It was pitch black but we knew they were coming fast by the approaching sound of men dying. They were calling their mothers and God, screaming, "I don't want to die!" Their full—to—the—bursting, panic—stricken, dilated eyes were suddenly looking into grinning, foreign faces with gun muzzles bursting out of the darkness, spitting death. With the grim, unforeseen, icy fingers of death gripping them with fear, they embraced the bullets with open-mouthed, full-throated pleading and defensive hands stiffened by fright. Despite their loud protests and pleading posture, they were ushered into eternity.

I yelled, "Lindsey, help me get this gun around!" as I glanced at my gun sergeant, pinned to the tent floor, grounded there by fear. He had dived there from a sleeping position as the first blast went off. As I turned to face the direction of the hammering flood of battle noise that assaulted my senses, I saw him in mid-dive towards the floor. He stayed there but another soldier crawled out to the X102, the advanced version of the old 105MM Howitzer and together we dragged that big gun around to point it in the direction of the incoming fire. My first thought was, "We need to see before we fire point-blank. I called for an illumination round.

Just as I stood up from a crouching position to load the round, the enemy fired an AK-47 assault weapon at me from about 20 feet away. (I found out later where the enemy soldier was hiding when he fired at me.) I can never forget the sound of incoming AK-47 rounds. They have a very distinctive whine when they go by. These bullets came so close; I heard four or five whooshes, along with their distinctive whine, as they went by my head. But one bullet, —one bullet—came so close to my left ear that it sounded like a firecracker went off in my ear. It could not have missed me by more than a millimeter. I said, "Whoa! They're shooting at me!" As I got back down, the artillery round was just partially in the breach block. I would not stand all the way up again but managed to push the round in. Sgt. Ramsey took a chance, came up enough and snatched the breach lever, closing the breach block. Lindsey elevated the gun and someone else pulled the lanyard, firing the round. It was supposed to rise up and open with a flare and illuminate the battlefield. It did not deploy.

Someone lowered the gun tube; we were running out of time. Still squatting, I loaded a high explosive round and Sgt. Ramsey closed the breach block and fired. It landed well beyond the field of battle against a mountain located to the rear of us where the attack came from. I called for another round as someone else lowered the tube of the gun to fire closer. Pvt. Starcher brought another round over and it was pushed to me by a set of unseen hands under the trails of the gun. I loaded the round. Pvt. Starcher had given me a beehive round.

A beehive round is an anti-personnel round. When fired from an artillery gun, it is deadly. The round is packed full of metal darts. They fan out and fly out in a zone 100 yards deep and 75 yards wide. It is called beehive because of the buzzing sound the darts make when flying through the air. All you see when it is fired is a big red tracer down the middle of the firing track. We fired one that night. Then we fired another high-explosive round. When we fired, we heard the simultaneous sound of the gun and the flash bang in a tree less than 75 feet away, along with the screaming of some of our protecting infantry troops, who yelled, "To the left! To the left!" We fired again and again.

It was becoming light now. The enemy had broken off the fight and there was no more incoming fire. We continued to fire. We had just fired another round when suddenly I felt something I could not see "step" out of my body and rise upward and away.

I fell down between the trails of the gun, stunned and suddenly almost paralyzed by fear. I was not afraid of what just happened with this being leaving my body. I was afraid because this angel (I know that now) took with him all the bravado and fearlessness that I had exhibited in the battle with him when he left. Just minutes ago I was not afraid. I was yelling orders and working along with my fellow warrior soldiers of the 2nd and 320th Artillery in the 101st

Airborne Paratrooper Division. Now, I was shaken, frightened and stunned.

I could go on and on, telling you more about that night but it was the revelation of God's intervening power through this angel that has remained with me to this day. That powerful demonstration of God's love on the battlefield that night was the beginning of God's revelation concerning His love for me.

Despite all that I would later go through in life, much of it by my own choices, God's love is still being revealed to me in spite of myself.

As we gathered our dead, the infantry reinforcement helicopters along with medevac helicopters, arrived. We shared what happened as individuals. What a night! So many stories of death, near-death experiences and heroism!

War is more terrible than you can imagine. Had it not been for the divine intervention of God via His angel, I would be dead. That story I just shared with you is one of seven distinct times I know of that God saved my life in Viet Nam. This is how it was recorded by the Army, but the victory is God's:

On December 17, 1966, James Lamb received the Department of the Army's Award of the Army Commendation for Heroism in connection with military operations against a hostile force. According to the award signed by Major AGC Adjutant General, J. G. Brown, *"private first class Lamb distinguished himself by exceptionally valorous actions near Tong Binh, Republic of Vietnam."*

I want to share with you three other times when my life was spared. One is when I had been sent to the combat rear area with symptoms relating to possible malaria.

Every man in my first gun crew was maimed in some way by a muzzle burst just moments before I returned from the rear. A muzzle burst happens when the artillery gun is fired and the round that is supposed to go to the target some miles away explodes as soon as it leaves the muzzle of the gun.

One fellow soldier and a friend of mine who was hit pretty badly called me over. I talked to him as they were putting others I knew on the medevac helicopters. He told me what had happened to him and to everyone else. I mentioned that I was sorry about his foot being blown off and he said, "At least I am going home alive."

I was the only one spared. I was not there. The others, each of them in my gun section, were hurt and maimed and I never saw them again.

Another time, we were riding down a road, truck packed with equipment, with our legs dangling off the side of the ¾ ton truck. We were suddenly run off the road and sideswiped a tree. We hit the tree right where my feet were. It smashed my left foot, breaking it and throwing me up in the air. We were blessed to have hit a tree because, if we hadn't, the truck would have rolled over on us. We were towing a 5,000-pound 105MM Howitzer and it also hit the tree, bounced back on the road and was bucking on and off the road from one wheel to another.

As I was thrown up in the air, I saw my M16 fly off me and then I saw myself headed for the howitzer. I fell just in front of the howitzer as it bucked on one wheel and I watched it go over my head, all 5,000 pounds of my potential death sailing right over me. It all happened so fast but I can remember every moment of that episode. Once again, I was spared.

I arrived in Viet Nam the day after Christmas and I was stationed at Phan Rang. Not long after that, we went on our first mission. While setting up our fire base and improving our position, it was normal for helicopters to land in the area and take off again so frequently that we really did not pay much attention unless they were carrying ammunition, hot meals or mail.

This last event I want to share with you happened the day an observation helicopter was landing in our area. It was landing off to my right as I was walking across the gun base area. As I looked to the right, noticing the chopper landing, I saw a lieutenant walking toward me also from my right side.

Observation helicopters carried two M60 machine guns, one on each top side of the landing struts. Just as the chopper hit the ground for the landing, the lieutenant crossed directly in front of the chopper in between my position and the landing helicopter. One of the machine guns fired a single shot. I saw the round hit the ground and saw the lieutenant stop in his tracks, dead still, his eyes rolled up in his head, his back arched as he fell over. For a moment, everyone froze. Medics and others ran over to help. I saw the helicopter pilot getting out of the chopper and standing there with his mouth open, a look of absolute panic and distress etched on his face. That bullet was headed directly for me. Had that lieutenant not stepped in its path, I would have been hit.

I never knew what happened to him. He was rushed out on a medivac helicopter. One reason I never found out what happened to him was that he was in the infantry that was performing perimeter security for our guns. A day or so after the incident, we moved to another area by truck with a different security unit guarding our perimeter, but I have no doubt that God protected me and spared my life again.

I will never forget Viet Nam. I salute all veterans no matter where or when you have served. To those of us who served in combat roles and faced death, it is we only who know the distinct horror and the honor of that kind of service.

In this book, *The Revelation of Power*, you will read about several spiritual events in my life similar to the angelic intervention on the battlefield of Viet Nam. Some of these spiritual events may amaze you, depending on the level of God's personal revelation to you. If you have been exposed to the supernatural realms in your relationship with God through Jesus Christ and the Holy Spirit, you will be able to identify with these testimonies. If you have not been exposed to events of a supernatural nature, you may experience disbelief and think what I am sharing with you could not possibly have happened. Let me say this to you: everything about these events is true as I relate my experiences to you. They are intended to give you faith that a close relationship with God is possible and that these events have happened, and do happen, to people as they expose themselves to the revelation of God's love. Why not you?

John 3:16 For God so loved the world, that He gave his only begotten Son, that whosoever believeth in Him should not perish, but have everlasting life.

Chapter 1

Knowing Self

Knowing self is the key to understanding how to have power over self. If you are really, really tired of you, then now, perhaps now, you will learn about you.

The original *Power to Change* was written primarily without using Biblical scriptures to reinforce spiritual and universal law. This is because *The Power to Change* was written at a time when many programs, including the one in which I work, that received government funds came under spiritual attack. Clients began to file lawsuits, saying that they were being forced into religious settings where they were being required to pray.

Many programs, like the one in which I work in the prison setting, were coming under attack because of the structure we used, which was based on faith in God and a 12-step model. So, unfortunately, much of the material we used including the Big Book of Alcoholics Anonymous, the twelve steps and twelve traditions and many videos which were Christian-based had to be removed from the program.

The Power to Change was written under these restrictions. However, *this* time I refuse to publish this material without giving the glory to God and including Biblical references along the way. The original idea for *The Power to Change* and *The Revelation of Power* came to me during an inspirational moment while reading the Bible.

If you are out of control or want more control and power, then you need to understand you! This book is about you. This book is a revelation of you and the universe you live in.

Unless you understand you and the universe you live in, things may get worse. What have you got to lose? Have faith and enter into *The Revelation of Power.*

Genesis 1:26 And God said, Let us make man in our image, after our likeness...

God created us in His image and likeness. Just what is His image? What is our likeness to God?

Contained in this book is a revelation of how we are like God. It begins with our ability to create through the power of invisible thoughts and words. We create our circumstances and surroundings through our thinking and our speaking. We create, just as God created, with His Word. He spoke light into existence and we also have created and continue to create our lives with our words. Whatever the circumstances in which we now find ourselves, we created them. We have the power of creation. It is a gift from God, and look at what kind of a personal world we have created for ourselves with this power.

The greatest revelation about my personal addictions was to finally come to the conclusion after years of denial that I alone had created the circumstances of my life. When I finally admitted this to myself, I began to think, how did I get myself to this position in life?

If you are wondering how you have arrived where you are in life right now, this book will show you. If you are looking for a door into a new future, you have the right book. You hold in your hand one of the most powerful books ever written about recovery! This book is not designed and written to show you just how to recover. This book is a revelation of how to live with power, peace and prosperity.

Do you want to change? How many times have you prayed? How many times have you promised? How many times have you begged for another chance? Are you ready to change? How many programs have you been in? How many times have you failed? What do you really, really want to do with your life? If you really want to change your life, you will read, love and cherish this work.

The real question is: Do you want to learn about power that can change your life? If the answer is yes, then this method of change is for you. The information contained in this book is capable of showing you the way to complete, continued and long-lasting recovery. Your past life is gone; today is a new day and a new beginning. However, your past will be investigated and talked about so you can utilize the power that is in your past for your new future.

The knowledge presented here is to be viewed as inspirational and motivational. The information in this book is information based on personal research, experience, scientific research and known facts. It is designed to help you focus your internal power into *The Revelation of Power*.

The stimulation of your mind and emotions to a high level of activity and awareness in a positive direction is the purpose of using *The Revelation of Power*. Yes, we are God's work. He is working for us when we decide to let Him in and if we allow Him, through His Spirit and His word, to work on us and in us. This sometimes is the forgotten point: we must work with God by acting on His Word. We forget all about our own responsibility and believe that it is all up to God Almighty to fix us. This was my problem. He was supposed to fix me.

The intent of using this constructive power contained in *The Revelation of Power* is to have your negative thought conditions become so stimulated by positive thoughts from the Word of God that you as a person will begin to consider yourself an ongoing work of art. You, hopefully, will take the paintbrush of power that moves the intellect and emotions, using God's Word to create a new you. *Ephesians 2:10 For we are **his** workmanship, **created** in Christ Jesus unto good works, which God hath before ordained that we should walk in them.* The attainment of mastery over your own self through use of the Word of God and through inspiration of *The Revelation of Power* is an essential step in the process of total liberation for those of you who are victims and who wish to end the oppression of any addiction and regain self-respect and mental well-being.

*Proverbs 16:32 He that is slow to anger is better than the mighty; and **he that ruleth his spirit** than he that taketh a city.*

Prepare yourself to study and think about what you are reading. If you have wanted to change and did not know how, then prepare yourself for a deep level of change as you absorb this information with patience and endurance. My promise to you is that you will change if you follow what is written in this book. I know these laws and principles work because they worked for me and have been working for me for over twenty years.

I have come from being out there, in a life that was completely lost in alcohol, drugs and criminal behavior. I have come from actually living in an abandoned car with three other men to going to college, attending Seminary, becoming a pastor and becoming the supervisor over all alcohol and drug treatment in the prison where I work. What I learned about that negative-to-positive progression is that I did not know myself or how confused I had become. I was mentally and spiritually bankrupt and did not understand how I got there.

So, I am very aware of the internal struggle to break free from that kind of dysfunctional lifestyle and stay free. This is the reason I have written this book—to share knowledge and give hope and understanding to those who struggle with addictions. It is for my brothers and my sisters who are still not free—some in prison, jails, hospitals and some lost in the prison that exists in their own mind. I know I have found a way to be completely free and I now offer this to you. I have never experienced a greater pleasure than to see others know the peace and serenity that I have found through *The Revelation of Power.*

Start reading this material with high hopes. Make up your mind that you are going to set aside time to study every day if possible. Do not be afraid to get a dictionary when you need it. This book is not designed for you to read it and just put down. With thought, study, patience and reflection, you will see the need to go back over the material again and again. Also, at some point in your spiritual and mental journey toward recovery, you may begin to realize that, through this study material, you can have such a sudden creative act or idea, so inspired by this revelation of power to change, that you can begin a steady expedition to new success.

If you want to recover from addictions then you must begin the process of identifying and letting go of the things that you do not want in your life and replacing them with the positive things that you do want. This will take time. But, when you begin this process, you will begin to appreciate knowing that each step you take is leading you in the right direction for positive, continued, healthy change.

Inspiration is an act of allowing stimulation and power into your life. When you expire you die. When you are inspired you take in life. You will begin to look for and absorb the power to change your mind. That will give you the knowledge and guidance in life you have desired. This revelation will show you how to alter your mind to seek true wisdom and power.

Also, expect that this revelatory power will alter your mind in positive ways. Start with this: Your mind must adjust to this new reality. As long as you are alive and in reasonably good health, these four things do not change: thinking, action, behavior and consequences. Of course, there is always what *you* thought would happen. However, thinking, action, behavior and consequences will not change as a continual life process.

The inspirational information contained in this book is designed to affect and guide you by identifying and arousing hidden potentials within you, thus enlivening and exalting your emotional levels in positive ways. Study and mediate on this revelation you hold in your hands in order to stimulate yourself into positive action. The internal revelation of spiritual, mental and factual evidence will elicit and arouse motivational aspects of your conscious and subconscious mind toward positive change.

How many times in our addiction and misguided efforts have we desired a new direction to follow but felt we needed someone or something to breathe new life into us and stimulate energies that would be explosive in nature and bring about a major change? You will learn that every moment is extraordinary. Make a choice now that you will do whatever is necessary to change. Believe that, speak that, declare that and stand on that.

Proverbs 18:21 **Death** *and* **life** *are in the power of the tongue: and they that love it shall eat the fruit thereof.*

The past exists only in our memory. The future is only our expectations. The only time that we have is the now. Let *The Revelation of Power* breathe new life into your particular set of circumstances.

I promise you that *The Revelation of Power* is intended to energize and galvanize your thought patterns and provoke powerful change. *The Revelation of Power* is conceived with the idea that we need to be our own cheerleaders, to be proactive and to encourage ourselves toward change. You will be surprised how your knowledge of *The Revelation of Power,* with the help of the Holy Spirit, will transform your life, nourish your soul and open doors to unlimited possibility.

I know there are many of you who have questions. How do we give ourselves the courage to change? How can we rally ourselves and stir up the urge to change? How can we exert pressure upon ourselves to start walking in the right direction and to keep walking? Where is the call to action that will stir the embers of our inner fires and call forth the strength that will thrust us into fanning the flames of our passion to be free? What will touch our heart, arouse our emotions and not only set on fire our passion but electrify us and raise to a fevered pitch our intensity to be free? How can we challenge ourselves with a vision and imagination that will whip up and invite an enthusiasm that will lead into a never-ending pathway of excitement? How can we transport into our lives hope and a new work ethic, based on becoming a man or woman of principle?

*Matthew 19:26 But Jesus beheld them, and said unto them, with men this is impossible; but with God **all things are possible**.*

This instructional book of acquired knowledge is based on scientific facts and is designed to help students bridge the gap between the information given in any seminars, groups, lectures and videos and turn it into a powerful force for change. This information will work with any other program of recovery because it is based on universal principles that do not change.

This new understanding of method will enable students to turn presentations into actual and factual energy. You can, with patience, turn this presentation material into positive student action. The goal is for the student to understand his or her personal power to become self-actualized, self-aware, self-empowered and, as a consequence, oriented in a positive direction.

Each step in the process will allow students to more fully understand how to focus their personal energy and thoughts in order to obtain new thought patterns and habits of action. The result will be that the student's behavior will change also. At each level, every student will be taught how to harness his or her personal energy to appropriate the daily skill levels in understanding how the brain generates power. *The Revelation of Power* is all about how you can tap into that stream of thought energy in order to direct that power into positive change.

Things do not change; we change.
Henry David Thoreau

He who cannot change the very fabric of his thought will never be able to change reality.
Anwar Sadat

Even God is limited if you are limited in how you think.

Psalms 78:41 Yea, they turned back and tempted God, and **limited** *the Holy One of Israel.*

Chapter 2

What is The Revelation of Power?

Consider this carefully: What is *The Revelation of Power*? Is there power that will actually change us? Are there extraordinary powers of the mind and spirit that have been discovered through an investigative search of scientific facts and principles? Have secrets of the universe and their use in our own daily life been hidden from you? Are you looking for secrets that will open the door to achieving the health, wealth and happiness, which is what every heart longs for?

- You have already used and been exposed to these universal laws and mental principles.

- *The Revelation of Power* provides you with stunning new revelations of knowledge, showing you how to stimulate your personal ability.

- You will learn how to employ your will power and to choose to move in concert with universal laws.

- You will learn how to apply these universal laws and principles to your own, everyday life experience for your personal benefit.

- You can achieve the positive dreams and visions that are yours to choose from.

- No longer do you have to be held captive and a slave to powers of habit that have controlled your life.

Through committing yourself to a life of discipline and learning, along with daily practice, you too can have a new

17

existence. *Don't be afraid! You can do this.* You now have the opportunity to choose a new pathway for yourself, starting today. Yes, there is power to change us, yet many are unaware of its presence and potential.

To be aware of this power and how we can harness this power/potential for our positive use is one of the many subjects covered in this material. Amazingly, this power is unknown to some, but you and others will continue to use this power every day. You alone are the only one who can choose whether or not to change for the positive lifestyle available through this book. The fact of the matter is that we change every day, every minute and every millisecond. Today, choose to read study and observe this material and always use these powerful mental and spiritual tools for the good of yourself and others.

As we start to study the physical brain and the invisible mind, you will begin to understand the awesome power that operates at all times inside us and around us. Finally, we shall learn how to manipulate this power to build new dreams, visions and new, healthy lives. Some of the descriptions of the brain and how it works are given in medical terms and can be very complex in nature. I am asking that you take the time to try and understand the overall picture of how powerful the mind/brain connection is. As you gain understanding of your own brain functions, you will gain new faith that change is actually taking place within you when you make the choice to begin your journey toward recovery.

Addicted humans are complex beings and each area of our lives is affected by our addictions. *The Revelation of Power* is a workable concept, based on scientific facts and years of research—all designed to help you look at and understand how the inner reality we live in produces our outer reality. We are both surrounded by this complex mental/energy force and involved in the invisible internal human existence of force and power that affects our external reality.

By understanding the outer and inner forces of energy and the force that we exist in, we have the opportunity to direct these forces and have more control over the results of our continued exposure within this present reality. Our reality, simply put, is one of constantly changing energy. In the words of Einstein "Energy can neither be created nor destroyed, it simply changes form." *All living things are made up of energy.* It can change from one form to another, but it cannot really be destroyed. All living things have the ability to put out energy or take in energy. The universe is impartial. The universe is pure energy, which is constantly shifting and changing.

This process of *The Revelation of Power* is based on restructuring your thinking process for your own benefit. I believe that our reality, as we create it, moves from the invisible realm of thought to the visible realm of our outer reality. Take a moment to realize that there is nothing around you that was not once just a thought. The chair you are sitting on, the bus you are riding in, or the home in which you live. You are at present intimately involved with someone's or group of people's past thoughts, which have become physical reality. You are sitting on thoughts, riding in thoughts and interacting in a world of past thought and your present reality. Learning how to take charge of these invisible realities of thought is the objective of this course.

The term for this process is "positive cognitive restructuring." It leads to the constructive ability to change. Cognitive change involves all the mental aspects of thinking and reasoning. When you change your thinking, your conceptual intellectual capacity is changed and we, together, can move into a more positive, self-conscious awareness of our thinking power and potential.

Being addicted to drugs, criminal thinking and behavior, our emotional, cerebral and intellectual capacities have been negatively affected. This continues to produce a mind that creates more negative emotional upheaval and chaos as both the conscious and subconscious mind continue to use negative thoughts to promote a dysfunctional, subjective, perceptual and psychological living process.

These perceptions, words, ideas, concepts and theories are many times repressed into unconscious levels and are actually an entire world of ideas, yet they are treated as though they do not exist. Certain perceptions, thoughts and energies may exist that are never acknowledged or uttered as a concrete form of mental reality—*ever!* However, this repressed information base becomes the substratum from which the forces of habit are formed and unleashed.

In this attempt to explain in a few words the dilemma facing those who are addicted to drugs, we have just briefly explored our areas of focus for this process. And, most importantly, the process just described uses the very power that we use every day as humans and will continue to use until the process of this human life for us stops. We use power to live every day.

The purpose of *The Revelation of Power* is to let you understand how to harness this power for your positive use. To understand the principles behind this power, which we as humans are subject to in this present world, again let me say that you will need to study this material—not just read it and forget it, but study and refer back to it from time to time. No one is excluded from the invisible authority of universal principles—*and that means you!*

Chapter 3

How the Brain/Mind Works

The mind has within it the capacity to be *goal-directed.* This area is the collective area of focus where goals and all that we learn through this material will come to a point of convergence.

A number of phenomenal cerebral happenings appear to be connected one to another as elements in an intelligent, goal-directed system. Our sense organs are stimulated by events in our environment. By the quality of this stimulation, we perceive things about the external world. Then, we use this information, as well as information we have remembered or inferred, to guide our actions in ways that further our goals. Goal-directedness is the holographic quality of the mind that allows us to use inner vision and imagination to create our lives.

Being goal-directed means, having more control over the direction of your personal mind as a powerful instrument and precious gift to be valued. Many things enter our mind, but we determine what stays there and what we let out through the mechanism of our mouths. If you allow just anything to invade your mind and do not set goals, you will not know where you are going. By not setting goals, you could end up anywhere. Nothing can hold you captive to negative thoughts and behavior without your consent and cooperation. Remember this: you can break free from past conditions since your mind will respond to what you give it on a daily basis. When goals and thoughts are positive, you must take the time to value that and work to preserve that direction. When goals and thoughts are negative, get rid of them by replacing them with new goals and dreams.

Do not be afraid to decide what your dreams and goals are going to be. Take authority over your thought patterns, which inform your vision and imagination. Reinforce that process by writing down specific goals. Use your creative imagination to develop a plan of action to reach your dreams. Make up your mind that you will not allow anything or anyone to impede your progress. Determine, on a daily basis, that nothing will get in the way of you and your goals. That does not mean that you are not open to instruction and help from others. What should happen is that when your mind is trained to look for the positive knowledge and information that can help you, the *who* is talking is not as important as the *what* that is being said. You do not know who the teacher will be until you listen to the message. You just want to make sure that whatever you accept will enhance what you are trying to accomplish along positive lines and train yourself to look for knowledge, wisdom and understanding. Or you can continue to maintain the kinds of negative goals that led you to where you are right now.

Goal-directedness is the holographic quality of the mind that allows us to use inner vision and imagination to create our lives. The mind is constructed in such a way that we can view different aspects of whatever we are placing in our vision and imagination. Always remember that the most wonderful thing about setting goals in this area is that the moment you set a positive goal you will begin to feel a sense of control. As you use this holographic quality of the mind to plan, you can begin to "see" yourself accomplishing goals by imagining the most important tasks that must be completed to achieve your goal. You will feel a flow of energy as the brain works exponentially to bring in other thoughts as a response from the universe of potential energy that is around you all the time. You will experience the thrill of millions of neurons beginning to carry this new message with increasing power. You will know what it is to be inspired and motivated by this new burst of energy. Your self-esteem will be elevated as you see yourself making progress.

*Philippians 1:6 **Being confident** of this very thing, that he which hath begun a good work in you will perform it until the day of Jesus Christ:*

Have you ever bought a lottery ticket? What happened to your thinking? Did you think about all the things you could do with those millions? For a while you felt pretty good—just the thought of winning put a smile on your face. That was just one example of how one thing can change your thinking and responses. Do not underestimate the power that is in you to change direction.

Nothing can hold you captive to negative thoughts and behavior without your consent and cooperation.

*Isaiah 54:17 **No weapon** that is formed against thee shall prosper; and every tongue that shall rise against thee in judgment thou shalt condemn. This is the heritage of the servants of the LORD, and their righteousness is of me, saith the LORD.*

Do not be afraid to decide what your dreams and goals are going to be. Take authority over your thought patterns, which inform your vision and imagination.

Creativity and Freedom are two of the most important characteristics of the mind that we want to focus on, especially the higher functions of our mind, imagination and vision. In short, we want to explore the use of higher consciousness and how we can best use these areas to change our lives for the better. Harnessing these capacities for choice and imagination simply cannot be overemphasized. Rather than automatically converting past influences into future actions, individual minds are capable of exhibiting creativity and freedom. This freedom from negative influences is crucial to our ability to recover and flourish in new ways. We can imagine new things we have not experienced and can act in ways that no one would expect or could predict of us. The question is: will it be now?

Immediately stop all self criticism based on what you have done. Criticism will not change anything. Refuse to criticize yourself over and over. And, as you do learn to stop the negative influences, your daily experience will change. Accept yourself just as you are, realizing that what you did is not who you are, nor is it a true statement of who you will become. Everything changes daily, moment-by-moment. Stop terrorizing yourself with your own thoughts. Stop the brain from continually reproducing negative thoughts. Stop being stuck in a torrent of negative thoughts. That is a terrible way to live, being caught in a life of negative images and mental torture. Be gentle, kind and firm with yourself. Take control of your imagination and use your creative vision to create freedom for yourself.

*Romans 8:1 There is therefore now **no condemnation** to them which are in Christ Jesus, who walk not after the flesh, but after the Spirit.*

If you are a born-again Christian, accept that reality and stop mentally condemning yourself. When you become free in your mind you create freedom of thought around you. That freedom is the door into creativity unbound by negative addictions. Every day we encounter both positive energies and negative energies in our mind. Most of these energies are not external to us, but come from our own thoughts.

Throughout each day, we have good thoughts and bad thoughts—a memory of a happy time we had with someone special, the anticipation of something enjoyable we are going to do in the evening or a bad memory of when we felt we were done *wrong,* a memory that we can't seem to prevent mentally dragging ourselves through again and again in our own mind. Or we may continue to entertain violent thoughts in reaction to a perceived insult in the present. Those things seem to continually nag us until we are miserable.

What we continually forget is that most of our lives occur in our minds, and we can learn to have control over our minds. We don't have to be unhappy. If we are unhappy, if we are plagued with bad thoughts, it is because at some point we have accepted that we deserve that punishment, which we don't deserve. Isn't it funny how we always seem to be able to forgive others much more generously and quickly than we forgive ourselves? In the final analysis, we are the only ones who can take control of our creative potential and create peace. We may have to use any number of sources to "feed" our minds with good information, but the opportunity is there because this capacity lies within our mind and a better use of our brain.

An aware consciousness is a gift. Consciousness is the phenomenal experience of knowing you are alive and are aware of that fact. Consciousness may be the closest term we have for describing what is special about us as humans. Minds are sometimes referred to as consciousness, yet it is difficult to describe exactly what consciousness is. Although consciousness is closely related to inward accessibility and subjectivity (that means consciousness is personal and subjective to each person), these very characteristics seem to hinder us in reaching an objective, scientific understanding of just what, precisely, that is. What can truly be said is that we are aware that we are alive.

You can send your consciousness into the future, explore the past and even embrace the present. Right now you can focus your consciousness on your big toe, on your left foot or anywhere else you decide to go through your conscious awareness. You can visit the past through your memory or look into the future through your vision and imagination. You are alive and aware in the universe.

Inward Accessibility is perhaps the most important characteristic of our mind, for it is there that the spark of creation and inspiration can lead us to a new life.

*Proverbs 2:10-13 When wisdom entereth into **thine heart**, and knowledge is pleasant unto thy soul; Discretion shall preserve thee, understanding shall keep thee: To deliver thee from the way of the evil man, from the man that speaketh froward things; Who leave the paths of uprightness, to walk in the ways of darkness...*

Our inner mental and emotional world is accessible and available to us through introspection. We can know our own mind and get to know ourselves much better by being honest with what we see inside. Look at our multiple sensations, thoughts, memories, desire and fantasies. Each of us is a walking, living universe of thoughts and feelings.

In a direct sense, the power of internal reflection is the doorway into the realm of creation. We also have the ability to know our mental states in a way that no one else can. In other words, we have privileged access into our own mental states, which no one else can see.

However, no one can make us look inside ourselves if we are afraid or unwilling to do so. Inward accessibility means that you have access to all the different aspects of your mind and personal psychology. You have the ability to go within and make the necessary changes!

Your consciousness and inward accessibility are your personal gateway into exploring your emotions and behaviors. One way of exploring deep within is to ask questions about yourself and be honest in terms of what you see and what you believe. Are you calm and serene or are you full of anger, anxiety and worry? Are you striving toward more positive action with clear ideas about where you are going? Or are you confused and depressed about your present situation? Do you experience doubt about your future in recovery? Are you envious of others who seem to be doing well? Or are you experiencing joy and kindness in your newfound lifestyle?

The brain is the portion of the central nervous system that is enclosed within the cranium, continuous with the spinal cord. It is the primary center for regulating and controlling bodily activities, receiving and interpreting sensory impulses and transmitting information to the muscles and body organs. It is also thought to be the seat of consciousness, consisting of, but not limited to, thought, memory and emotion.

The mind is the human consciousness that is thought (by man) to originate in the brain and is manifested especially in thought, perception, emotion, will, memory and imagination.

In the Bible, the heart or the center of man is where issues come from. We will study this more carefully later in this revelation.

The collective conscious and unconscious processes are thought to originate in the mind, which directs and influences mental and physical behavior. Inside the physical brain is the invisible mind. The mind is invisible and yet the mind is the principal seat of intelligence, where the spirit of consciousness is now regarded as an unseen aspect of reality. This is where the faculty of thinking, reasoning and the application of knowledge moves from the invisible to the visible energy and chemical reactions that are interpreted by the brain.

*Isaiah 26:3 Thou wilt keep him in perfect peace, whose **mind** is stayed on thee: because he trusteth in thee.*

*Matthew 22:37 Jesus said unto him, Thou shalt love the Lord thy God with all thy heart, and with all thy soul, and with all thy **mind**.*

Comprehensive thinking is greatly assisted in this respect by a very powerful memory. It is conventional wisdom that once one learns how to ride a bicycle, one never forgets. The ability and knowledge is stored in the subconscious memory as a habit, and it may remain there for a lifetime. This is true for many relatively complex skills. Typing, for example, requires knowledge of letters and of a complex set of finger movements necessary to produce such symbols. Nevertheless, over time, the knowledge of typing enters one's subconscious memory, and the activity becomes a habit. When this happens, one no longer has to give attention to the question of which keys produce which letters. The conscious mind is free to give its full attention to the thoughts one is trying to capture and the words that will best represent them.

The subconscious also, I believe, plays a critical role in many of the special powers of comprehensive thought. The speed of comprehensive thought, for example, certainly depends on information from subconscious mental activity. The exhilaration that we feel when goals are reached arises in part from the fact that we cannot fully account for our success. Subconscious mental activity likewise plays a critical role in the capacity of comprehensive thought to account for a variety of factors at once.

A football player does not consciously consider every factor that enters into his effort to elude defensive backs and catch a pass. He visualizes the result that he hopes to achieve, and his subconscious mind in a variety of ways bends his efforts toward the desired result.

Let's look at how your own conscious, comprehensive thinking and subconscious mind work together to allow you to grow develop and create your life. Your conscious mind is your *awareness.* It is your communication center. It thinks, reasons, calculates, plans, directs deliberate actions of your body, determines results and makes decisions. It is creative, it registers pain, fear, happiness and it sets goals (both long-term and very short-term goals). In order for the conscious mind to be able to do all of these things, it must have a place to pull information from—a storage area. The subconscious mind is our data storage bank. When our conscious mind asks for answers our subconscious mind delivers.

To get rid of the old, incorrect ideas or any negative information based in our subconscious, we must replace this negative information with positive and beneficial ideas. There are ways to do this. The most widespread way is through the use of positive affirmations. Your subconscious mind is most affected by the thoughts you most frequently indulge in and the words you most frequently use.

The conscious mind is where we organize facts and discriminate between alternatives, applying logic to the thinking process. Our active memory is utilized when making logical decisions and applying critical thinking, keeping in mind our concepts of reality. We try to control emotions by using our conscious minds.

The conscious mind is a beehive of activity. It avoids silence and reflection and can become comfortable with negatives. Our conscious awareness understands the movement of time and deals in the past and can project or envision the future through foresight and imagination.

The conscious mind maintains the illusion of control and our ego keeps us separated from the truths that exist in the subconscious but the subconscious is the more powerful of the two. This is how people can swear by all they know that they will do one thing and, over time, will end up doing what has been formed as a long-standing habit. But, habits can be changed.

Do you want to start again? You can become new by accepting Jesus as your savior and then the gift you receive is the unfolding revelation of what God has done in you through Jesus.

*2 Corinthians 5:17 Therefore if any man be in Christ, he is **a new creature:** old things are passed away; behold, all things are become new.*

There will come a time when you believe everything is finished. That will be the beginning.
Louis L'Amour

All glory comes from daring to begin.
Eugene F. Ware

Most of the important things in the world have been accomplished by people who have kept on trying when there seemed to be no hope at all.
Dale Carnegie

Chapter 4

The Loins of Your Mind

For the purpose of more effectively understanding and using your own mind, I want to share this revelation of the six major areas discovered in the Bible: "the loins of your mind."

Another one of the reasons this book has been written is because I am now in recovery after years of pain and I want to share my liberating experiences with you.

From the age of 23 until I went into The Delancey Street Foundation treatment center, I went down a rapidly descending spiral staircase of bad choices, pain, lost jobs, marital infidelity, madness, heroin, crack and cocaine addition, numerous hospitals, drug and alcohol programs, accidents, attempts at recovery, frequent trips to jail, until, finally, I called my brother and he took me to the hospital after an attempted overdose had failed.

Years of suffering and untold self-inflicted pain drive me to write so that others may learn how to live free. Repeated failure, even after knowing the Lord, forced me to look for answers. Having received power from God, why was I still failing over and over? This struggle, which lasted for years, caused me to search the Word of God for some answers.

I was desperately searching for reasons about why my life was in such a mess. Why, after so many years, was I still such a failure and completely given to alcohol and drug addiction?

After what I call an *awakening moment,* I realized at a very deep psychological level that I was creating the chaos in my own life. It was not anyone else—not my mother or my background. It was not racism or authority figures. I was creating my own miserable life while blaming everyone else. Well, if I was doing it, *how* was I doing it?

It took some time to move past powerful, ingrained years of denial, but I finally realized I was creating my own problems. If I was creating this ongoing problem and allowing it to continue, how was I doing that? I began to look into the Bible with some questions, looking for some answers. What am I creating and how can I stop creating chaos in my life? One day after prayer, this scripture really caught my attention:

*1 Peter 1:13 Wherefore gird up the **loins of your mind,** be sober, and hope to the end for the grace that is to be brought unto you at the **revelation** of Jesus Christ;*

In *1 Peter 1:13* for some reason my eyes and mind focused on the phrase, *"loins of your mind."*

As you know, the loin area in men and women is the creative area (remember the loincloth). So if there are creative areas of our mind, what are they? In my search I ran across the six creative areas of the mind in the Bible, which began my quest for a revelation of how I created my own living hell. In this Christian version of *The Power to Change,* called *The Revelation of Power,* I have added a sixth creative area, called the heart.

Now this powerful truth is revealed in *The Revelation of Power.* This book is a labor of love. We can now create a new life with the help of God. The following are some of the many scriptures that refer to these six creative areas of the mind. Some are used in a negative context. Nevertheless, they can be used in a positive way.

For those of you who have read *The Power to Change*, you will find a great deal of this material is the same as it is in that book. I have re-written much of the material and added what I thought would enhance the book. It is my hope and desire that you be blessed by *The Revelation of Power*.

Six is the number of man according to many scriptures. Man was made on the sixth day. His appointed days of labor are six. A Hebrew slave was to serve for six years. For six years the land was to be sown and then left to rest during the seventh year. The kingdoms of this world are to last for six thousand years. Moses was compelled to wait for six days on the Mount before God revealed Himself. For six days the Children of Israel compassed the city of Jericho. There were six steps to Solomon's throne. Goliath's height was six cubits. The image of gold was six cubits high. The number of the beast is 666. There are six creative areas within man that I use in this book. Two of the creative areas, Vision and Imagination, look into the future.

1. Vision:

Vision is the combination of thoughts, focused into a picture or goal of the future. It is the area of the mind that holds a more complete representation and illustration of the future, using all of the other areas of the mind, namely: perceptions, emotion, your will, memory, knowledge and imagination. These areas allow for planning and forethought of action. The area called vision is a place of mental thought pictures, preparation and predetermination. When used skillfully, it is a place of intelligent anticipation. It is foresight.

Vision is also another area of creation in man. In Isaiah 28:7 not only does the Bible speak about the capacity within man to use vision but if strong drink and wine is the object of your continual vision it brings about errors in judgment. The importance of having a positive vision is made clear by the scripture in Proverbs 29:18. The lack of a positive vision means you are headed toward death. If you do not know where you are going through the use of vision, any road will get you there, dead in trespasses and sins.

*Isaiah 28:7 But they also have erred through wine, and through **strong drink** are out of the way; the priest and the prophet have erred through **strong drink,** they are swallowed up of **wine,** they are out of the way through **strong drink;** they err in vision, they stumble in judgment.*

*Proverbs 29:18 Where there is no **vision,** the people perish: but he that keepeth the law, happy is he.*

2. Imagination:

Imagination is the area of the mind where the formation of a mental image takes place. The difference between vision and imagination is that your imagination of something can be perceived as real or not. And it is not present to the five senses; it is an internal sense. It is the essential area of the mind where the ability to create takes place. You can imagine anything. Your imagination is a testing ground for the more focused vision, where the ability to confront and deal with the possibilities of reality is born. Various problems presented in reality can be handled with the use of the imagination. The imagination is an ability to look into the future in multiple ways. We are equipped with this ability to carefully imagine future accomplishments and circumstances and we are able to turn those ideas into reality by formulating these random ideas into a vision for the future.

*Genesis 6:5 And GOD saw that the wickedness of man was great in the earth, and that every **imagination** of the thoughts of his heart was only evil continually.*

*Genesis 8:21 And the LORD smelled a sweet savour; and the LORD said **in his heart,** I will not again curse the ground any more for man's sake; for **the imagination of man's*** *heart is evil from his youth; neither will I again smite any more every thing living, as I have done.*

*Genesis 11:6 And the LORD said, Behold, the people is one, and they have all one language; and this they begin to do: and now nothing will be restrained from them, which they have **imagined** to do.*

*1 Chronicles 29:18 O LORD God of Abraham, Isaac, and of Israel, our fathers, keep this for ever in the **imagination** of the thoughts of the heart of thy people, and prepare their heart unto thee:*

3. Knowledge:

*Hosea 4:6 My people are destroyed for lack of **knowledge**: because thou hast rejected knowledge, I will also reject thee, that thou shalt be no priest to me: seeing thou hast forgotten the law of thy God, I will also forget thy children.*

There are many kinds of and uses for knowledge. For the purposes of viewing knowledge in terms of what we need for recovery we can use this definition: knowledge is information that changes something or somebody both by becoming the basis of new actions or by making an individual capable of different or more useful achievement.

Our past acquaintance with facts, personal knowledge, truths or principles that we stood for has placed us in positions where we need a whole new knowledge base. All the so-called body of truths, the sum of what we know, all our so-called facts accumulated over the course of time, all our profound studies of life have brought us to where we are now. Are you satisfied with where you are? If you are not happy and satisfied with where you are in life, study and read on.

Knowledge is a result of learning something and acquiring skills over time. It leads to and becomes the truth of the experience. It is being aware through experiences or studies of the sum or range of what has been perceived as truth and that now has become truth and knowledge.

Knowledge can be acquired or learned in a moment of clarity or possibly over a lifetime. Knowledge is the broadest range of information acquired. It includes facts and ideas along with understanding, as well as the totality of what we have come to know.

New information helps us reshape past information refining it into knowledge. Information is usually considered to be narrower in scope than knowledge; it often implies a collection of facts and data. Information can bring understanding and, along with experience, it can produce knowledge. This knowledge relates to the six areas of the mind because a person's judgment and actions cannot be better than the information on which he or she bases his or her understanding.

Both imagination and vision are limited to personal acquired knowledge and information. This knowledge and information can be projected into the future when we plan. Knowledge is added to our experience each day. The acquisition, intensity and focus of the knowledge received are determined by the mind that seeks it or lets it in.

Knowledge must be challenged over time to make sure our information base is as current as possible. This means that continued study and testing of our knowledge base is important. New information can change what we know and therefore change our knowledge.

Knowledge is also a third area from which we create our reality. The purpose of this revelation is to add to your knowledge base, giving you the building blocks necessary to create a new, more powerful you. There is a clear indication that strength of character can be increased with proper knowledge. The term knowledge is also related to the thinking processes of perception and communication. Knowledge also means confident understanding of any subject with the ability to use it for a specific purpose when appropriate. These two following scriptures clearly show that precious things and riches can be gained through knowledge.

*Proverbs 24:4 And by **knowledge** shall the chambers be filled with all precious and pleasant riches.*

*Proverbs 24:5 A wise man is strong; yea, a man of **knowledge** increaseth strength.*

4. Memory:

Memory is the area of the mind where the mental faculty of retaining and recalling past experience is located. It is part of the invisible world of the mind and cannot be observed directly. We do, however, realize that we have a memory containing a collection of past experiences. Those memories can be good or bad, negative or positive or any combination of those elements. Many people have pleasant childhood memories and others have memories of abuse and dysfunctional family experiences. You see the world through your memory. If you did not have a memory, you could not remember how to wash your face, brush your hair or clean up. As a matter of fact, if you could not remember how to do anything such as talk or walk (and the list goes on), you would not be able to function at all.

Memory is another area that creates our present reality. In *Proverbs 10:7*, we find that living in a state of being justified by God will lead to having a blessed memory, no doubt full of sweet memories and gracious deeds done over time. In *Corinthians*, Paul talks about how important the use of the memory is, especially as we continue to keep it refreshed in the Gospel.

*Proverbs 10:7 The **memory** of the just is blessed: but the name of the wicked shall rot.*

1 Corinthians 15:1 Moreover, brethren, I declare unto you the gospel which I preached unto you, which also ye have received, and wherein ye stand;

*1 Corinthians 15:2 By which also ye are saved, if ye keep in **memory** what I preached unto you, unless ye have believed in vain.*

5. Conscience:

Conscience is the inner awareness of right and wrong. It is a moral and ethical aspect that is applied to one's behavior, together with the urge to prefer doing what is right over doing what is wrong. The common phrase is to let your conscience be your guide. And *if* your conscience is based on good moral and principled footing, it can be a source of correct moral decisions and right ethical judgment.

Conscience can warn us in the present before we move forward with action. Many lessons, warnings and cautions in the conscience can give us advance notice about the wisdom of our present choices. It is information that can counsel us with object lessons from the past. The danger signals that alert and warn us become more pronounced as we become more aware of our inner qualities and spiritual tools. Effective use of the conscience can prevent future disasters. You grow to use this area correctly or fail to use it and dull or silence its voice at your own peril.

*John 8:9 And they which heard it, being convicted by their own **conscience,** went out one by one, beginning at the* *eldest, even unto the last: and Jesus was left alone, and the woman standing in the midst.*

1 Timothy 3:9 Holding the mystery of the faith in a pure **conscience.**

1 Timothy 4:2 Speaking lies in hypocrisy; having their **conscience** *seared with a hot iron...*

In the book of Hebrews we also find information about the fifth area of creation called conscience. The book of Hebrews speaks of the conscience being cleansed by the blood of Christ and Timothy indicates that faith and a pure conscience need to be joined together. We will look much more closely at these important areas of memory and conscience later in this book. It is because of the destructive potential that lies in a negative use of the conscience and memory that we will explore this later, in detail. One powerful reason for discussing this subject in greater detail is that the negative use of these areas results in self-condemnation and a poor self-image.

Hebrews 9:14 How much more shall the blood of Christ, who through the eternal Spirit offered himself without spot to God, purge your **conscience** *from dead works to serve the living God?*

1 Timothy 3:9 Holding the mystery of the faith in a pure **conscience.**

6. Heart:

The Bible gives us information regarding the heart of man. When we talk about the heart in man, we are not talking about the heart that pumps blood. We are talking about the heart or center of men and women. Out of the center of men and women come all of the issues of life. In my opinion, the center of men and women is where all of the other creative areas find their focus.

Both the Hebrew *"leb"*—feelings, the will, even the intellect, the center of things—and the Greek *"kardia"* speak of the center of anything, the thoughts and *even the mind.* These expressions give God's meaning and definition to the fact that the heart is a creative area.

The heart or center of man is the sixth area of creation in man. All six of these areas are invisible yet powerful and are the source from which we co-create our lives.

Much earlier in my life I heard a pastor say that as a man thinks in his heart. I thought to myself, everyone knows that a man thinks with his mind with the use of his brain or so I thought at the time. The heart just pumps blood. But when I looked up the word "heart" and discovered what it meant in the Greek, I had a much fuller understanding. The heart is the center not only of spiritual activity but of all the operations of human life. The heart is the *home of the personal life,* and hence a man is understood and known according to his heart. Humans look at actions. God looks at the heart of men and women. The Bible says the heart is naturally wicked.

And again, *Genesis 8:21 And the LORD smelled a sweet savour; and the LORD said in his heart, I will not again curse the ground any more for man's sake;* **for the imagination of man's heart is evil from his youth;** *neither will I again smite any more every thing living, as I have done.*

Because the heart is naturally wicked, it contaminates the whole life and character of a person. Yet it is with this same heart or center of man that he or she must commit in order to accept Jesus for salvation. Because of sin, mankind is corrupt at the core or center, called in the Bible the heart. It is at the heart of the matter where the issue of salvation is settled. At the very core of a person is where the decision is made to believe God and to have faith in God's Word. The word faith is used only twice in the Old Testament. The word believe(d) is used for faith.

*Genesis 15:6 And he **believed** in the LORD; and he counted it to him for righteousness.*

*James 2:23 And the scripture was fulfilled which saith, Abraham **believed** God, and it was imputed unto him for righteousness: and he was called the Friend of God.*

*Proverbs 23:7 For as he thinketh in his **heart**, so is he ...*

*Matthew 15:19 For out of the **heart** proceed evil thoughts, murders, adulteries, fornications, thefts, false witness, blasphemies ...*

*Romans 10:10 For with the **heart** man believeth unto righteousness; and with the mouth confession is made unto salvation.*

*Proverbs 4:23 Keep **thy heart** with all diligence; for out of it are the issues of life.*

*Matthew 12:34 O generation of vipers, how can ye, being evil, speak good things? for out of the abundance of **the heart** the mouth speaketh.*

*Matthew 12:35 A good man out of the good treasure of **the heart** bringeth forth good things: and an evil man out of the evil treasure bringeth forth evil things.*

*Mark 7:21 For from within, out of **the heart** of men, proceed evil thoughts, adulteries, fornications, murders ...*

*Psalms 44:21 Shall not God search this out? for he knoweth the secrets of **the heart**. But:*

*Proverbs 15:13 **A merry heart** maketh a cheerful countenance: but by sorrow of the heart the spirit is broken.*

*Proverbs 15:15 All the days of the afflicted are evil: but he that is of **a merry heart** hath a continual feast.*

*Proverbs 17:22 **A merry heart** doeth good like a medicine: but a broken spirit drieth the bones.*

Chapter 5

Habit Force

In my opinion, the main problem with continued, sustained recovery is in this area of breaking bad habits. It was my biggest problem. I just could not understand why, if I said I was going to change, the change just did not happen and continue to happen. I have found the following is the reason.

People do not maintain their recovery because of energy, in the form of negative information that is stored in various invisible areas of our real self. The energy of thoughts and emotions is stored in us everywhere—*we are energy*. But one place where these thoughts and emotions do the most damage is in our habits.

The force of habit causes many a positive life to get sidetracked by one thought that reaches into our old habits and starts a torrent of old thought patterns that emerge and choke out new life. Here is something to think about:

A habit is behavior that is acquired over a period of time and that becomes a pattern of almost involuntary, impulsive actions. If you go back far enough in examining these habits of thought, speech and action, you will find that at some point you made a decision about a set of circumstances, accepted as truth and repeated as a personal response.

If you have decided to study this book, it took some courage to make that decision. If you continue reading and studying this book, it should demonstrate that you have the courage to change and fully experience *The Revelation of Power*. Once one habit is brought under control, you will experience the rush of making some progress and success toward a more complete change of habits.

Habits are really any actions or behaviors that you continue to do over and over. Some habits are bad, like smoking tobacco, drugs and overindulgence in alcohol. Some habits, like brushing your teeth, combing your hair and fixing yourself up for the day, are good habits.

When you look into the complex workings of the brain, you will more fully appreciate the battle it will take to change your habits.

Once I was working a job where I had to walk down several flights of stairs. When I got to the bottom floor, I noticed that I had a brown powder all over my pants. I could not figure out what it was. When I went back upstairs, I noticed that on the top three floors the handrail had been sanded in preparation for painting. It was dried paint particles that had gotten on my pants. I said to myself that I just wouldn't touch the rail again.

How many times do you think I did that again? Well, it was at least twice more until I had to concentrate, think about it before I went upstairs and then remind myself after I got up there not to touch the railing.

I was successful a few times but as soon as I took my mind off the railing and began to think of something other than the rail, I did it again.

That is just a small example. Actually, it surprised me how many times I had to pay attention. Over time, I had developed a powerful habit and I had to focus in order to create and form a new habit.

If you want to change some habits that have held you hostage for years, then take time to make a list of habits you would like to change and those you would like to get rid of.

Take time to list those habits that could directly apply to your life and bring direct benefit over time. Start the day off with some inspirational reading and meditation. Start a book of ideas and keep a journal of your key life points of change and success or failure. Most people do not choose their future; they choose their habits and their habits determine their future. So carefully begin to search out your habits and determine to work on them.

Select a habit, take a week and work on it. Make a change every day and be aware of the change. It is impossible to change everything at once and you will never really change your life until you work on and change your habits on a daily basis. Bad habits were my most difficult problem to solve.

Don't overload yourself. Take your time and work on yourself a little each day. Soon you will start to feel the rush of reward for your efforts. We all fail. Don't waste time focusing on the mistakes you have made; take note of the mistake and move on. Time and life are too short for you to plunge into self-recrimination because you made a mistake.

Confront your problem habits and remember: what you refuse to master today will master you tomorrow. What you do on a habitual and permanent basis determines what you will continue to become on a permanent basis. You already know what bad habits can do to your life. Through the material in this book you can confront your habits. You will never correct what you are unwilling to confront in your life.

In the beginning you will need discipline. Discipline is forcing yourself to do what is necessary and right because it's the right and best thing for your positive progress. There is a difference between discipline and habit. While forcing yourself to do something that is right may be difficult, discipline's purpose is to bring you to a point where you love the results of what you have created through developing a new, more positive habit.

New habits are the children of discipline. When you attack a goal or a purpose with discipline and it becomes a habit, you then have a sense of purpose that will allow you to maintain your motivation through hard times. Remember: this is a struggle and a fight but certainly a fight that others have won. Why not you?

*Ephesians 6:13 Wherefore take unto you the whole armour of God, that ye may be able to **withstand** in the evil day, and having done all, **to stand**.*

*Ephesians 6:14 **Stand therefore**, having your loins girt about with truth, and having on the breastplate of righteousness;*

Remember this quotation: "I am your constant companion; I am your greatest helper or heaviest burden. I will push you onward or drag you down to failure. I am completely at your command. Half the things you do you might just as well turn them over to me and I will be able to do them quickly and correctly. I am easily managed—you must merely be firm with me. Show me exactly how you want something done and, after a few lessons, I will do it automatically. I am the servant of all great men and, alas, of all failures as well. Those who are great, I have made great. Those who are failures, I have made failures. I am not a machine, though I work with all the precision of a machine plus the intelligence of a man. You may run me for profit or run me for ruin—it makes no difference to me. Take me, train me, be firm with me, and I will place the world at your feet. Be easy with me and I will destroy you. Who am I? I am habit!"

Author Unknown

Chapter 6

Holiness and Scientific Discoveries

*Romans 5:19 For as by one man's disobedience many were made sinners, so by the obedience of one shall many be **made righteous.***

We now want to look at the word holiness. And we want to look at it in two ways. One way is to know that, because of the sacrifice of Jesus on the cross, we **have been made holy**. That was God's responsibility and promise to us. Have faith in the fact that you were *made* holy and separated from sin. You are holy because God said so. We have been *made right* because God said so. No matter who attempts to judge us, we shall be able to condemn their accusation now and forever because God promised it and said we are right because of Him. He cannot lie. While we strive to live right and make mistakes or sin, we are still right with God. Sin will separate us from a pure fellowship but confession renews the pure relationship.

*Ephesians 2:8 For by grace are ye saved **through faith**; and that **not of yourselves**: it is the gift of God...*

*1 John 3:9 Whosoever is born of God **doth not commit sin;** for **his seed remaineth in him**: and he cannot sin, because he is born of God*

It is the seed of the Word of God that declares you righteous and sinless as your state of being and present standing before God. Our sins, present and future, are nailed on the Cross.

*Colossians 2:14 Blotting out the handwriting of ordinances that was against us, which was contrary to us, and took it out of the way, **nailing it to his cross**...*

That is our judgment for all time. As Saints of God, we are judged for our works as far as rewards or losses are concerned. Our souls cannot be lost unless we do not believe or have faith in what God has said and done. Do you believe God or the devil?

*2 Corinthians 5:10 For we must all appear before the **judgment seat of Christ;** that every one may receive the things done in his body, according to that he hath done, whether it be good or bad.*

1 Corinthians 3:11 For other foundation can no man lay than that is laid, which is Jesus Christ.

12 Now if any man build upon this foundation gold, silver, precious stones, wood, hay, stubble;

13 Every man's work shall be made manifest: for the day shall declare it, because it shall be revealed by fire; and the fire shall try every man's work of what sort it is.

*14 If any man's work abide which he hath built thereupon, **he shall receive a reward.***

*15 If any man's work shall be burned, he shall suffer loss: **but he himself shall be saved;** yet so as by fire.*

*Isaiah 54:17 No weapon that is formed against thee shall prosper; and **every tongue** that shall rise against thee **in judgment** thou shalt condemn. This is the heritage of the servants of the LORD, and **their righteousness** is of me, saith the LORD.*

How we are going to look at holiness now is different. Now we focus on the fact that it is our responsibility to walk in holiness. *Our standing before God is holy.* Our responsibility is to eliminate everything that is wrong and prevents us from enjoying the fullness of joy and peace, one day at a time.

Now we want to narrow the meaning of the word holiness to apply to our thoughts and actions in everyday, practical living. This by no means takes away from the true and complete meaning of the word holiness. However, this book you are reading is designed to break down just how various aspects of God's Word apply to specific areas of our need. Then, when we enter worship service, we can observe the other aspects of what is holy. This leads us to have reverence for others who are also separated to God and present ourselves in more wholesome ways of total consecration to God in purity of thought, praise and action.

It is absolutely necessary that you see the reason for these two ways to see holiness. Holiness is for a calm state of mind, for living and for worship. In order to worship properly and live successfully we must learn to live in separation from our old life. Holiness is separateness in thought, action and deed. This is the highway of holiness or the highway of separated living where we cannot fail because God's will is to do whatever it takes to correct and help us while we are on this road. The Bible says you can be foolish and trust in God's gift and not err because *in God's eyes, our standing is holy.*

Isaiah 35:8 And an <u>highway</u> shall be there, and a way, and it shall be called **The way of holiness***; the unclean shall not pass over it; but it shall be for those: the wayfaring men,* ***though fools****, shall not err therein.*

As long as you learn and use the material presented in this book you will not fail. That means you will stay on a positive journey down the highway of separate living. You will be in the process of refining your spiritual footsteps by obeying and using the invisible laws and principles of the universe presented in a step-by-step process in this book. What we are striving for is right (holy and separate from wrong) thought and right (holy and separate from wrong) action providing (holy) positive results.

What God is doing when He sends His Word to heal you is to separate you from your wrong action or sin. God's Word in you is meant to create different actions by you. Because we live under a major universal law called reciprocity, you reap what you sow. What goes around comes around. What goes out from you comes back to you, multiplied. Thus, you must change your bad thinking and bad actions leading to continual behavior problems.

Refine your actions, modify your behavior, take positive action and reap the benefits of a separated, holy way of living. We are going to do this by the careful examination of God's word, combined with the contemporary language of today, to change your thinking and action. Of course, what you do with this information is up to you. If you choose to work on change then perhaps, if you will learn to understand more about you and the world you live in, you just might be willing to separate yourself from your old life.

Take a break now and read the 8th chapter of Romans and think about what it means. That chapter is one of my favorite chapters in the Bible. Stop beating yourself up!

This is important for our daily progress so I will say it again: What we want to do is to separate ourselves from a life of bad thinking, bad action, bad behavior and bad consequences. Holiness also means to be cut or separated from something. That something is sin, error and bad living. So the separation of a person from errors in thinking and actions means to become holy and separated from the profane and to set you aside for divine use. Separation is the keyword in relation to our thinking and actions. We want to separate ourselves from wrong living. Being declared separate and being separated by God is what holiness means. Thus, God is holy, and people—including their actions— may be holy by lining up their thinking with the thoughts of God. Holiness may also include the ideas of consecration to God and purity from what is evil or improper. Separation from thoughts that are negative and actions that result in negative consequences is the process of becoming holy and separated for God's use.

This is a holy war against all that would seek to hurt you and others. All the material in this book is designed to help you separate yourself from bad thoughts and actions. All the symbols, words and metaphors are a guide to show you the way toward true holiness: separation from sin by the operation of God's Word and other positive words of faith. They will guide you to the peace you seek. Peace is the absence of sin and error, combined with the indwelling presence of the Holy Spirit. The more positive energy that can be created within you as you evolve into a righteous warrior of faith and power is the process of *The Revelation of Power*. The more you grow in power, faith and the presence of God, the greater becomes the kingdom of God within your temple. Every negative thought must be brought under control. Your body is the temple of the Holy Spirit.

2 Corinthians 10:3 For though we walk in the flesh, we do not war after the flesh:

2 Corinthians 10:4 For the weapons of our warfare are not carnal, but mighty through God to the pulling down of strong holds;

*2 Corinthians 10:5 Casting down **imaginations**, and every high thing that exalteth itself against the knowledge of God, and bringing into captivity **every thought** to the obedience of Christ ...*

Our physical brain is part of our "flesh." It is physical and can be seen. A war is taking place in the invisible realm. Our warfare is in the realm of thought. The weapons we are using are mighty because they are God's words. God's anointed words are encouraging and designed to help us and are the mighty weapons of our warfare.

Imagination is in the invisible area of the mind. Everything that exalts itself against God is no more than negative, destructive thoughts. Words and thoughts are invisible but they are potentially powerful. This is why the war must take place in the invisible realm of thoughts. It is a war of thoughts, imaginations, visions, actions and consequences.

Every negative thought must be transformed by the power of God's positive words and rendered powerless. The energy of the negative can be brought into bondage and servitude. That means the negative can be changed to serve the purposes of God by being transformed. You can learn to do this and train your brain to carry out your positive instructions, using the Word of God and the material in this book. And you are not limited to just that.

Any books with positive material, designed to help you overcome problems and errors in living, are positive symbols, metaphors and potential knowledge and power that you can use to become more separated and holy. Every thought changes your mind inside your physical brain. What are you waiting for? Work on killing your old self, the self you have created through your choices, which are now determined to kill you. Every new thought must be attacked and brought into submission to the greater good and intent of your divine purpose to serve the living God. That is the true meaning of humility: destroying your old self.

James 4:10 **Humble** *yourselves in the sight of the Lord, and he shall lift you up.*

*1 Peter 5:6 **Humble** yourselves therefore under the mighty hand of God, that he may exalt you in due time*

The Revelation of Power is designed to give you the tools to enter the war that has been waged against your divine purpose. This is why we go into the invisible areas of the mind. Because these weapons, although unseen by human eyes, can be seen by the *"seven-spirit" power of God.* This power allows you to "see" in the invisible realm where the war is being waged for your soul.

*Isaiah 11:2 And the **spirit of the LORD** shall rest upon him, the **spirit of wisdom** and **understanding**, the **spirit of counsel** and **might**, the **spirit of knowledge** and of the **fear of the LORD** ...*

*Revelation 5:6 And I beheld, and, lo, in the midst of the throne and of the four beasts, and in the midst of the elders, stood a Lamb as it had been slain, having seven horns and **seven eyes, which are the seven Spirits of God** sent forth into all the earth.*

These divine **seven eyes** and **seven** (aspects of) the one **Spirit of God** were upon Jesus when he walked on the earth. They were described in Isaiah's prophecy and these same aspects of the Holy Spirit are in and upon us. These unique aspects of the Holy Spirit allow us to "see" as we are tutored and led into all truth. These seven aspects of the spirit will mature and develop the new you!

Remember: everything that is against God, every thought, must be revealed and defeated by the anointed Word of God. You have already won the war if you have accepted Christ. Now you want to be the victor in *every* battle. But, to give the full glory of your life back to God and live out the complete power of salvation, you must engage in warfare every day, one day at a time.

*1 Timothy 1:18 This charge I commit unto thee, son Timothy, according to the prophecies which went before on thee, that thou by them mightest **war a good warfare** ...*

*James 4:1 From whence come **wars and fightings** among you? Come they not hence, even of your lusts that war in your members?*

*Psalms 27:3 Though an host should encamp against me, my heart shall not fear: **though war should rise against me**, in this will I be confident.*

*Psalms 27:4 One thing have I desired of the LORD, **that will I seek after**; that I may dwell in the house of the LORD all the days of my life, to behold the beauty of the LORD, and to enquire in his temple.*

It is important to note: All of the previously mentioned six creative areas of the brain/mind, vision, imagination, knowledge, memory, conscience and your heart—use electrical energy and chemical changes to function. Also, this electrical energy and chemical action supports many or all of the ways we feel about anything going on in these areas.

That is why holiness is such an important subject to study with regard to how we decide to grow and create our new lives before a loving God.

When you have a positive goal on which to focus your mind, your thoughts, actions and behavior will be different. Depending upon the importance of the goal you have in mind, when passion and inspiration are involved you have more power.

Inspiration can be felt when passion for a goal is implemented and maintained. You begin almost to operate outside yourself. It is no longer work but passion that causes you to spring out of bed in the morning. Inspiration lights a fire inside you that, when properly fueled with new exciting information, will take you to your goal.

When you feel inspired you are more likely to be operating in the law of magnetic force and control. If you act when you feel inspired to do so, your success through the law and principle of manifestation is guaranteed. Why? Because when you are truly inspired and full of passion to reach your goal, you are forcefully connected to the creative energy of the universe at a subatomic level where creation starts.

Have you ever been in the presence of an inspired and passionate person? You could feel his or her power, passion and intent. Didn't that person make you want to get involved with his or her project? Well, such people have honed their skills and energized themselves around their goals and beliefs so that you can feel the emanation from the vibration of their very essence. The reason why inspirational speakers are so effective is because their vibration is so powerful it stimulates the thoughts and emotions of those around them. Such people who use this invisible force find it a lot easier to recruit the people and resources needed to accomplish their goals.

When your thoughts become focused and your intentions are completely on what you really want, to the point where you can almost taste it, you will feel relaxed, exhilarated and on point. There will be an almost elated feeling of true optimism about your goal. Your work production will increase. The more joyful you are, the more easily you are able to work, and the more powerful and effective your actions become to the point where what you are doing is no longer work but the fruition of an unfolding dream.

What does it mean to you to become empowered and to be able to sustain a high degree of internal power to complete any goal? It means understanding that the law of the universe is delivering *The Revelation of Power* into your life.

*Ephesians 6:15 And your **feet shod with** the preparation of the **gospel of peace** ...*

For me, the living, experiential revelation is that you can become so filled with the power of the Holy Spirit and the good news of peace that you change the atmosphere of a room when you walk in. Believe me. I know.

Remember that the law of reciprocity is designed to support any and every decision you make that is sustained over time and that brings a return. It means that, in order to become empowered, you must make a decision to become empowered at the level of your essence, which is the vibratory power in your inner self. A part of you must become power. Once that decision is made, all thought, emotion, action and manifestation will inevitably follow. This is the most important and powerful phase of the manifestation process: to become power, to become peace, to become love!

What is most important about becoming power are the metaphors and words we attach to those energy clusters. For example, mental pain or despair is just a phrase used to describe what we feel. Simple words and vibrations enable us to relate to present mental energy. Everything is energy. All matter, regardless of where it is or what it is, in the final analysis is energy.

We eat vegetables to grow strong and have energy. We are told to get eight hours of sleep to have proper levels of energy for the next day. Energy gives us the ability to do work. Energy is everywhere in the universe Energy is in the wind, the water, plants and animals. We use energy every day.

Our bodies are made up of several different groups of matter. There are major organs and various kinds of cells and tissues. But, mainly, the body is made up of water and even that water is made up of molecules and atoms. These atoms and molecules break down even further into smaller elements. If you break down the atoms, you will find that each atom contains particles of energy. These energy particles move so fast that they make the atom seem solid although it is not. If the nucleus of an atom were the size of a tennis ball, the electrons that circle it would be from two to ten miles away. Atoms are mainly made up of space.

Quantum theory has changed everything scientists think about how we now view the universe. Many scientists have given their lives to the Lord as a result of this new understanding. Through experiments, science finally admits that the simple act of observing atoms, electrons and neutrons changes the result of any experiment and, as a result, the new conclusion is that the observer and the observed object are not separate.

In the late 19th century, what scientists discovered is that subatomic particles were not particles at all. They behaved like particles when they were measured but they traveled like waves. What were once thought of as elementary physical entities, such as atoms and their components—electrons, protons and neutrons—have a duality. They behave like waves when they are not observed but behave like particles when observed.

These whirling electrons and photons are clouds of possibilities. This is very important and I do not want you to miss this point. You are, at the level of atoms, pure potential.

Experiments have been set up to determine the speed of subatomic particles when atoms are smashed. Scientists can detect this speed. The same experiment that is used to find the atomic particle's location can be set up to determine the speed of the particle but it must be done separately. In other words, you cannot simultaneously locate the particle and track its speed. This is because electrons, photons and subatomic particles appear to change, depending on how we set up the experiment.

Two conclusions can be derived from this. Particles and subatomic particles exist both in the form of a particle and in a moving wave. They are both there and not there. They have the potential to be in either a particle or a wave, depending on how we set up the experiment. Let me say this again: At the smallest levels of reality, particles are both there and not there, they are both matter and energy.

Many now say that whatever we may be conscious of as an individual, the sense of consciousness is something we all share. This consciousness is the one truth many scientists now say they cannot deny.

*Acts 17:28 **For in him** we live, and move, and have our being; as certain also of your own poets have said, For we are also his offspring.*

In conclusion: Matter is both thought/energy and physical substance. The universe is, at some level, pure potential. How you think this fact affects what is created in the invisible realm until it is manifested in the physical realm?

No wonder I can still hear that song from Walt Disney: "When you wish upon a star, makes no difference who you are. *Anything* your heart desires will come to you."

Look around you now. You are living in past thought that has become present, material reality. Start shaping your new reality now!

*Mark 11:24 Therefore I say unto you, What things **soever ye desire,** when ye pray, **believe** that ye receive them, and ye shall have them.*

*Matthew 7:7 Ask, and it shall be given you; seek, and ye shall find; knock, and **it shall** be opened unto you:*

*Matthew 21:22 And all things, **whatsoever** ye shall ask in prayer, believing, **ye shall receive.***

*John 14:13 And **whatsoever ye shall** ask in my name, that will I do, that the Father may be glorified in the Son.*

*John 14:14 If ye shall **ask any thing in my name,** I will do it.*

*John 15:7 If ye abide in me, and my words abide in you, ye **shall ask what ye will,** and it shall be done unto you.*

Because you reap what you sow and because whatever comes out of you—thoughts, words, actions and behavior—comes back to you, multiplied, in a sense everything you do is a prayer. Since you act based on some internal belief, whether that belief is right or wrong, you exercise faith. We are created to use faith. We cannot *not* use faith. You act based on what you believe.

Do you believe God? Do you believe his Word? Do you believe His promises? If not, you will believe something else. Nevertheless, whatever comes out of you comes back to you. That is why faith, belief and trust and the Word of God are so important in your prayers, because whatever goes out from you comes back.

Now you know why it is so important to conquer your mind with the Word of God. Your mind, your faith and your words create your reality in the universe.

*Hebrews 11:1 Now faith **is the substance** of things hoped for, the evidence of things not seen.*

What is the substance? If faith is the substance, then what is that substance? What can look into the future? What can you use to hope for in the future? Hope means to believe in something that has not happened yet, so your hope is for something in the future. What is the only thing that can go into the future and create something that cannot yet be seen? Well, I believe that it is thought. Yes, thought. Our thoughts are energy that can affect the invisible creative realm of subatomic particles and, when we believe, our belief begins the process of making our hope a reality. Remember: everything around you was once a thought before it became physical reality. Even before there was anything, God spoke and the invisible became reality! He has given us this same power to create. Use it wisely and have faith in God. Without believing God, it is impossible to please Him.

*Hebrews 11:6 But without **faith** it is impossible to please him: for he that cometh to God **must believe** that he is, and that **he is a rewarder of them** that diligently seek him.*

Faith can affect these particles of energy traveling at incredible speed, along with other particles that have subatomic particles called quarks. (That is my belief, based on prayer and study.) Gases, liquids and solids are all made up of microscopic particles, but the behaviors of these particles differ, depending on the state they are in. Particles in a gaseous form will vibrate and move more freely at higher speeds than they would in a liquid or solid state. Liquids vibrate and move about freely but not as freely as they would as a gas. The particles still have the ability to slide past each other and change position. Solids still vibrate but do not move from place to place unless heat or some other property is introduced to start a reaction.

The whole universe is alive with energy vibrations on many levels. This energy comes in many forms: light, chemical, heat, electric, atomic and sound. Some forms of energy can be seen and other forms are invisible to the human eye. You cannot see the wind but you can feel it and see what it does. We, as spirits living inside these human forms, are at the smallest level of our existence, living vibrations and energy. That, in my opinion, is who and what we actually are in the universe. You are words, vibrations and emotional energy. That is a powerful combination when focused in the right direction.

Einstein's laws of thermodynamics are the laws that other laws in the universe depend on. According to Einstein, there is a balance or symmetry in the universe. That proportion or balance never changes. His laws say that there is conservation or saving of energy. That saving or conservation happens because all processes, no matter what they are, involve the transformation of energy. Matter is a form of energy. If you boil water, it changes to steam. If you freeze water, it becomes ice. If you burn wood, it becomes several gases and gives off light and heat. I hope this is enough information to help you to understand this crucial point.

Energy can be changed from one form to another! Thoughts can be changed! Negative thoughts and vibrations can be changed into positive thoughts and vibrations. It is all just energy. Pain is energy. With my mind, I can create a positive metaphor for pain. I can choose to use the energy of pain to read and study or anything else I need to do to create a positive outcome. I can use pain. I can use my pain as energy, chemical reactions, thoughts, actions and behaviors and, ultimately, my consequences. That is the law of the universe: everything changes. I can use my past pain to change my present and future.

Let us learn to dance the transforming dance of the universe, the dance of energy. No matter what I have done in the past that has produced bad thoughts and feelings, I can use that as energy. Use the Word of God for positive purposes through the transforming power of the mind. If I can use the negative thoughts and energy inside me for positive action, what can possibly stop me? Now I can understand the following scripture with a clarity not seen before. I hope you can understand it, too.

*Romans 8:28 And we know that **all things work together for good to them that love God,** to them who are the called according to his purpose.*

Thoughts create feelings. Do you want to change your feelings? Remember: emotions are just energy in motion. The feelings they generate can be used to our advantage when we learn to use the energy of a negative memory. By assigning a different metaphor or word to that energy you can learn to act positively in the present.

Daily, you must learn to transform the negative energy of bad memories in your past into powerful forces for the present and future in the imagination. When you visualize future possibilities all things become possible and work for you. This process takes practice on a daily basis and an awareness of what is necessary to turn negative energy or thoughts into positive energy and a positive force. There will be more about this transformation process when we explore the use of positive affirmations.

The negative things we have done produce pain and we must fearlessly look at that pain. However, the same negative energy and pain that had us under its control can be used to cause you to go to the library, make new plans to go to school or to pursue any other worthwhile endeavor.

Let's face it: the greater the pain, the bigger the supply of energy that is at your disposal for positive use in the areas of "visualization" and imagination. We cannot change the past but we can use the energy and examples of the past to energize the present with positive action.

Remember: at some level, thoughts, memories and feelings are just energy and energy is fuel. What words and metaphors are you going to attach to the energy in your life so you can use energy to promote positive action?

If you can imagine it, you can achieve it; if you can dream it, you can become it.
William Arthur Ward

Courage is not the absence of fear, but rather the judgment that something else is more important than fear.
Ambrose Redmoon

You gain strength, courage, and confidence by every experience in which you really stop to look fear in the face. You must do the thing which you think you cannot do.
Eleanor Roosevelt

All serious daring starts from within.
Harriet Beecher Stowe

If you lose hope, somehow you lose the vitality that keeps life moving, you lose that courage to be, that quality that helps you go on in spite of it all. And so today I still have a dream.
Martin Luther King, Jr.

One isn't necessarily born with courage, but one is born with potential. Without courage, we cannot practice any other virtue with consistency. We can't be kind, true, merciful, generous, or honest.
Maya Angelou

Obstacles are those things you see when you take your eyes off the goal.
Hannah More

Chapter 7

A Short History of Mind/Matter

History informs us just how far we have come in the understanding of this wonderful and complex physical body that connects us to physical reality and realms of understanding that we are only now becoming aware of.

The ancient Greeks were divided as to the respective roles of the heart and the brain. Some philosophers, such as Homer and Aristotle, believed that the heart was the center in which intelligence resided. This idea persisted for many years—even into the seventeenth century.

Descartes felt that the flow of blood from the heart to the brain served the purpose of producing "animal spirits" that animated the body. Descartes proposed two categories: *mind* and *matter*. The matter category related to the physical brain, the mind category to thinking.

These philosophers and scientists thus distinguished the physical operation of the brain from the thought process. While the physical part was thought to be useful for scientific study, consciousness was excluded from the scientific worldview.

It is only recently that researchers have begun to challenge this mind/matter split with evidence that many human qualities traditionally associated with the mind/brain, such as personality, are, at least in part, determined by biochemistry.

Galileo, in 1623, put forward the view that science should be concerned only with the primary qualities, those of the external world that could be measured or weighed. So-called secondary qualities, such as love, beauty, meaning and value, were said to lie outside the realm of science.

A major motivation for the study of the physical workings of the brain came in 1791, when it was *shown* that electricity existed as a force within the body—in fact, this electricity was found inside the brain cells. It was shown in a sequence of experiments that it was possible to control the motor nerves of frogs using electrical currents. In 1850, the discovery was made that neurons emit pulses of electricity that travel at around 200 mph.

In 1870, the observation was made that there were literally billions of neurons in the central nervous system. It was also established that the neurons in the brain send information to the motor nerves and that the sensory nerves send information to the brain for analysis.

In the early 1900s, it was found that the electrical pulses within the neurons cause chemicals to be released. It was also discovered that messages are sent to other neurons, using the connections between them, and that takes one-thousandth of a second for the neuron to recharge after this firing process has taken place.

Subjectivity is the area of the mind that we generally call experiences, and they have a subjective nature. This means that they have certain characteristics we become aware of when we reflect. For instance, there is a particular sensation when we feel pain, or have an itch or see something orange. These characteristics are considered to be subjective because they are accessible only to the subject of the experience, the person who has the experience, but not to others. Sometimes, we project this inner experience onto others, believing that what we feel is what they feel.

Subjective thinking and perception are both internal processes and proceed from within a person's mind, often unaffected by the external world. Subjective thinking is a introspective point of view, based on and existing only in the mind. It is part of the illusory world existing only within the mind of the person having the experience.

Psychology is the emotional makeup and behavioral characteristics of an individual, a group or a group activity such as the psychology of war. It is also a science that deals with the mental processes and behavior. For example, we may possibly use our mental, emotional and behavioral characteristics to influence others through argument or subtle manipulation, thereby using psychology to sway others' opinions or behaviors.

Psychological and mental defenses of the human ego are universal features of the human mind. These features operate on a conscious and subconscious level to protect the human ego from painful experiences, words and events.

The psychology of the addicted person is hidden behind the concrete wall of denial. If you are addicted, you tend to deny the addiction and deny what is at the root of the addiction. This denial keeps you in a severe disruption of reality. It keeps you locked in a reality that you yourself create because you want to keep using and feeding the cravings of your brain/body.

You set up defenses to block any corrective influences such as logic, positive information or the opinions of others. Denial is not lying or dishonesty. The addicted person's viewpoint is built on a foundation of a misconceived and unshakable private version of reality that is totally shut off from any positive outside influence.

Our personal dysfunctional psychology causes us to keep hearing our own messages, based on our past experience, and that keeps us from growing emotionally. The ingrained messages in our personal psychology dictate what to believe and what life should be like. Our personal psychology is founded on attitudes, opinions and values we hold onto that are out of touch with the reality of the normal world around us. We hold onto scripts of negative, habitual responses especially when we are faced with stressful events or situations, generally surrounding our drug use. These thoughts, ideas, feelings, emotions, beliefs, ways of thinking, negative attitudes, prejudicial ways of seeing things and other values we may have been raised with or acquired earlier in our lives keep us acting in self-defeating ways. We have become so accustomed to using these habitual responses when facing any problems that we use them even when they are not productive, problem-solving responses.

These self-defeating ways of thinking, acting and speaking may on the surface seem ok, but in reality they result in negative consequences. Habitual ways of thinking must be examined so that we can determine for ourselves that these habitual ways of responding to the pressures of life are ineffectual.

If you apply yourself to introspection, this harmful psychology of painful addictive behaviors will cause you to look at the pack of lies that surrounds you, the complete distortions of reality and the almost psychotic denial to fend off any corrective cognitive and behavioral attempts directed at you. You, the addict, have previously existed for one purpose only: to carry out the desires and demands of the brain/body addiction.

Every normal human resistance to this process of recovery has been suppressed, overridden or pushed aside by this uncontrollable desire to continue using. But, if you apply yourself, and despite having an elaborate and often a very sophisticated array of mystifying and obscuring defenses set in place, you will finally discover the truth. The final result of denial is jails, institutions and death.

The human psyche functions as the center of thought, emotion, and behavior and, consciously or unconsciously, adjusts or mediates the body's responses to the social and physical environment. In essence, for lack of a more proper metaphor, the human psyche sometimes has been called spirit or soul.

The meaning of the Greek word *psyche* suggests a totality of inner experience. There are similar words in other cultures, such as the Chinese *Chi*, referring to inner power, and the Egyptian *Ka*, speaking of a person's energy force or eternal inner being. All these words are metaphors (symbols representing something else), in this case the invisible "I" in each of us represented by force and power with multiple gifts and talents. Therefore, perhaps *psyche* owes its significance to our subjective (inner) sense that we are in possession of an invisible force. We cannot directly apprehend the *psyche* in others the way we appreciate it in ourselves, not even by using our five senses.

William James, an American philosopher and psychologist, introduced psychology to the United States in the late nineteenth century. James used the word "consciousness" instead of "psyche." All of the terms I have discussed represent small insights into our invisible force.

Perception in psychology is the recognition and interpretation of sensory stimuli, including feelings based chiefly on memory. Also, we need to understand the neurological processes by which the recognition and interpretation of these memories and feelings affect our overall understanding of reality. Perception is insight, intuition or knowledge gained by observing. The capacity for such insight is based on memory and past experiences. It is clearly our perceptions as individuals that allow us to have our own particular view of reality.

The word "psychology" is the combination of two terms - study (ology) and soul (psyche) or mind. Thus, cognitive psychology is the psychological science that studies cognition (thinking) the mental processes that underlie behavior, including thinking, deciding, reasoning and, to some extent, motivation and emotion. This covers a broad range of research domains, examining questions about the workings of memory, attention, perception, knowledge representation, reasoning, creativity and problem solving.

Ego

Ego is what we use to falsely protect our negative self. We *E*ase *G*od *O*ut: EGO

The ego is a self-justifying historian which seeks only that information that agrees with it, rewrites history when it needs to, and does not even see the evidence that threatens it.
Anthony G. Greenwald

I count him braver who overcomes his desires than him who conquers his enemies; for the hardest victory is the victory over self.
Aristotle

It is not the mountains that we conquer, but ourselves.
Sir Edmund Hillary

Your vision will become clear only when you look into your heart. Who looks outside, dreams. Who looks inside, awakens.
Carl Jung

Chapter 8

The Mind/Brain and Deeper Levels

The Modern Brain

Before you begin this chapter, remember that, while these terms may seem difficult to understand, it is important that you be aware of these marvelous things happening inside you. And, even when you do not physically feel or see change, change is happening.

Now let us consider the brain, which is probably the most complex structure in the known universe; complex enough to coordinate the fingers of a skilled surgeon or those of an artist who can create a three-dimensional landscape from light that falls on a two-dimensional retina, demonstrating the holographic capacity of the mind.

As you read about the brain, remember that most of the discoveries about the brain and how it functions have been made in the last few years. These recent discoveries have paved the way for modern neuroscience, which in recent years has yielded enormous amounts of information about the physical functions of the brain.

The brain functions by means of a complex set of nerve cells that act like connecting circuits. Communication between neurons is both electrical and chemical and always travels from the dendrites of a neuron, through its soma (the cell body) and out its axon to the dendrites of another neuron.

Dendrites of one neuron receive signals from the axons of other neurons through various chemicals known as neurotransmitters. The neurotransmitters set off electrical charges in the dendrites, which then carry the signal electrochemically to the soma. The soma integrates the information, which is then transmitted electrochemically down the axon to its tip.

One neuron may communicate with thousands of other neurons, and many thousands of neurons are involved with even the simplest behavior. It is believed that these connections and their efficiency can be modified by experience.

There are three major classes of neurons. The *sensory* neurons run from the various types of stimulus receptors, such as touch, smell, taste, sound and vision, to the spinal cord.

The next major class of neuron is called *interneurons*. These are found exclusively within the spinal cord and brain. They are stimulated by signals reaching them from the sensory neurons, other interneurons or sometimes both.

Interneurons are also called *association neurons* because of the interaction between the neuron carrying the information from the senses. It is estimated that the human brain contains 100 billion (10^{11}) interneurons, averaging 1000 synapses on each; that is, some 10^{14} connections. This represents a tremendous amount of energy and power that can be channeled along positive and logical lines of thinking.

The interneuron contains a great diversity of structural and functional types of cells. In fact, it is not known how many different kinds of interneurons are present in the human brain.

The last class of neuron is called *motor neurons*. These transmit impulses from the central nervous system to the muscles and glands of the body that carry out the responses.

The word neurology means the logical study of neurons and their pathways that carry information around the body through the brain and spinal cord. It is my contention that our neurons can be charged positively or negatively by our thinking.

It is important that you realize that, with focus, the electrical energy passing through the brain can be increased many times. Just think of the potential involved in this process of moving from one thought with limited power to many powerful thoughts, moving and drawing other thoughts like themselves into a powerful torrent of positive energy.

In many ways, neurons act like minicomputers. They can receive messages, process those messages, increase or decrease the intensity of the messages and send out the results as new messages to other cells. These messages, which consist of chemicals, interact with the outer surface of cell membranes. This chemical interaction with the cell membrane causes chemicals within the receiving neuron to be released so the message can be altered. I submit to you that passion and inspiration are the keys to increasing the power of the messages in your brain for positive change.

Why is this important information? Because when you are in recovery, especially in the beginning, you do not necessarily "feel" any changes. The pleasure/pain center perhaps has been damaged to the point where you cannot *feel* an overall sense of accomplishment by doing what is right. Having this information allows you to know that change is taking place inside your brain, and a powerful change it is.

Drugs can damage your intellectual ability and capacity by blocking nerve impulses, thus preventing neuron transmissions from getting where they are supposed to go, or by producing too many or too few in neuron transmissions. As a result, neurons may be either over stimulated or not stimulated at all, crippling the nervous system's ability to carry out its normal functions. Drugs can damage the complicated circuitry of nerve pathways in your mind and body.

Treatment for addiction to drugs stops this negative, destructive cycle through abstinence. Your body and brain are made up of a network of very intricately designed nerves and neural pathways that allow you to reason, imagine, compute, remember and dream. That is truly incredible and it is not something to be taken lightly. So, why continue to injure yourself? Stop damaging your brain and get help now. Reading this book can be the beginning of a new life but always remember you need a brain to recover.

One of the most important functions of our brain is the creation and recall of memories. It is difficult to imagine how we could function without both short and long-term memory. The absence of short-term memory would render most tasks extremely difficult if not impossible—life would be chaotic, punctuated by a series of one-time images with no logical connection between them. Equally, the absence of any long-term memory would ensure that we could not learn from past experience. Indeed, much of our impression of self depends on remembering our past history.

Our memories function in what is called an associative or content-addressable fashion. That is, a memory does not exist in some isolated fashion, located in a particular set of neurons. All memories are in some sense strings of memories. You remember people in a variety of ways—by the color of their hair or eyes, the shape of their nose, their height, the sound of their voice or perhaps by the smell of a favorite perfume. Thus, memories are stored in *association* with one another. These different sensory units reside in completely separate parts of the brain, so it is clear that the memory of the person must be distributed throughout the brain in some fashion.

Notice also that it is possible to access the full memory (all aspects of the person's description for example) by initially remembering just one or two of that person's characteristic features. We access the memory by its contents—not by where it is stored in the neural pathways of the brain. This is very powerful; given that, even from a poor photograph of that person, we are quite good at accurately reconstructing the person's face. This is very different from a traditional computer, where specific facts are located in specific places in the computer's memory. If only partial information is available about this location, the memory (a person's face) cannot be recalled at all.

The brain is a powerful tool that you can use for positive change. Never underestimate the power of a focused mind. Remember: every moment that the brain is working, it is using energy and thoughts. Tap into this powerful flow of energy and begin to carefully reshape your thinking, actions and the consequences of your behavior.

New research has led scientists to entertain the idea that the quality of the brain that distinguishes it from any modern computer is its adaptability. In other words, the brain is a computer that learns.

The brain is much more flexible and dynamic than first believed. Although it was once thought that the brain was in a "fixed" position by age 2 or 3, it has been demonstrated through our ability to trace the electrical activity in the brain that it remodels itself constantly in response to experience, aging, hormones, illness, injury, learning and countless signals from the world. Growth is a newfound feature of the brain.

Research has come across striking evidence of neural flexibility. CAT (stands for Computerized Axial Tomography) scans of the brain show that parts of the brain normally used for special tasks can be re-routed to perform other tasks in place of other damaged areas of the brain. This new view has come partly from the advances in neuron-imaging techniques that allow scientists to see inside the living brain and map its shifting territories. Images from the processes of positron emission topography (PET) and functional magnetic resonance imaging (MRI) enable scientists to track changes in the brain even as they occur. It is important for you to know that brain plasticity is a reality and that you can build new neural passageways.

The activated areas of the brain light up during these scans, revealing increased blood flow and electrical energy. This evidence has led to the belief that how you use your brain determines how your brain is organized.

The human brain has up to 100 billion nerve cells or neurons, of which about 10 billion are in the neocortex, the outer layer of gray matter responsible for all forms of conscious experience. Altogether, there are 148,000 neurons beneath a square millimeter of cortical surface, roughly a hundred million per square inch. These neurons are often organized into little minicolumns of about 100 neurons per column. Those, in turn, are sometimes organized into macrocolumns of perhaps 300 minicolumns, each containing 30,000 neurons. Brainpower comes from these cells' connections. The synapses are where messages, in the form of electrical pulses, leap across gaps to help the brain make sense of the world. Each neuron can form thousands of links, giving a typical brain 100 trillion synapses.

Neurons are the fundamental elements of the central nervous system. The central nervous system is made up of about 100 billion neurons (10 to the power 11, as stated before, to demonstrate and highlight the tremendous potential you have). Neurons are similar to other cells in the body in their general organization and their biochemical systems. However, they also possess unique features, which are crucial to the functioning of the central nervous system. In essence, a given neuron may both receive and send signals to neighboring neurons in the form of electrical pulses, reinforced with use, forming intricate circuits of knowledge and memory. The more cells get together and fire together, the greater the power and potential outcome of these connections. The more connections in an active adult brain, the more numerous, complex and sophisticated it becomes, thus demonstrating that the human gets smarter as the brain becomes more complex in its neural wiring.

The evidence of the brain's built-in adaptability and flexibility helps us understand that the brain will respond to new demands and will "grow."

When the brain tries to make up for an injury to one part of itself by shifting the operations of the damaged area to an unaffected area, the potential compensation gained sometimes comes at a cost. This action causes, for lack of better terms, a kind of neurological traffic jam.

As we age and remain mentally active, the connections between nerve cells become more numerous and far-reaching. The intertwining of neurons becomes more intricate and they become wider. You could compare this process to widening a country road into a multi-lane highway. This is perhaps what keeps some older people reinventing themselves throughout long, productive lives.

The increase in connections between nerve cells as we age gives the mind of an adult more reach and richness, thus a larger view of the world. So as you age you may lose some of the details but you get a bigger picture. Perhaps this is the brain's physical representation of the intangible quality of what we call wisdom. Why is it necessary to discuss the physical brain in such detail? *So you can know beyond a shadow of a doubt that you can continue to teach your brain new things throughout your lifetime.*

*Psalms 92:12 The righteous shall flourish like the palm tree: he shall **grow** like a cedar in Lebanon.*

*Ecclesiastes 11:5 As thou knowest not what is the way of the spirit, nor how the bones do **grow** in the womb of her that is with child: even so thou knowest not the works of God who maketh all.*

Our cerebral cortex is continually assaulted by information coming from our eyes, ears, nose and other sensory organs. Out of this flow of information, the amygdala has the ability to turbocharge the frightening or other highly emotional stimuli, thus bypassing other, less important information.

For example, if you are watching television and your child is about to put a paperclip into the electrical outlet, your attention is diverted and impulses are sent to your voice box and feet, if necessary, in order to respond to the immediate danger. If the situation is more urgent, the brain sends information to your feet and necessary muscles involved in your getting to your child quickly, bypassing the cortex altogether. In other words, you move before the information reaches the cortical regions that make you conscious of your physical actions. Those milliseconds that give you a head start on your reaction time may mean the difference between life and death. So, the more urgent the need, the more quickly the brain responds.

How urgent is it for you to change? How badly do you want this recovery? Is your freedom important? Then make it an urgent priority each and every day until you have burned in new neural pathways, creating powerful new habit forces.

Much of the lower and midbrain areas are relatively simple systems, which are capable of registering experiences and regulating behavior largely outside of any conscious awareness. We don't have to think to remember to breathe! In a sense, the human brain is like an archeological site with the outer layer composed of the most recent brain structure, and the deeper layers consisting of older, more primitive structures.

Changing the configuration of various neuron-transmitter chemicals can increase or decrease the amount of stimulation that the firing axon imparts to the neighboring dendrite. Altering the neurotransmitters can also change whether the stimulation is excitatory or inhibitory.

Because addictions produce a life that is sometimes based on feelings and emotions and responses to them, it is important to understand that change is taking place despite possible feelings to the contrary. You need to face the fact that sometimes you must walk through the pain, knowing by faith that God will prepare a table of rejoicing in the presence of all your enemies of bad habits, choices and consequences. Pain may last for a while but joy is coming.

Psalms 30:5...weeping may endure for a night, but ***joy*** cometh in the morning.

Psalms 23:4 Yea, though I walk through the valley of the **shadow of death,** *I will fear no evil: for thou art with me; thy rod and thy staff they comfort me.*

5 Thou preparest a table before me **in the presence of mine enemies:** *thou anointest my head with oil; my cup runneth over.*

Isaiah 61:1 The Spirit of the Lord GOD is upon me; because the LORD hath anointed me to preach good tidings unto the meek; he hath sent me to **bind up the brokenhearted,** *to*

*proclaim **liberty** to the captives, and **the opening of the
prison to them that are bound**...*

*Isaiah 61:3 To appoint unto them that mourn in Zion, to give
unto them **beauty for ashes**, the oil of **joy for mourning**, **the
garment of praise** for **the spirit of heaviness**; that they might
be called trees of righteousness, the planting of the LORD,
that he might be glorified.*

*The greatest revolution of our generation is the discovery
that human beings, by changing the inner attitudes of their
minds, can change the outer aspects of their lives.*
William James

*To change your life: start immediately; do it flamboyantly;
no exceptions.*
William James

*I have learned over the years that when one's mind is made
up, this diminishes fear.*
Rosa Parks

Have a vision. Be demanding.
Colin Powell

*Proverbs 139:14 "I will praise thee; for I am fearfully and
wonderfully made: marvellous are thy works; and that my
soul knoweth right well."*

Chapter 9

Screaming and Praise

Why do we scream? Because it hurts? No, not exactly. We scream because we are receiving pain signals from our neural connections. This is the brain's way of trying to divert attention to some other area. In other words, it is the brain's automatic way of trying to ease the signals of pain. If you are sedated and your foot was on fire you would not feel the pain. Signals would be sent to your brain but your "asleep" brain would not be able to interpret the signals so you would not feel any pain.

This is one of the reasons that getting motivated and passionate is so important. This is why stating what you will do with force and power is so important. You override normal signals of defeat and, with passion, excitement and enthusiasm, change the negative signals into positive signals. This is why praise is so important. Some people do not think so, but God made us and God always knew that praises override other negative signals resulting from pain, depression and sin. That is why some people who are really hurting scream, moan, cry and cry out before God. While some of the more sophisticated, elite thinkers do not believe praise is appropriate in the church setting, God thinks it's really important and the Bible is filled with scripture about praise. I am not saying that you are required to shout and cry out loud, but the Bible is and God is saying:

Psalms 22:22 I will declare thy name unto my brethren: **in the midst of the congregation will I praise thee.**

*Psalms 33:1 Rejoice in the LORD, O ye righteous: for **praise is comely for the upright***.

*Psalms 147:1 Praise ye the LORD: for it is good to sing praises unto our God; for it is pleasant; and **praise is comely***.

The word **comely** in Hebrew is <na'veh>. This means that it is suitable, beautiful and seemly. Seemly, to follow up and give additional definition and meaning to the word comely so there is no doubt, means appropriate, fitting, decent, proper, becoming and right.

I know that, for some, praise in a church setting is difficult but you can be at home, in your car or anywhere you feel comfortable and let your praise go and give God the glory due His name. Sometimes, it's a sacrifice because of how you feel. The whole point is to praise your way into feeling differently!

*Hebrews 13:15 By him therefore let us offer **the sacrifice of praise to God continually**, that is, **the fruit of our lips** giving thanks to his name.*

*Jeremiah 33:11 The **voice of joy**, and the **voice of gladness**, the voice of the bridegroom, and the voice of the bride, the voice of them that shall say, **Praise the LORD of hosts**: for the LORD is good; for his mercy endureth for ever: and of them that shall bring the **sacrifice of praise** into the house of the LORD. For I will cause to return the captivity of the land, as at the first, saith the LORD.*

Solomon appointed Levites to **praise** and minister under the oversight of the priests. That was their job in: to praise God.

*2 Chronicles 8:14 And he appointed, according to the order of David his father, the courses of the priests to their service, **and the Levites to their charges, to praise and minister***

before the priests, *as the duty of every day required: the porters also by their courses at every gate: for so had David the man of God commanded.*

Chapter 10

The Subconscious Mind

The subconscious mind is where mental activity also occurs and it is another striking characteristic of comprehensive thought power. How this energy of thought is used is uniquely different from wakeful conscious thinking.

Among other things, use of the subconscious frees our present, individual thought patterns from the mental demands of our routine activities. Thus, we regularly do things without the intervention of words or commands or even our conscious attention. When we put on a coat, for example, we don't talk to ourselves about it—even silently. Indeed, we may not even think about it. Our conscious thoughts may be devoted entirely to our plans for the day or evening. Our ability to transfer tasks, such as putting on a coat, to the control of the subconscious permits our wakeful, thinking consciousness to work on other things.

The subconscious mind takes in everything we learn in our entire lifetime. It begins at birth (the Bible says before birth), soaking up information like a sponge, accumulating data as we grow and experience life. In some ways, this is another area that is like God, who does not sleep. Our subconscious is always aware.

*Psalms 121:4 Behold, he that keepeth Israel shall **neither slumber nor sleep.***

The subconscious mind along with the autonomic system of the brain repairs the body and maintains working organs, keeping them in good condition. It circulates your blood, regulates your heartbeat and blood pressure. It also operates your lungs and breathing, even while you are asleep, without your conscious awareness.

The subconscious controls the hearing, seeing and feeling centers in your brain, including the control of the entire glandular system of your body, and regulates the amount of secretion that each gland releases into your bloodstream These are just a few of the automatic functions of your subconscious mind. All these things and many more do not require any help from you, nor do you have to pay conscious attention to such details. The subconscious also begins forming beliefs, based on what we learn and what we experience, that determine how we react to everything in our life. The older we become, the more strength and momentum these beliefs gain.

The subconscious mind does not make moral or ethical choices; it accepts everything, good and bad, positive and negative. The conscious mind, however, does make choices, almost every minute of our lives. The amazing thing about your subconscious mind is that, despite its power, which is really superior to the conscious mind, it will take orders from your conscious mind. Since everything has its equal and opposite such as day and night, love and hate, abundance and lack, our lives are a matter of choice, *our conscious choice*. All these habitual conscious choices are made with the information we have amassed in our subconscious mind over our lifetimes.

Conscious Mind

1. Is sometimes inactive (sleep)
2. Organizes
3. Discriminates (choices moral ethical)
4. Has an active memory
5. Makes logical decisions
6. Is able to exercise critical thinking
7. Deals with concepts
8. Tries to control emotions
9. Avoids silence and reflection
10. Can be made comfortable with negatives
11. Understands time—past, present & future
12. Maintains illusion of control
13. Maintains illusion of separateness
14. Is generally in control and, when active, closes down the subconscious

Subconscious Mind

1. Is active from before we were born (I believe)
2. Governs instincts and habit force
3. Shows uncritical acceptance and literal interpretation
4. Stores long-term and forgotten memories
5. Bases its preferences on emotions
6. Believes everything it is told, good or evil
7. Deals primarily in images
8. Is the seat of emotions

9. Creates internal psychological responses

10. Does not differentiate between positive or negative

11. Sees everything in the present

12. Is more powerful than the conscious mind but stays in the background

13. Is the gateway to the power of the higher self

14. Records what is important and what is not important

15. Develops insights during restful hours, relaxation and sometimes upon awakening

Remove negative ideas and thoughts as soon as you identify them in your thought process. The way we think becomes a pattern and a matter of habit. Negative thinking will grow and multiply if not dealt with quickly and swiftly. Be responsible and take charge of yourself. Remember: the subconscious is a power for you to use. Also, be very aware that, when you begin to push yourself towards your goal, there will be resistance. The subconscious is there for the sole purpose of growth and is designed to serve you and strengthen you with positive power. Without resistance, you cannot grow subconsciously. Resistance requires positive power to change the subconscious.

The subconscious is more powerful than the conscious, aware mind because the beliefs of the subconscious are always in the present.

The conscious mind maintains the illusion of control and our ego (who we think we are) keeps us separated from the truths that exist in the subconscious, namely, that the subconscious is the more powerful of the two.

In order to reprogram your subconscious mind, your most frequent prevailing positive thoughts need to take authority over other, negative thoughts.

With enough repetition, positive affirmations are eventually absorbed and accepted into and by our subconscious mind, which is where we want them to be. Knowing this gives you the ability to influence your subconscious mind by suggesting anything you desire and, when you do this persistently and with passion, you will eventually see your positive thoughts manifesting themselves in your life.

Sometimes, positive affirmations might seem like lies but they are really just a set of projections and instructions for future reality, as we desire it. But those instructions are a lie *only* to our conscious mind. Our subconscious is perfectly willing to accept them as truth. Statements spoken to you like "I can be different," "I can change" and "I am becoming a capable person," are powerful. The list can be endless.

For example:

- I am an intelligent person and I can improve and become more intelligent.

- I am a worthwhile person and I can and I will begin to act that way.

- Today, I can dare to take a positive risk and know that I am entitled to receive good things in my life as I give good things to others.

- I have the choice to be happy despite what is happening around me because happiness is a state of mind and I can practice every day to remain happy despite outer negative circumstances.

- I have the privilege to ask for what is right and proper and expect to get it because I am doing what is right and proper for others and for me.

- I am an unlimited being and I am growing every day and from now on I choose to grow in the right direction.

If you begin to act and think like a successful person you will begin to speak as though you are already successful. Adapt a successful attitude. Even before success has come to you, begin to act as though you have already achieved your goal, living your dream of success. Our subconscious mind does not know the difference between reality and fantasy. You can prove this to yourself by thinking about how you react at movies. If a movie is sad, we cry; if it's funny, we laugh. There is a part of us that knows that it is only a movie, yet we react as if it's real. Our subconscious mind will accept anything presented to it as real. The impressions that are now coming alive within you reach a point where those who might be in a position to help you will notice your new inner and outer radiance. You can now see how this will impress people you come in contact with who might be able to aid you in the fulfillment of your dream.

Affirmations actually become real after they are accepted by our subconscious mind and—make no mistake—many repetitions are necessary to accomplish this. How many repetitions? Thousands upon thousands, and there's a reason for this. To understand why, we must understand how our subconscious mind is reprogrammed, one thought at a time. Talk to yourself using power-producing words. Discuss your future, not your past. Think and talk about your victories, not your defeats. Never say anything that you do not want someone to believe about you. Remember: words create pictures in your mind on a continuous basis. Those are the pictures that ultimately decide what you believe. What you look at the longest in your mind will determine what will affect you the most in the long run.

Say to yourself, "I am successful and I am happy," despite what you may feel. Tell yourself "I will attract all the right conditions into my life thus giving me a sense of power. I will take advantage of every situation that comes my way in my day-to-day experience that will bring me the happiness, success and the peace of mind that I deserve." Sooner than you think, you will have built such a reserve of positive conscious and subconscious conditions that your positive attitude will become a habit, like a reflex. The conditions you once just thought about will become a living reality.

The average person talks to him/herself in a negative way. As much as 94 percent of your inner dialogue tends to be about the things you fear, your worries, the people you're angry with, your problems and your concerns. If you want to be successful in life, you have to consciously keep your words and your inner dialogue consistent with what you wish to accomplish.

The simple conclusion is that, if you are dissatisfied with anything in your life, you must do something that will work at altering or changing those beliefs in your subconscious mind...because the quality of your life is directly related to the quality of your thinking.

Nothing will happen to change your life until you consciously and with great, continued effort, step in and start to work with the subconscious mind. If you are not aware of or not exercising *The Revelation of Power,* you will continue in the same pattern of growth without being in control of yourself. It is not what happens to you but what you *do* with what happens to you.

We all have dreams. But in order to make dreams into reality, it takes an awful lot of determination, dedication, self-discipline, and effort.
Jesse Owens

Science and research indicate that the subconscious mind has always been active from the day we were born. The Bible declares that we are known and chosen by God even before we leave the womb.

*Jeremiah 1:5 **Before** I formed thee in the belly **I knew thee**; and **before** thou camest forth out of **the womb** I sanctified thee, and I ordained thee a prophet unto the nations.*

The subconscious, I believe, carries within it instincts and habits that, over time, become what I refer to as habit force. The subconscious mind is uncritically accepting of whatever information it is given, positive or negative. It takes any information given it and awaits its retrieval. The subconscious, in my opinion, is one of the areas where the power of faith or belief rules.

The power that helps break records and accomplishes the seemingly impossible is located in the subconscious part of man. The subconscious is more powerful than the conscious, aware mind; in its beliefs about reality, everything is in the present. By contrast, the conscious mind can sometimes be inactive or asleep.

The subconscious mind can change. It is changing and evolving all the time.

You are the only person who can change, who can eventually master the changes you need to make and sustain them long enough to completely change your life. The predominant thoughts you have learned over time, harbored within the subconscious mind, have superior influence on what you do. In essence, we are talking about the mastery of your self through the use of the subconscious mind.

In order to reprogram your subconscious mind, you must let your positive thoughts take authority over your negative thoughts. It takes daily practice to develop this skill. Practice makes one better, not perfect, although we strive for perfection. Affirmations are simply positive thoughts or ideas that we want to manifest in our lives. By repeating positive affirmations over and over again, verbally and in our minds, we observe that they gradually begin to take effect in our lives. The things you say, the things you do, what you read, write and think most frequently are imprinted on the subconscious mind and the more repetitions you can use the better. It is not so much the volume of words as the repeated use over time that creates a superior quality of change. For added effect, you can also keep a running list of handwritten affirmations that you can review several hundred times per day. Affirmations are put into action by our conscious mind; that is, it is our conscious mind that decides to use affirmations as a way of changing our thinking and our lives. With enough repetition, positive affirmations are eventually absorbed and accepted by our subconscious mind, which is where we want them to be.

Knowing this revelation of power gives you the ability to influence your subconscious mind by suggesting anything you desire and, if you do this persistently and with passion, eventually you will see your positive thinking become a reality in your life, springing forth from the invisible into the visible.

*Mark 11:24 Therefore I say unto you, What things soever ye desire, when ye pray, **believe** that ye receive them, and ye shall have them.*

Philippians 1:6 Being confident of this very thing, that he which hath begun a good work in you will perform it until the day of Jesus Christ:

You can be creative with your list of positive statements because you can create anything you want in your mind, we have done this before but today you can make a choice to grow in the right direction. I can and will become the master of my being and an active co-creator of my life along with God and those who will become my teachers.

John 14:26 But the Comforter, which is the Holy Ghost, whom the Father will send in my name, he shall teach you all things, and bring all things to your remembrance, whatsoever I have said unto you.

Romans 8:37 Nay, in all these things we are more than conquerors through him that loved us

Here's one way to visualize how your subconscious mind is reprogrammed: imagine a clear pond of water, with one stream flowing into it and another stream flowing out of it. If, somewhere along in the flowing stream of water, some mud and industrial waste were to flow down from a factory and get into the stream, the stream would become muddy and toxic, eventually killing the fish and other life in the pond.

To clear the pond, we would first have to locate the source of the factory and the source of the problem, which is the toxic waste that is sliding down the bank into the stream. Next we would have to somehow stop this flow of toxic waste into the stream. After this had been done, the stream would eventually be clear again. The pond would not immediately become unpolluted and clear. The clear, inflowing water would first have to dilute or displace the water in the pond, and then, after a while, we would have a nice, clear pond once again. Depending on how toxic the water in the pond was, it could take quite a while before the pond was noticeably clearer.

John 4:14 But whosoever drinketh of the water that I shall give him shall never thirst; but the water that I shall give him shall be in him a well of water springing up into everlasting life.

You can liken the toxic water to some old, poisonous ideas and mistaken information existing in you. The clear water is the new, clean ideas you want to put in your mind. The sooner the flow of clearer, cleaner water enters the toxic pond, the sooner it will clear up. This means that the more repetitions your subconscious mind hears, the sooner it will displace the old ideas.

Isaiah 41:10 Fear thou not; for I am with thee: be not dismayed; for I am thy God: I will strengthen thee; yea, I will help thee; yea, I will uphold thee with the right hand of my righteousness.

The sooner you change the collection of old information, the sooner your habits and thinking will change and the sooner your life will improve.

Isaiah 41:13 For I the LORD thy God will hold thy right hand, saying unto thee, Fear not; I will help thee.

You can change the direction in which you are heading by declaring that, affirming that, standing on that and taking action to bring that new you into reality.

Deuteronomy 31:6 Be strong and of a good courage, fear not, nor be afraid of them: for the LORD thy God, he it is that doth go with thee; he will not fail thee, nor forsake thee.

Deuteronomy 31:8 And the LORD, he it is that doth go before thee; he will be with thee, he will not fail thee, neither forsake thee: fear not, neither be dismayed.

We have the power to create whatever we want in our lives. We can now make positive choices and all we have to do is envision what we want and use our subconscious to create that new life for us. The subconscious becomes a willing servant to help guide us to realize the unlimited possibilities, rich opportunities and new adventures that await us.

There is a newfound joy in being capable, for the first time, of having what we want with joy and serenity and using that awareness to project and perceive new levels of understanding in our next goal. We can now avoid negative thinking traps that have held us hostage and that continue to create doubt in our minds about whether or not you can achieve success. If you can look beyond today, with the intense purpose and passion of re-creating your conscious and subconscious mind, you can create a better tomorrow.

Ephesians 4:23 And be renewed in the spirit of your mind...

Flushing out the old ideas can be achieved with both written and spoken declarations and affirmations, but you must do this on a daily basis.

Matthew 6:11 Give us this day our daily bread.

The continued use of positive affirmations can release us from these self-imposed mental prisons.

There is another way of reprogramming and changing the subconscious mind. I, for example, have made my own self-help tapes, taken from numerous books and articles. The powerful change that continues to happen as I meditate through the use of this self-hypnosis (self-correcting) or meditation tapes is awesome. I have also purchased such tapes; if they are good, positive tapes, they produce faster results, with less effort. There are several reasons why this is so. The prime reason is because the best tapes of this sort first get us into a very deep state of relaxation. This deep state of relaxation is called the Theta level of the brain's electrical activity and is the level of consciousness we are in just before we fall asleep. Our brain waves slow down to around 2 to 4 cycles per second.

When we are in this very deep state of relaxation, we are better able to access our subconscious mind. This part of our mind can then more easily recall information for us, and it can also more easily accept or record new information for us. So, if appropriate messages are put on the tape, and we listen to them when we are very relaxed, they are more quickly absorbed by our subconscious mind, producing the results we want. And this produces quicker results in the changing of our thinking, actions, behavior and habit force.

On some tapes of this kind, affirmations are repeated at regular and high-speed intervals, so that the number of repetitions that you will hear is greatly increased. This produces even faster results. Also, with tapes of this kind, you can visualize your goals or the objectives you want to achieve while in this relaxed state, and this further increases the reprogramming effect.

Another thing about using these tapes is that they are pleasant and easy to use. No special effort or concentration is required. You simply lay back and relax, and let the tape do the work. These tapes also provide tremendous stress-reduction. Reducing stress has benefits such as allowing your digestive and immune systems to function better. When you are less stressed, you think more clearly and you react more calmly and logically in stressful situations.

You now have another way of understanding how your subconscious mind works, and how it can be reprogrammed with the beliefs you want it to have. Using this knowledge can radically change your life for the better.

*Proverbs 2:6 For the LORD giveth **wisdom**: out of his mouth cometh knowledge and understanding.*

*Proverbs 3: 13 Happy is the man that findeth **wisdom**, and the man that getteth understanding.*

The mouth of wisdom is closed, except to the ears of awareness. Author unknown

*Exodus 31:3 And I have filled him with the spirit of God, in **wisdom, and in understanding, and in knowledge**, and in all manner of workmanship ...*

Exodus 35:31 And he hath filled him with the spirit of God, **in wisdom, in understanding, and in knowledge,** *and in all manner of workmanship ...*

Psalms 111:10 The fear of the LORD is **the beginning of wisdom***: a good understanding have all they that do his commandments: his praise endureth for ever.*

Proverbs 15:14 The heart of him that hath understanding **seeketh knowledge:** *but the mouth of fools feedeth on foolishness.*

Proverbs 15:21 Folly is joy to him that is destitute of wisdom: but **a man of understanding walketh uprightly.**

Self-discipline begins with the mastery of your thoughts. If you don't control what you think, you can't control what you do. Simply, self-discipline enables you to think first and act afterward.
Napoleon Hill

Men are not prisoners of fate, but only prisoners of their own minds.
Franklin D. Roosevelt

Galatians 6:7 Be not deceived; God is not mocked: for whatsoever a man soweth, that shall he also reap.

Chapter 11

Positive Affirmations

Affirmations of faith are statements that describe a desired condition or situation you want manifested in your life, and, when they are repeated, positive changes can take place. Although affirmations consist of words, they routinely and subconsciously call up mental images. These mental images, if repeated often enough, are brought into reality by the power of the mind through the principle of manifestation that is explored later in this book.

The basically responsible-acting person has a life that consists of hard work, fulfillment of obligations and a consideration for the feelings of others. A normal responsible person who acts normally may lie, but lying is not his or her way of life. A normal-acting person may drink alcoholic beverages, but drinking is not his/her way of life. Normal, healthy people quite often discard thoughts about wrong choices because those thoughts and actions are not a part of their view of life, so they disregard those influences. They do not need any special effort to eliminate negative thoughts and actions. We, on the other hand, need a genuine self-critical look at our thoughts, words, actions and the consequences we paid for having them and acting on them. Self-examination is absolutely essential to the change process. Positive affirmations are a powerful way of changing at the deepest levels of self.

The reason that using faith affirmations in the shaping of self is so effective is because those statements motivate. They become a part of your personal success program because such powerful statements keep the mind focused on a goal. Affirming words, powerfully spoken with conviction, enter the subconscious mind. The power of these positive affirmations reaches out into the universe and helps you to achieve what you repeatedly ask for by thought, action or habit. Self-help groups are powerful because you are able to discuss and acknowledge what is continually repeated in your mind, your words and your actions, and the group also suggests methods and ways to help you. This is why, in a group setting, sometimes you are able to hear exactly what you need to help you make some progress in your life without your having said anything during the group meeting. The continual neural firing and energy produced in the mind influences your inner world and requires responses from the outer world you live in. What you continually focus on inside produces your outside reality.

Faith-filled, positive affirmations are positive sentences that describe a desired set of circumstances and that are repeated many times, in order to impact the subconscious mind and energize it into positive action. Let me say this again: in order to ensure the effectiveness of positive affirmations, you must repeat them with enthusiasm, confidence, awareness and desire.

But, before we can become self-affirming, we need to learn about the effects of being negative—not just thinking negatively, but believing and speaking into existence our negative belief—and what that does in our lives. What are the negative things we say to ourselves that lead to us actually *be* negative?

Most of the time, people go over and over in their minds a lot of negative sentences and statements concerning the daily situations and events in their lives and, consequently, bring upon themselves unwanted situations. Such negative sentences and statements work both ways, to build or to destroy. It is the way we use them that determines whether they are going to bring positive or self-destructive results.

Think about it: we very often mentally repeat negative statements, without even being aware of what we are saying, thinking of the progression that results. We repeatedly paint mind pictures when we tell ourselves that we cannot do something because we are too lazy, or when we actually believe we are going to fail by repeating to ourselves thoughts of failure. Remember: the subconscious mind always accepts whatever we give it and follows what we tell it, whether it is good or bad for us, so why not choose only positive statements to reshape your mind?

The negative things that you entertain in your mind are beliefs you have about yourself and that you remind yourself of on a daily basis. This way of thinking continues to create anxiety and worry. Since everything grows and expands in the universe as well as in the personal world of your mind, the process moves from your mind to your conversation. Negative statements in your mind are statements you believe about yourself or begin to use in your everyday conversations. This promotes doubt. Doubt is just one word; however, this continued process increases the force of energy in the area of your life where doubt resides. Every neuron that transmits information that supports doubt supports this process of creating a negative self-image. Eventually, a tiny doubt has become a mountain of doubt. Negative remarks are the words you speak or the thoughts you have that continually put you down. These remarks begin to influence your behavior and your beliefs. The process expands into other areas that are self-destructive. Before you know it, doubt has created self-pity.

When you begin to give negative descriptions of yourself and what you do, you must remember that these beliefs have their origin in things that may have been said by members of your own family. These things may have been said to you in a dysfunctional family setting or they may have come from groups of negative friends and peers when you were much younger. When you become diligent and search out the sources of these beliefs through a personal search of yourself, you will discover that those statements, which you still hold onto, have been growing and expanding throughout your life, to this very day.

This shows you how the universal principle of growth and expansion creates low self-esteem because these negative beliefs grow in power and intensity over time. It could be some negative feedback that you got from your spouse, your boss, your teacher or others that you take personally and continue to incorporate into your personal belief system and continue to repeat to yourself. Over time, this can create self-doubt and shame. If you continue to visualize dysfunctional, negative self-images you have of your body, your looks, your face, weight, coloring, hair, feet, or other parts of your body, they will continue to influence your presentation of yourself to others. This negativity can make you resentful of others because, to you, everyone else seems to be better in every way. These thoughts and feelings of jealousy you continue to harbor toward others who you feel (in reality or in your imagination) are more successful, prettier, luckier, better liked, smarter, more talented, more creative and generally better off than you create continual feedback information that you are not worth much at all. But know that the reverse of this process will bring higher self-esteem to the forefront as you train your mind.

Any completely negative assessment you have made of yourself—about your skills, your ability, your accumulated knowledge, your lack of intelligence, your lack of creativity or your lack of any common sense—are self-destructive. What makes this analysis really bad is that you agree with all these negative self-assessments because you continue to act and speak this way without any self-correction.

In short, over time, you have hypnotized your subconscious self and your personal psychology to believe that you really *are* worth nothing. A continual stream of negative stories about your past behavior, your personal failures or damaging performances that you systematically and continually run over and over in your mind and that continues to influence your current conduct without any relief in sight will keep you in a mental prison.

Destructive attitudes that you have harbored for your entire life about the possibility of your personal achievement, your personal fear of the future concerning any individual success in your life—these and many other things like them influence your motivation. Your personal effort in the present determines your overall drive to attain your future goals. Unconstructive imaginings and visualizations you have of your current status in life, such as feelings of anger, resentment and hostility or rage you feel toward others for real or imagined past or present mistreatment, will keep you producing those same results in your present life. As a matter of fact, this continual negative flow of information so immobilizes you over time that your emotional growth becomes stunted and you feel negatively about both yourself and life in general. Feelings of guilt for actual or imagined devastating wrongs you have committed—feelings that prevent positive self-valuing thoughts make you think that you *deserve* to be punished.

Depressing prophecies that you and others have made about yourself, your future, your possible success, your relationships, your family or your health keep haunting you as you face a daily battle to *win* in the struggles of life. This ongoing, relentless process unleashes self-fulfilling prophecies, which you now unleash upon yourself as you speak them into a universe that is prepared to give you what you say through the principle and right to decree. Remember: feelings of failure that you harbor about real or imagined mistakes in the past and your certainty of continuing to fail are projected into the future only to return on the cycle of return and reciprocity. The dread and fear you have and continue to develop when facing your future and the internal belief system that you developed say that you do not have what it takes to survive or to be successful in whatever circumstances you face—all this negativity keeps you returning to jails, institutions and death.

Self-affirmations are:

Healing, positive, self-affirming statements that you begin to give yourself will counter your negative personal psychology. These affirmations are vehicles by which you can free yourself from the overdependence on others' opinions, attitudes or feelings about you and help you to feel good about yourself. It takes time to become aware of the positive changes and how they affect your self-esteem, but you must start somewhere. Start using your imagination to visualize a new order of direction and a new sense of power developing in your life, using the principle of faith. You can now take personal responsibility and exhibit control over your mental health and emotional stability. You, with newfound authority and personal power, give yourself permission to grow, to change, to take risks, to rise up and to create a better life for yourself, knowing that abundance will come.

Now you can boldly work toward achieving real goals and a life of continued and sustained recovery. *The Revelation of Power* teaches us about being aware that everything is energy. Your thoughts are energy. Therefore, you can change negative thoughts, feelings and energy into positive scriptures, thoughts, feelings and words. This allows you to develop the "mind of Christ."

*1 Corinthians 2:16 For who hath known the mind of the Lord, that he may instruct him? But we have **the mind of Christ.***

103

You can transform the negative emotional baggage you have been carrying into new, powerful, positive emotions. Only then will you be able to deal with life as it happens and your own personal life in a realistic and positive manner. Your goal of your new, developing self is the transformation of emotions and feelings from the past so that you can face the present with a clearer view of yourself and your newfound power. Having a reservoir of powerful, positive statements about yourself is to know that the information, knowledge and energy that is within you is greater than the information, knowledge and energy that is coming against you. I like to place these positive affirmations in this order: I *can* (pure potential), I *will* (statement of force) and I *am* (statement of actual being that you stated, willed toward and, in reality, became).

I can: A proclamation of your possibilities

Philippians 4:13 **I can do all things** *through Christ which strengtheneth me.*

This is a positive declaration of your ability to accomplish goals. It is a statement of your confidence in your power to develop, to change and to help yourself.

I can be compassionate	I can grow
I can be assertive	I can be supportive
I can be considerate	I can be wonderful
I can become whole	I can have courage
I can help my children	I can have staying power
I can gain self-confidence	I can inspire others
I can be honest	I can talk about my feelings
I can control my temper	I can change my way of thinking

I can be a winner	I can walk with dignity
I can lose weight	I can be positive
I can be strong	I can stop smoking
I can laugh	I can solve my own problems
I can be valiant	I can let go of my fears
I can let go of my guilt	I can take risks
I can erase self-doubt	I can stop being stubborn
I can stop being lazy	I can stop being irresponsible
I can stop projecting	I can stop being selfish
I can stop being in denial	I can stop having a negative attitude
I can take proper action	I can be successful

I will: An announcement of positive change in your life

Hebrews 10:35 Cast not away therefore your confidence, which hath great recompence of reward.

This is a positive affirmation of a change you want to achieve. It is a positive statement of what you want to happen. It is a "success prophecy." *I will* statements are developed after you have set your priorities for your short-term goals. Examples include:

I will believe in myself more each day.

I will challenge myself to change today.

I will gain mental strength each day.

I will smile more today.

I will become more honest each day.

I will maintain more self-control each day.

I will control my temper today.

I will grow emotionally stronger each day.

I will take a risk to grow today.

I will offer a helping hand today.

I will teach my children today.

I will feel better about myself today.

I will sleep better tonight.

I will feel less and less guilt each day.

I will face my fears with courage today.

I will manage my time better today.

I will handle my finances wisely today.

I am: A positive statement of who you are

Matthew 19:26 But Jesus beheld them, and said unto them, with men this is impossible; **but with God all things are possible.**

Mark 10:27 And Jesus looking upon them saith, with men it is impossible, but not with God: for **with God** *all things are possible.*

John 15:7 If ye abide in me, and my words **abide in you***, ye shall ask what ye will, and it shall be done unto you.*

This is a positive affirmation of a real state of being that exists in you. You can achieve a full list of *I am* statements by taking a personal, positive inventory of your attributes, strengths, talents and competencies. Examples include:

I am creative   I am smart

I am talented   I am sharing

I am open   I am loyal

I am forgiving

I am a good person

I am trusting

I am a loving person

I am courageous

I am magnificent

I am awesome

I am knowledgeable

I am courteous

I am energetic

I am strong

I am intelligent

I am beautiful

I am caring

I am responsible

I am outstanding

I am incredible

I am extraordinary

I am helpful

I am kind

I am marvelous

I am considerate

I am determined

I am remarkable

I am fantastic

I am enthusiastic

I am relaxed

I am joyful

I am generous

I am persistent

Positive Biblical Affirmations

I am: in Christ and have the mind of Christ.

1 Corinthians 2:16: But we have the mind of Christ.

I am: Forgiven of all my sins and washed in the Blood.

Ephesians 1:7 In whom we have redemption through his blood, the forgiveness of sins, according to the riches of his grace...

Hebrews 9:14 How much more shall the blood of Christ, who through the eternal Spirit offered himself without spot to God, purge your conscience from dead works to serve the living God?

Colossians 1:14 In whom we have redemption through his blood, even the forgiveness of sins...

1 John 1:9 If we confess our sins, he is faithful and just to forgive us our sins, and to cleanse us from all unrighteousness.

I am: A new creature in Christ.

2 Corinthians 5:17 Therefore if any man be in Christ, he is a new creature: old things are passed away; behold, all things are become new.

I am: God's child for I am born again of the incorruptible seed of the Word of God.

1 Peter 1:23 Being born again, not of corruptible seed, but of incorruptible, by the word of God, which liveth and abideth for ever.

I am: Delivered from the power of darkness and translated in God's kingdom.

Colossians 1:13 Who hath delivered us from the power of darkness, and hath translated us into the kingdom of his dear Son...

I am: Holy and without blame before Him in love.

1 Peter 1:16 Because it is written, Be ye holy; for I am holy.

Ephesians 1:4 According as he hath chosen us in him before the foundation of the world, that we should be holy and without blame before him in love:

I am: Crucified with Christ.

Galatians 2:20 I am crucified with Christ: nevertheless I live; yet not I, but Christ liveth in me: and the life which I now live in the flesh I live by the faith of the Son of God, who loved me, and gave himself for me.

I am: **Sealed with the Holy Spirit of promise.**

Ephesians 1:13 In whom ye also trusted, after that ye heard the word of truth, the gospel of your salvation: in whom also after that ye believed, ye were sealed with that holy Spirit of promise...

I am: **The temple of the Holy Spirit.**

1 Corinthians 6:19 What? know ye not that your body is the temple of the Holy Ghost which is in you, which ye have of God, and ye are not your own?

I am: **Justified, completely forgiven and made righteous.**

Romans 5:1 Therefore being justified by faith, we have peace with God through our Lord Jesus Christ...

I am: **Redeemed from the curse of the law of sin and death.**

1 Peter 1:18-19 Forasmuch as ye know that ye were not redeemed with corruptible things, as silver and gold, from your vain conversation received by tradition from your fathers;

1 Peter 1:19 But with the precious blood of Christ, as of a lamb without blemish and without spot ...

Galatians 3:13 Christ hath redeemed us from the curse of the law, being made a curse for us: for it is written, Cursed is every one that hangeth on a tree ...

I am: **Blessed.**

Deuteronomy 28:2-12 And all these blessings shall come on thee, and overtake thee, if thou shalt hearken unto the voice of the LORD thy God.

3 Blessed shalt thou be in the city, and blessed shalt thou be in the field.

4 Blessed shall be the fruit of thy body, and the fruit of thy ground, and the fruit of thy cattle, the increase of thy kine, and the flocks of thy sheep.

5 Blessed shall be thy basket and thy store.

6 Blessed shalt thou be when thou comest in, and blessed shalt thou be when thou goest out.

7 The LORD shall cause thine enemies that rise up against thee to be smitten before thy face: they shall come out against thee one way, and flee before thee seven ways.

8 The LORD shall command the blessing upon thee in thy storehouses, and in all that thou settest thine hand unto; and he shall bless thee in the land which the LORD thy God giveth thee.

9 The LORD shall establish thee an holy people unto himself, as he hath sworn unto thee, if thou shalt keep the commandments of the LORD thy God, and walk in his ways.

10 And all people of the earth shall see that thou art called by the name of the LORD; and they shall be afraid of thee.

11 And the LORD shall make thee plenteous in goods, in the fruit of thy body, and in the fruit of thy cattle, and in the fruit of thy ground, in the land which the LORD sware unto thy fathers to give thee

12 The LORD shall open unto thee his good treasure, the heaven to give the rain unto thy land in his season, and to bless all the work of thine hand: and thou shalt lend unto many nations, and thou shalt not borrow.

Galatians 3:9 So then they which be of faith are blessed with faithful Abraham.

I am: A Saint.

Romans 1:7 To all that be in Rome, beloved of God, called to be saints: Grace to you and peace from God our Father, and the Lord Jesus Christ.

1 Corinthians 1:2 Unto the church of God which is at Corinth, to them that are sanctified in Christ Jesus, called to be saints, with all that in every place call upon the name of Jesus Christ our Lord, both theirs and ours...

Philippians 1:1 Paul and Timotheus, the servants of Jesus Christ, to all the saints in Christ Jesus which are at Philippi, with the bishops and deacons ...

***I am:* The head and not the tail, above and not beneath.**

Deuteronomy 28:13 And the LORD shall make thee the head, and not the tail; and thou shalt be above only, and thou shalt not be beneath; if that thou hearken unto the commandments of the LORD thy God, which I command thee this day, to observe and to do them ...

***I am:* The Elect of God.**

Colossians 3:12 Put on therefore, as the elect of God, holy and beloved, bowels of mercies, kindness, humbleness of mind, meekness, longsuffering...

Romans 8:33 Who shall lay any thing to the charge of God's elect? It is God that justifieth.

***I am:* Established to the end.**

Romans 1:11 For I long to see you, that I may impart unto you some spiritual gift, to the end ye may be established...

***I am:* Made near to My Heavenly Father by the Blood of Christ.**

Ephesians 2:13 But now in Christ Jesus ye who sometimes were far off are made nigh by the blood of Christ.

***I am:* Set free.**

John 8:31-33 Then said Jesus to those Jews which believed on him, If ye continue in my word, then are ye my disciples indeed;

32 And ye shall know the truth, and the truth shall make you free.

33 They answered him, We be Abraham's seed, and were never in bondage to any man: how sayest thou, Ye shall be made free?

I am: **Strong in the Lord.**

Ephesians 6:10 Finally, my brethren, be strong in the Lord, and in the power of his might.

I am: **Dead to sin.**

Romans 6:2 God forbid. How shall we, that are dead to sin, live any longer therein?

Romans 6:11 Likewise reckon ye also yourselves to be dead indeed unto sin, but alive unto God through Jesus Christ our Lord.

1 Peter 2:24 Who his own self bare our sins in his own body on the tree, that we, being dead to sins, should live unto righteousness: by whose stripes ye were healed.

I am: **More than a conqueror.**

Romans 8:37 Nay, in all these things we are more than conquerors through him that loved us.

I am: **Joint heir with Christ.**

Romans 8:13 For if ye live after the flesh, ye shall die: but if ye through the Spirit do mortify the deeds of the body, ye shall live.

I am: **In Christ by His construction.**

1 Corinthians 1:30 But of him are ye in Christ Jesus, who of God is made unto us wisdom, and righteousness, and sanctification, and redemption...

I am: **Accepted in the Beloved.**

Ephesians 1:6 To the praise of the glory of his grace, wherein he hath made us accepted in the beloved.

I am: **Complete in Him.**

Colossians 2:10 And ye are complete in him, which is the head of all principality and power ...

I am: **Alive in Christ.**

Galatians 2:20 I am crucified with Christ: nevertheless I live; yet not I, but Christ liveth in me: and the life which I now live in the flesh I live by the faith of the Son of God, who loved me, and gave himself for me.

I am: **Free from condemnation.**

John 5:24 Verily, verily, I say unto you, He that heareth my word, and believeth on him that sent me, hath everlasting life, and shall not come into condemnation; but is passed from death unto life.

I am: **Reconciled to God.**

2 Corinthians 5:18 And all things are of God, who hath reconciled us to himself by Jesus Christ, and hath given to us the ministry of reconciliation...

I am: **Qualified to share in His inheritance.**

Colossians 1:12 Giving thanks unto the Father, which hath made us meet to be partakers of the inheritance of the saints in light ...

I am: **Firmly rooted, built up, established in my faith and overflowing with thanksgiving.**

Colossians 2:7 Rooted and built up in him, and stablished in the faith, as ye have been taught, abounding therein with thanksgiving.

I am: **The righteousness of God.**

2 Corinthians 5:21 For he hath made him to be sin for us, who knew no sin; that we might be made the righteousness of God in him.

1 Peter 2:24 Who his own self bare our sins in his own body on the tree, that we, being dead to sins, should live unto righteousness: by whose stripes ye were healed.

I am: **Born of God and the evil one does not touch me.**

1 John 5:18 We know that whosoever is born of God sinneth not; but he that is begotten of God keepeth himself, and that wicked one toucheth him not.

I am: **His faithful follower.**

Revelation 17:14 These shall make war with the Lamb, and the Lamb shall overcome them: for he is Lord of lords, and King of kings: and they that are with him are called, and chosen, and faithful.

Ephesians 5:1 Be ye therefore followers of God, as dear children ...

I am: **A fellow citizen with the saints of the household of God.**

Ephesians 2:19 Now therefore ye are no more strangers and foreigners, but fellow citizens with the saints, and of the household of God ...

I am: **Built upon the foundation of the apostles and prophets, Jesus Christ Himself being the chief cornerstone.**

Ephesians 2:20 And are built upon the foundation of the apostles and prophets, Jesus Christ himself being the chief corner stone ...

I am: **Overtaken with blessings.**

Deuteronomy 28:2 And all these blessings shall come on thee, and overtake thee, if thou shalt hearken unto the voice of the LORD thy God.

Ephesians 1:3 Blessed be the God and Father of our Lord Jesus Christ, who hath blessed us with all spiritual blessings in heavenly places in Christ ...

I am: **His disciple because I have love for others.**

John 13:34-35 A new commandment I give unto you, That ye love one another; as I have loved you, that ye also love one another.

35 By this shall all men know that ye are my disciples, if ye have love one to another.

I am: **The light of the world.**

Matthew 5:14 Ye are the light of the world. A city that is set on an hill cannot be hid.

I am: **The salt of the earth.**

Matthew 5:13 Ye are the salt of the earth: but if the salt have lost his savour, wherewith shall it be salted? it is thenceforth good for nothing, but to be cast out, and to be trodden under foot of men.

I am: **A partaker of His Divine Nature.**

2 Peter 1:4 Whereby are given unto us exceeding great and precious promises: that by these ye might be partakers of the divine nature, having escaped the corruption that is in the world through lust.

I am: **Called of God.**

2 Timothy 1:9 Who hath saved us, and called us with an holy calling, not according to our works, but according to his own purpose and grace, which was given us in Christ Jesus before the world began ...

I am: **An ambassador for Christ.**

2 Corinthians 5:20 Now then we are ambassadors for Christ, as though God did beseech you by us: we pray you in Christ's stead, be ye reconciled to God.

I am: **God's workmanship created in Christ Jesus for good works.**

Ephesians 2:10 For we are his workmanship, created in Christ Jesus unto good works, which God hath before ordained that we should walk in them.

I am: **The apple of my Father's eye.**

Deuteronomy 32:10 He found him in a desert land, and in the waste howling wilderness; he led him about, he instructed him, he kept him as the apple of his eye.

I am: **Healed by the stripes of Jesus.**

1 Peter 2:25 For ye were as sheep going astray; but are now returned unto the Shepherd and Bishop of your souls.

Isaiah 53:6 All we like sheep have gone astray; we have turned every one to his own way; and the LORD hath laid on him the iniquity of us all.

I am: **Being changed into His image.**

2 Corinthians 3:18 But we all, with open face beholding as in a glass the glory of the Lord, are changed into the same image from glory to glory, even as by the Spirit of the Lord.

Philippians 1:6 Being confident of this very thing, that he which hath begun a good work in you will perform it until the day of Jesus Christ ...

I am: Christ's friend.

John 15:15 Henceforth I call you not servants; for the servant knoweth not what his lord doeth: but I have called you friends; for all things that I have heard of my Father I have made known unto you.

I am: Chosen and appointed by Christ to bear His fruit.

John 15:16 Ye have not chosen me, but I have chosen you, and ordained you, that ye should go and bring forth fruit...

I am: A servant of righteousness.

Romans 6:16 Know ye not, that to whom ye yield yourselves servants to obey, his servants ye are to whom ye obey; whether of sin unto death, or of obedience unto righteousness?

I am: Constrained to God.

Romans 6:22 But now being made free from sin, and become servants to God, ye have your fruit unto holiness, and the end everlasting life.

I am: A son/daughter of God.

Romans 8:14-15 For as many as are led by the Spirit of God, they are the sons of God.

15 For ye have not received the spirit of bondage again to fear; but ye have received the Spirit of adoption, whereby we cry, Abba, Father.

Galatians 4:6 And because ye are sons, God hath sent forth the Spirit of his Son into your hearts, crying, Abba, Father.

1 Corinthians 3:16 Know ye not that ye are the temple of God, and that the Spirit of God dwelleth in you?

1 Corinthians 6:19 What? know ye not that your body is the temple of the Holy Ghost which is in you, which ye have of God, and ye are not your own?

I am: **A member of Christ's Body.**

1 Corinthians 12:27 Now ye are the body of Christ, and members in particular.

Ephesians 5:30 For we are members of his body, of his flesh, and of his bones.

I am: **One in Christ.**

Galatians 3:26 For ye are all the children of God by faith in Christ Jesus.

Galatians 3:28 There is neither Jew nor Greek, there is neither bond nor free, there is neither male nor female: for ye are all one in Christ Jesus.

I am: **An heir of God since I am a son/daughter of God.**

Galatians 4:6-7 And because ye are sons, God hath sent forth the Spirit of his Son into your hearts, crying, Abba, Father.

7 Wherefore thou art no more a servant, but a son; and if a son, then an heir of God through Christ.

I am: **Righteous and holy.**

Ephesians 4:24 And that ye put on the new man, which after God is created in righteousness and true holiness.

I am: **A citizen of heaven and seated in heaven right now.**

Philippians 3:20 For our conversation is in heaven; from whence also we look for the Saviour, the Lord Jesus Christ...

Ephesians 2:6 And hath raised us up together, and made us sit together in heavenly places in Christ Jesus ...

I am: **An expression of the Life of Christ because He is my life.**

Colossians 3:4 When Christ, who is our life, shall appear, then shall ye also appear with him in glory.

I am: **Chosen and dearly loved by Christ.**

Ephesians 1:4 According as he hath chosen us in him before the foundation of the world, that we should be holy and without blame before him in love ...

1 Peter 2:9 But ye are a chosen generation, a royal priesthood, an holy nation, a peculiar people; that ye should shew forth the praises of him who hath called you out of darkness into his marvellous light ...

I am: **A son/daughter of light and not of darkness.**

1 Thessalonians 5:5 Ye are all the children of light, and the children of the day: we are not of the night, nor of darkness.

I am: **A holy brother/sister, partaker of a heavenly calling.**

Hebrews 3:1 Wherefore, holy brethren, partakers of the heavenly calling, consider the Apostle and High Priest of our profession, Christ Jesus ...

I am: **One of God's living stones and I am being brought up as a spiritual house.**

1 Peter 2:5 Ye also, as lively stones, are built up a spiritual house, an holy priesthood, to offer up spiritual sacrifices, acceptable to God by Jesus Christ.

I am: **A child of God.**

John 1:12 But as many as received him, to them gave he power to become the sons of God, even to them that believe on his name...

Romans 8:16 The Spirit itself beareth witness with our spirit, that we are the children of God ...

I am: **A temple of God. His Spirit dwells in me.**

1 Corinthians 3:16 Know ye not that ye are the temple of God, and that the Spirit of God dwelleth in you?

I am: **A chosen race, a royal priesthood, a holy nation, a people for God's own possession to proclaim the excellence of Him.**

1 Peter 2:9-10 But ye are a chosen generation, a royal priesthood, an holy nation, a peculiar people; that ye should shew forth the praises of him who hath called you out of darkness into his marvellous light ...

10 Which in time past were not a people, but are now the people of God: which had not obtained mercy, but now have obtained mercy.

I am: **An alien and stranger to this world in which I temporarily live.**

1 Peter 2:11 Dearly beloved, I beseech you as strangers and pilgrims, abstain from fleshly lusts, which war against the soul ...

I am: **The enemy of the Devil.**

1 Peter 5:8 Be sober, be vigilant; because your adversary the devil, as a roaring lion, walketh about, seeking whom he may devour ...

I am: **Now a child of God. I will resemble Christ when He returns.**

1 John 3:1-2 Behold, what manner of love the Father hath bestowed upon us, that we should be called the sons of God: therefore the world knoweth us not, because it knew him not.

2 Beloved, now are we the sons of God, and it doth not yet appear what we shall be: but we know that, when he shall appear, we shall be like him; for we shall see him as he is.

I am: **Reconciled to God and I am a minister of reconciliation.**

2 Corinthians 5:18-19 And all things are of God, who hath reconciled us to himself by Jesus Christ, and hath given to us the ministry of reconciliation;

19 To wit, that God was in Christ, reconciling the world unto himself, not imputing their trespasses unto them; and hath committed unto us the word of reconciliation.

I am: Joined to the Lord and I am one with him.

1 Corinthians 15:10 But by the grace of God I am what I am: and his grace which was bestowed upon me was not in vain; but I laboured more abundantly than they all: yet not I, but the grace of God which was with me.

I am: Dead with Christ and dead to the power of sin's rule over my life.

Romans 6:1-6 What shall we say then? Shall we continue in sin, that grace may abound?

2 God forbid. How shall we, that are dead to sin, live any longer therein?

3 Know ye not, that so many of us as were baptized into Jesus Christ were baptized into his death?

4 Therefore we are buried with him by baptism into death: that like as Christ was raised up from the dead by the glory of the Father, even so we also should walk in newness of life.

5 For if we have been planted together in the likeness of his death, we shall be also in the likeness of his resurrection:

6 Knowing this, that our old man is crucified with him, that the body of sin might be destroyed, that henceforth we should not serve sin.

I am: Dead, I no longer live for myself but for God.

2 Corinthians 5:14-15 For the love of Christ constraineth us; because we thus judge, that if one died for all, then were all dead:

15 And that he died for all, that they which live should not henceforth live unto themselves, but unto him which died for them, and rose again.

I am: **Bought with a price. I am not my own. I belong to God.**

1 Corinthians 6:19-20 What? Know ye not that your body is the temple of the Holy Ghost which is in you, which ye have of God, and ye are not your own?

20 For ye are bought with a price: therefore glorify God in your body, and in your spirit, which are God's.

I am: **Sanctified and I am one with the sanctifier, Christ. He is not ashamed to call me brother/sister.**

Hebrews 2:11 For both he that sanctifieth and they who are sanctified are all of one: for which cause he is not ashamed to call them brethren...

I am: **Established, anointed and sealed by God in Christ.**

2 Corinthians 1:21 Now he which stablisheth us with you in Christ, and hath anointed us, is God ...

I am: **Given the Holy Spirit as a pledge, a guarantee of my inheritance.**

Ephesians 1:13-14 In whom ye also trusted, after that ye heard the word of truth, the gospel of your salvation: in whom also after that ye believed, ye were sealed with that holy Spirit of promise,

14 Which is the earnest of our inheritance until the redemption of the purchased possession, unto the praise of his glory.

I am: **Crucified with Christ and it is no longer I who lives, but Christ who lives through me.**

Galatians 2:20 I am crucified with Christ: nevertheless I live; yet not I, but Christ liveth in me: and the life which I now live in the flesh I live by the faith of the Son of God, who loved me, and gave himself for me.

I am: **The peace of God which passes all understanding.**

Philippians 4:7 And the peace of God, which passeth all understanding, shall keep your hearts and minds through Christ Jesus.

I am: **Chosen in Christ before the foundation of the world.**

Ephesians 1:4 According as he hath chosen us in him before the foundation of the world, that we should be holy and without blame before him in love ...

I am: **Predestined and determined by God to be a son/daughter.**

Ephesians 1:5 Having predestinated us unto the adoption of children by Jesus Christ to himself, according to the good pleasure of his will ...

I am: Not the great "I AM," but by the grace of God I am what I am.

I have: **Received the Spirit of God into my life that I might know the things given to me by God.**

1 Corinthians 2:12 Now we have received, not the spirit of the world, but the spirit which is of God; that we might know the things that are freely given to us of God.

I have: **Been redeemed and forgiven. I am a recipient of His lavish grace.**

Ephesians 1:7 In whom we have redemption through his blood, the forgiveness of sins, according to the riches of his grace ...

I have: **Been raised up and seated with Christ in the heavenly places.**

Ephesians 2:6 And hath raised us up together, and made us sit together in heavenly places in Christ Jesus...

I have: **Christ Himself in me.**

Colossians 1:27 To whom God would make known what is the riches of the glory of this mystery among the Gentiles; which is Christ in you, the hope of glory...

I have: **Been firmly rooted in Christ and I am now built up in Him.**

Colossians 2:7 Rooted and built up in him, and stablished in the faith, as ye have been taught, abounding therein with thanksgiving.

I have: **Been buried, raised and made alive with Christ.**

Colossians 2:12-13 Buried with him in baptism, wherein also ye are risen with him through the faith of the operation of God, who hath raised him from the dead.

13 And you, being dead in your sins and the uncircumcision of your flesh, hath he quickened together with him, having forgiven you all trespasses ...

I have: **Been raised up with Christ. My life is now hidden with Christ in God, for Christ is now my life.**

Colossians 3: 1-4 If ye then be risen with Christ, seek those things which are above, where Christ sitteth on the right hand of God.

2 Set your affection on things above, not on things on the earth.

3 For ye are dead, and your life is hid with Christ in God.

4 When Christ, who is our life, shall appear, then shall ye also appear with him in glory.

I have: **Been given a spirit of power, love and self-discipline.**

2 Timothy 1:7 For God hath not given us the spirit of fear; but of power, and of love, and of a sound mind.

I have: **Been saved and called and set apart according to God's responsibility.**

2 Timothy 1:9 Who hath saved us, and called us with an holy calling, not according to our works, but according to his own purpose and grace, which was given us in Christ Jesus before the world began ...

I have: **A right to come boldly before the throne to find mercy and grace in time of need.**

Hebrews 4:16 Let us therefore come boldly unto the throne of grace, that we may obtain mercy, and find grace to help in time of need.

I have: **Been given exceedingly great and precious promises by God in which I am a partaker of His Divine Nature.**

2 Peter 1:4 Whereby are given unto us exceeding great and precious promises: that by these ye might be partakers of the divine nature, having escaped the corruption that is in the world through lust.

I have: **Obtained an inheritance.**

Ephesians 1:11 In whom also we have obtained an inheritance, being predestinated according to the purpose of him who worketh all things after the counsel of his own will.

I have: **The mind of Christ.**

Philippians 2:5 Let this mind be in you, which was also in Christ Jesus...

1 Corinthians 2:16 For who hath known the mind of the Lord, that he may instruct him? But we have the mind of Christ.

I have: **Overcome the world.**

1 John 5:4 For whatsoever is born of God overcometh the world: and this is the victory that overcometh the world, even our faith.

I have: **Everlasting life and will not be condemned.**

John 5:2 Now there is at Jerusalem by the sheep market a pool, which is called in the Hebrew tongue Bethesda, having five porches.

I have: **Received power to lay hands on the sick, see them recover, power to cast out demons and power over all the power of the enemy.**

Luke 10:19 Behold, I give unto you power to tread on serpents and scorpions, and over all the power of the enemy: and nothing shall by any means hurt you.

I may: **Approach God with boldness, freedom and confidence.**

Ephesians 3:12 In whom we have boldness and access with confidence by the faith of him.

I live: **By the law of the Spirit of Life in Christ Jesus.**

Romans 8:2 For the law of the Spirit of life in Christ Jesus hath made me free from the law of sin and death.

I walk: **In Christ Jesus.**

Colossians 2:6 As ye have therefore received Christ Jesus the Lord, so walk ye in him...

I can: **Do all things in Christ.**

Philippians 4:13 I can do all things through Christ which strengtheneth me.

My life: **Is hid with Christ in God.**

Colossians 3:3 For ye are dead, and your life is hid with Christ in God.

I shall: **Overcome because greater is He who is in me then he who is in the world.**

1 John 4:4 Ye are of God, little children, and have overcome them: because greater is he that is in you, than he that is in the world.

I shall: **Do even greater works than Christ Jesus.**

John 14:12 Verily, verily, I say unto you, He that believeth on me, the works that I do shall he do also; and greater works than these shall he do; because I go unto my Father.

Use of these "I" statements as often as you can. They are designed to counter a negative self-concept. Repeating them can result in a positive attitude, optimism, and can motivate you toward emotional growth and progress. I put many positive statements on a tape recorder and listened to them over and over. I also included excerpts from many self-help books. This allowed me plenty of time to listen to these tapes while driving or just before I went to sleep or even while sleeping, to activate the subconscious. Use your imagination and take advantage of a way to force-feed your mind with powerful statements that can change your life.

Making your mark on the world is hard. If it were easy, everybody would do it. But it's not. It takes patience, it takes commitment, and it comes with plenty of failure along the way. The real test is not whether you avoid this failure, because you won't. It's whether you let it harden or shame you into inaction, or whether you learn from it; whether you choose to persevere.
Barack Obama

Winning is a habit. Unfortunately, so is losing.
Vince Lombardi

Chapter 12

The Logical Mind

Logic is the study of the principles of reasoning, including the formal, guiding principles of disciplined thought. It is the psychological relationship between our human understanding and the entire world of objects, individuals, principles and events in our lives. Logic is used to provide a way of reasoning out an issue that can be looked at from several points of view. Logic, instead of just emotional responses, becomes the force of an argument. If we add some reason, some thinking and some rationality to our lives, that positive flow of thought becomes our logic.

Logic challenges the arguments we have against change. In other words, let us use the art of reasoning and a logical process and logical sequences to examine and to change our lives. We can come to some logical conclusions and generalizations about what our lives look like now and projections for our future life, based on logical thinking.

Logical thinking does not discriminate. Logical reasoning will allow us to look at the facts of our lives and come to some compelling choices. Logical thinking, based on both past and present behavior, will lead us to conclusions that we have no alternative, no other option whatsoever, *except* to change. If you do not choose to change the direction in which you are going, you will continue to go in the same direction in which you are currently traveling and the addiction grows. According to logical thinking, it is certain that this must be your destiny—continued addiction.

The predetermination of your *fate* is located in your mind. The pressure of events caused by the constant working of your mind to achieve its goals becomes a force of future real-life circumstances. These circumstances of thought, habit force and universal law take control over your life.

There is no escape without change—no freedom from the course your life is taking. There is only subjection to the physical necessity and the laws of nature that keep you going in the wrong direction. The compulsion of negative thought overrides every other thought and this dominant force of habit brings us to this necessary conclusion: jails, institutions and death. Do you want proof? Do you want a demonstration of this force of universal law? Ask any inmate who has been to prison over and over again after vowing that he or she would never return. That is the living, undeniable truth.

Make up your mind to educate yourself and learn to use *The Revelation of Power*. From a drop of water, we can understand the logic of moving from that drop of water to the power of a flood or the vast expanse of an ocean. From just one drop, even if it is microscopic, you can begin the journey to become a small drink of knowledge, which then will become a mighty torrent of explosive, powerful, positive oceans of wisdom and enlightenment in you.

The demonstration of the power of logic and the use of proper facts is in the living, walking, documented lives of thousands upon thousands who have turned their lives around. We offer them and many others as evidence that the truth, rigorously applied, establishes conclusive proof and confirmation. The final argument is simply this: that triumph over negative behavior and actions can be achieved with certainty, if you choose to change and maintain your goals over time. Learn to use *The Revelation of Power* until the manifestation of your new reality comes to fruition.

Remember: logic, filled with positive information and wisdom, creates order out of confusion. You must make an effort to seek new information and to gain new understanding that adds to your ability to be logical. As you proceed in a positive direction, your level of intelligence will grow along with your increased ability to be more creative and improve the quality of your life.

Matthew 11:28 Come unto me, all ye that labour and are heavy laden, and I will give you rest.

Matthew 6:33 But seek ye first the kingdom of God, and his righteousness; and all these things shall be added unto you.

The following information is rendered in a logical manner in order for you to understand precisely the results that can be achieved by following the laws we are going to describe. As these laws are defined and you are able to appropriate and incorporate these laws into your daily thoughts and mental projections, you will find yourself becoming better adjusted and more logical in your thinking.

Over time, you can become better adjusted and have a well-aimed, straightforward, approach to life that will allow you to become more centered in universal and scientific law. The result is that you will become more self-directed and gain increasing confidence. While you will make mistakes along this new pathway, the goals of inner peace through the power of logical thinking and action become an unerring lifetime destiny. The developed logic and constant, uniform daily discipline of learning and applying these laws will allow you to take advantage of time because time is now much more important than ever before. How many more chances will you get?

You will discover a logically right and correct way of living, which will bring the true riches of life—*peace of mind*. You will find that the feeling of being right with self and others is a more natural way to live. You can and will become closer to others in a positive way, realizing that we all suffer from some self-created pain.

You will become a more faithful representative of what is right, logical and helpful to yourself and to your loved ones. Love will no longer be just a word you use to express some feeling you have: your actions will demonstrate true love with respect, honor, a proper relationship with, and loyalty to, those you love. And in time, you will be able to love yourself. Only then can you love others the way you wish to be loved. Then and only then, at the point when true love becomes a living reality, will you understand the key to right living. You must give away what you really want and, when you do, in time you will receive exactly what you have given away. That is what has happened to you already if you are honest with yourself: you have received what you have given.

*Mark 12:31 And the second is like, namely this, Thou shalt love thy neighbour **as thyself**...*

If you do not know how to love and respect yourself, you cannot love and respect another person. You will love someone the way you love yourself. If you do not know the love of God, then you can give away only the level of love you have. If you do not love or understand that love means putting someone else's welfare above your own, then you will remain selfish. You must be changed so you can learn to love. Then you will love others as you are being loved.

As you engage these laws and principles of logic, the words become a living reality within you and you begin to move in the right direction—not every time but much more often than before and with greater consistency. You will begin to find that your mind will become more photographic, which means that you take in reality in greater depth and understanding more quickly than ever before. And you will

131

see, as this power increases you will be more attuned to the world around you and you will find that the wonderful things you notice—all the things that you once overlooked—are there for you.

You will find that you now possess a more delicate, sensitive mind that is attuned to an almost infinite variety of things. The increased speed and precision of your personal decision-making process will improve markedly. When a problem comes, you realize it is there specifically for you to solve it. Not only that, but you are becoming more capable and resourceful in using logic and universal law either to move through every problem or to accept life as it is. All of this allows you to feel more electrically charged as you realize the millions of neurons that are firing in tandem to create a powerfully charged brain that is moving you in the right direction. Finally, you, the former servant of a negative mind, become the master of a positive, logical, sturdy mind. What a rush! But you have to live to the point where you can get high on life itself and enjoy the rush.

A more logically exact and correct mind, anchored in scientific, universal laws, provides the answers for the correction of your life. One plus one equals two. Simple, and yet that scientifically exact process, religiously applied to our thinking pattern, will create peace. One problem plus one solution continued through life, equals peace. When each day is multiplied through successful problem-solving skills, it creates a sense of accomplishment and, over time, a newfound strength of character.

While this is really oversimplified, put another way it is the correct way to deal with life. *It is not what happens to you but what you do with what happens to you.* Day by day find solutions to every problem. Applying yourself to the demanding, painstaking and strict attention to gaining a powerful, positive mind is your goal.

Educating yourself in an ongoing process of change through choice is the most important factor in *The Revelation of Power.*

What I have just described is a demonstration of *The Revelation of Power*. We use this power every day. There is no way around this startling truth. You simply cannot, **not** use *The Revelation of Power*.

Now, to demonstrate why you cannot **not** use *The Revelation of Power*, I am going to take the same positive approach just discussed and add the negative elements of the addicted personality and see if this does not clearly show you how this reality happens step by step.

The following information is provided in a step-by-step manner in order for you to understand that exact, precise and definite results can be achieved by following the laws we are going to describe. As these laws are defined, you will be able to incorporate them into your daily thoughts and mental projections. As a result, you will find yourself becoming more negatively adjusted.

A direct, straightforward, negative approach to life will allow you to become more centered in universal and scientific law, thus becoming more selfish and self-confident. This will lead to more self-destructive behavior. It is true that, while you will make mistakes along this new pathway of becoming an addict, you will crush any attempts by teachers, clergy, parents and others who might really care about you. Peers and other addicts will set you back on the pathway toward jail, institutions and death. The goals of inner misery and the goals of a lifetime of lawbreaking and temper tantrums drive you to become a four-time loser and coming to prison becomes your destiny four times.

As you continue to develop along negative lines through a constant daily discipline of pursuing negative thinking, your actions will make you more determined than ever to continue on your present course of negative thinking and behaving. And, because the addiction is much more important than ever before in meeting the deep need for negative self-gratification created within, you push on past any help.

As a result, you will discover an incorrect way of living that will bring the true rewards for your efforts: jails, institutions, death and misery of mind. You will find that the feelings of being right on your course towards prison and being out of touch with yourself and others are your quest and have become a more natural way to live. You can and will become closer to other people who are just like you. And then, as you meet and mingle in prison settings in a negative way with others who are just like you, you can expand your information base by denying the suffering of *self-created pain* and look for new ways to carry on your criminal thinking and behavior, while swearing you will never come back to prison again. You will become more faithful in representing and being a representative of what is wrong and hurtful to yourself and others who you say you love. Love will be just a word you use to express some feeling you have, but your actions will demonstrate no love to those you say you love and, in time, you will love others the way you treat yourself—negatively.

Then and only then, when all your thoughts and actions become a living reality, will you declare that it is all someone else's fault that brought you to the point where you are in life. You have not given away what you really wanted, but eventually you have received exactly what you have given away. If you are honest with yourself, this is what has already happened to you.

Although you thought all this "getting high" would make you and your life much more important and exciting and bring you friends and acceptance, things have just not worked out that way. You reasoned that you could avoid anxiety and stress and you justified your behavior because of, so you say, some inner pressures or peer pressure. Even over time and bad experiences, you still believed that you would receive benefits...and you have!

As you engage these laws and principles and the words become a living reality within you, you begin to move even farther in the wrong direction—not every time but much more often than before and with greater consistency. You will find that your mind will become more photographic. That is, you take in reality in greater depth and understanding of how to do wrong more quickly than ever before. And you will notice that this power increases the fine tuning, the many things you notice that you once overlooked. The places to rob and the people to con are there for you. You will find that you now possess a more delicate, sensitive mind that is precisely attuned to your decision-making process to get your sick needs met.

When a problem comes, it is there specifically for you to solve it negatively. Not only that, but you are becoming more capable and resourceful in using scientific and universal law to move through every problem and obstacle to get your drugs. Learning never to accept life as it is, but to take what you want now becomes the only way of dealing with life, on your terms only. All of that allows you to feel more electrically charged with a sense of your own negative powers. You do not realize that the millions of neurons that are firing in tandem are creating a powerful, negatively charged brain, moving you in the wrong direction. Finally, you are the servant and slave of a negative, unhealthy mind.

I could go on describing this process in much greater detail, but I believe you see exactly what is being presented to you. If you will be honest and not make excuses, you know that what I have written is true. Now, let us explore the universal laws and principles.

*Proverbs 3:1 My son, forget not **my law**; but let thine heart keep my commandments...*

*Proverbs 4:2 For I give you good doctrine, forsake ye not **my law**.*

*Proverbs 7:2 Keep my commandments, and live; and **my law** as the apple of thine eye.*

*Isaiah 51:7 Hearken unto me, ye that know righteousness, the people in whose heart is **my law**; fear ye not the reproach of men, neither be ye afraid of their revilings.*

Believe in yourself! Have faith in your abilities! Without a humble but reasonable confidence in your own powers you cannot be successful or happy.

Never talk defeat. Use words like "hope," "belief," "faith," "victory."

Any fact facing us is not as important as our attitude toward it, for it is our attitude that determines our success or failure.

Stand up to your obstacles and do something about them. You will find that they haven't half the strength you think they have.

Imagination is the true magic carpet.

There is real magic in enthusiasm. It spells the difference between mediocrity and accomplishment.

Norman Vincent Peale

Chapter 13

The Laws and Principles of the Universe

A universal law is the only law that can never be changed. Universal laws are constant. They are the laws by which all things were and are created. These laws have existed long before man ever came into being. They were as true for the first humans as they are for us today, and will be for all future generations. To be universal, something must apply to all things, people or beings, at all times in history, regardless of nationality, race, age, religious or social beliefs, culture, upbringing, social or environmental status or factors, time or space. These laws are not man-made; they were not written down in man-made text for those first beings. Over time, they have been discovered and revealed and then passed on to future generations. But they were as evident then as they are now. They govern our every life experience.

First, make a commitment that you will study the following material. Even though this request has already been made, it is important that you go over your mental commitment again. Make an agreement within yourself again that you will realize your goal. Let that agreement with yourself be so strong that no obstacle, no criticism and no one else will keep you from obtaining positive results.

The Law of Consciousness is a law that almost defies description. It is easier to describe some of the elements that make up consciousness and make observations about what it is rather than saying it is one particular thing. Consciousness is as big as the universe or as small as your awareness of your left pinky toe. How can you define something so immense? Consciousness is the use of intellect and the demonstration of mind. It is the capacity to feel affection for someone or something, to exhibit resolve, will, understanding and comprehension. It includes thinking and powers of thought, intellectual faculties, rationality and reasoning power and all of everything else that makes us aware of ourselves. It is being alive and aware of self and the universe that surrounds and penetrates us.

The ability to reason and bring together an association of ideas allows us to shape our destiny, just as some conscious effort went into the creation of all that exists. The greatest single gift of life we have been given is to be self-conscious, that is, aware of oneself. Now, through revelation, we can create a stream of consciousness that allows us to create at higher levels of vision and imagination. The ability to have perception about reality and an appreciation for the various forms of life, including the insight to perhaps change and influence reality, is to be conscious. That is power: to be aware of the fact that you can create—even create your new self. That is power and consciousness.

Consciousness is the ability to exercise fair judgment and to carefully choose the correct path in life—or not. This great mental capacity of our brains, with all our senses, intelligence and genius, which continue to grow and evolve, is consciousness. This organ of thought, this sea of thought that is beyond describing is consciousness. Consciousness is the awareness of being aware.

To try to understand what consciousness is, we must ask ourselves, "What is the 'I' in all of us?" Are you your thoughts? Are you your feelings? Are you your brain, your nervous system or your body? We are all these things and more. The "I" is the person who is aware of all this inner working of the self yet is not any one of its components. Consciousness is the "I" who is aware.

For the selfish, addicted person, who tries to satisfy his/her physical and mental needs, there is a problem. As I see it, the addicted person's negative emotions and thoughts are always concerned with objects, sensations, power and personal security. These are the main motivations of the selfish person. As that kind of consciousness expands, the space for negative remembered events increases in our subconscious and therefore the continued behavior is transformed into a habit force that makes the "I" go out of control and allows the "I" to serve the force of bad habits. The negative person will defend his or her developed habit force, which has become how that person sees him or herself. He or she will justify his/her actions at all costs, believing—with the aim of convincing you—that is who he or she is. However, through education the "I" can be elevated not only to be aware but also to become the "I" of higher consciousness. That is, a person's consciousness can be elevated not only to be aware of the higher, invisible laws of the universe but to elevate his or her consciousness to exist in a state of continual higher awareness. When you are keenly aware of your own thoughts and actions, remember that new possibilities will open for you to begin to move in tune and in concert with the invisible laws of the universe, thus bringing an awareness of true power and peace. The purpose of all the words used to describe these invisible laws and realms of existence is not just for you to be aware of them but for you to *know* and *become* all those words and energies. By knowing, being aware and changing in positive ways, we begin the process of enjoying life. Only then, with continued progress on a daily basis, can you evolve into appreciating the wonderful new journey of life.

*Exodus 3:14 And God said unto Moses, **I AM THAT I AM**: and he said, Thus shalt thou say unto the children of Israel, **I AM** hath sent me unto you.*

*John 8:58 Jesus said unto them, Verily, verily, I say unto you, Before Abraham was, **I am.***

Since you are reading this and are alive and aware, then you have been blessed with consciousness.

The Law of Vibration is that nothing rests; everything moves; everything vibrates. This is the law of progressive movement and of endless rotation. This law explains the differences between manifestations of matter, energy, mind and the animated, invisible self. Some call the invisible self "spirit" or "the human spirit."

All that is in the known universe results largely from varying rates of vibration. All that exists is in constant motion. Atoms are held together in molecules because the negatively charged electrons in one atom are pulled toward the positively charged nucleus of another. But, at the same time, the electrons in one atom repel those in the other, and the protons in the nuclei do the same. In other words, they are pulled back and forth.

This constant push and pull creates a vibration, as if the atoms were connected by tiny elastics, causing constant motion. The vibration is unique for each possible arrangement of atoms in a molecule; each vibration has a characteristic "energy level." Atoms always vibrate with such great velocity that they seem motionless and solid to the natural eye. I believe that everything begins with the invisible spirit energy and moves toward physical reality, which is yet another form of energy.

Atoms are the basic building blocks of ordinary matter. Atoms are composed of particles called protons, electrons and neutrons. Protons carry a positive electrical charge, electrons carry a negative electrical charge and neutrons carry no electrical charge at all. The protons and neutrons cluster together in the central part of the atom, called the nucleus, and the electrons "orbit" the nucleus. A particular atom has the same number of protons and electrons, and most atoms have at least as many neutrons as protons.

Both protons and neutrons are composed of other particles called *quarks* and *gluons*. Protons contain two "up" quarks and one "down" quark while neutrons contain one "up" quark and two "down" quarks. The gluons are responsible for binding the quarks to one another. Inside each atom is tremendous power and all that power is in each one of us.

A word is an articulated form of something that is written or spoken. Spoken and written words give us a mental picture of what the words describe. Air coming from the lungs is forced up through the vocal cords. The vocal cords vibrate as the air passes through them. Muscles located within the larynx (often referred to as the voice box) control the pitch, high or low, of sound vibrations. These muscles control the expansion and contraction of the vocal cords. The lips, tongue and soft palate control articulation and formation of the sounds into words. The importance point here is that we communicate with vibratory sounds.

When we receive words from others the sound waves strike the sound-sensitive eardrum. Three small bones, the hammer, anvil and stirrup, move in direct response to the particular sound waves received. This motion is transmitted through fluid in the inner ear, to a group of hair-like cells. Attached to each cell is an auditory nerve fiber, which carries an electrical signal. The brain analyzes all these impulses and produces a mental picture from vibratory sound. There is great vibratory power in words, in fact great enough power to create, through your own words, either a positive or a negative life.

*Matthew 17:20 And Jesus said unto them, Because of your unbelief: for verily I say unto you, If ye have faith as a grain of mustard seed, **ye shall say** unto this mountain, Remove* *hence to yonder place; and it shall remove; and nothing shall be impossible unto you.*

*Mark 11:23 For verily I say unto you, That **whosoever shall say** unto this mountain, Be thou removed, and be thou cast into the sea; and shall not doubt in his heart, but shall believe that those things which **he saith** shall come to pass; he shall have whatsoever **he saith**.*

The Law of Expansion and Growth is the law of a gradual and explosive expansion of everything that exists, including the consciousness in man and the expansion of the universe itself. That expansion and growth is a constant. Even the galaxies are racing away from some central point in an ever-expanding enlargement of the universe itself. Astronomer Edwin Hubble discovered that the galaxies are, in fact, moving away from each other. Everything grows and everything expands. Recently it has been discovered by scientists and astronomers that the universe is increasing at an accelerated pace.

Everywhere in our existence we can see growth and progress in any number of areas. This observation of universal expansion should stand without question. Our conscious understanding will expand and grow. Negatively or positively, you will grow and expand as long as you live. The question becomes: will we broaden and expand in the right direction? Since growth and expansion are a constant, our conscious efforts toward development and escalation of positive growth lie in using the power that exists around and through us every day. Growing pains are what alert us to the progressive opportunities and steps necessary for growth.

Think of growth and expansion using this example. If a farmer plants corn, he expects to get corn. When he plants the corn and covers it up with dirt he no longer sees the seed. He goes out and waters the dirt, believing that something will take place. That something is the law of growth and expansion. The farmer *knows* that corn will grow. He may not know how but he certainly knows that, with proper soil, water and sun, corn will be produced. Now look at the size of the corn plant compared to the size of the seed that was planted. That is growth and expansion.

To acknowledge the law of our growth and expansion is to understand how to better use our personal power. Greater awareness and concentration on enhancing and raising our active participation in study and seeking knowledge allows us to *grow* in positive ways. Thus, greater opportunities to grow in the right direction in many ways are afforded us. This continued building and strengthening of ideas leads to the development of new mental and emotional tools that can be used with confidence for even more positive growth and expansion. When we "get into" the continual excitement and stimulation of these new ideas, the result is that this form of elevated focus accelerates the process of our learning. The resulting rising tide of new emotion and awareness has a cumulative effect of giving us a new habit force and a growing appreciation for *The Revelation of Power*. When you actually begin to see this power being demonstrated, then that power becomes yours.

Now you can look on the bright side of things, knowing that you are fully capable and creative. You are more hopeful and peaceful because you are becoming more successful each day as you become a capable problem solver. Your inner space is calmer and quieter so that you carry yourself in a more relaxed way. You are more responsible because you know that you are able to respond in a loving and caring way. You are aware that, as you continue to meditate, become quiet and study to know yourself, you are becoming more intelligent and a more enjoyable person to be around.

If you find yourself thinking in the past, the future or the present, try to think pleasant thoughts, take it easy and think wisely. Know now, as you awaken to the wonderful powers and gifts within you, that you can have fun while you become a winner in the game of life. You can dare to be different and seize each opportunity, no matter what it is. As you look for the principle of abundance to manifest in your life, now realize that you stood back, dared to be different and took action. Now you believe in yourself and trust yourself to do the right thing because it's the right thing to do. When you do this on a daily basis, you will never fail. You can now sit back, relax and enjoy your new inner strength to work intelligently and be more in control of your destiny.

You now realize that you are coming alive to new possibilities in every area of your life and that you are the best friend you have. You now are beginning to understand, on a deep psychological level, that you can be a winner. When problems come up now you can look into your past successes and know that you have solved problems like this before and you have the ability to handle this, whatever *this*, is. Remember: there will always be a *this* or a *that* to be dealt with.

You are a capable, skillful human being and you deserve to love and to be loved. You can show others that, despite past bad habits, you now set a good example. You are still working toward the future. You face each new day as a special race and, if you stumble, you have the inner strength to get up and keep running. You are not perfect, but you are learning how to practice a new way of life, every day and your family, your son, your daughter or whoever will thank you in the future.

Your children will now benefit from your healthy changes. You know beyond a shadow of a doubt that nothing is worth losing your sanity, your sobriety or your freedom over. You can now love yourself for who you are. You have now become responsible for your own feelings. You do not owe anyone any explanations for your behavior, which is legally, morally and ethically correct because you take charge of your life. Now, finally, there are beautiful things happening in your life on a daily basis, and you experience daily the newness of personal excitement because of positive personal growth. You are a deserving human being who believes in giving the best that you have to any worthwhile endeavor. You are finally aware that your possibilities in life are endless. There is nothing you cannot handle.

Matthew 13:30 *Let both **grow** together until the harvest: and in the time of harvest I will say to the reapers, Gather ye together first the tares, and bind them in bundles to burn them: but gather the wheat into my barn.*

Mark 4:27 *And should sleep, and rise night and day, and the seed should spring and **grow up**, he knoweth not how.*

Ephesians 4:15 *But speaking the truth in love, may **grow up** into him in all things, which is the head, even Christ ...*

Chapter 14

The Law of Momentum is best described by the following examples. I am sure you have heard a sports announcer say, "Going into the all-star break, the Lakers have the momentum." Then, later in the game, the tide turns and we hear the new cry, "The Spurs are gaining momentum." Many coaches pump up their teams at half-time saying, "You have the momentum! Use that momentum and lay that team to rest in the third quarter and knock them out in the fourth." A team that has the momentum seems to be really moving as if by an unseen force and it is going to take some effort by the other team to stop it.

Momentum can be described as a snowball rolling down a hill. As it picks up more snow, becoming bigger, it has more mass and picks up speed. The bigger it gets, the harder the snowball is to stop.

Momentum is a term used in physics. It refers to the amount of motion that an object has. A basketball team that has the momentum is said and observed to be moving with force. In so many words, if an object or a team is in motion, then it has momentum. Momentum can also be defined as "mass in motion." All objects have mass, so if an object is moving, then it possesses momentum. The amount of momentum that an object has is dependent upon two quantities: how much material is moving and how fast the material is moving.

From the definition of momentum, it becomes obvious that an object has a large momentum if either its mass is large or its velocity is great. Both variables are of equal importance in determining the momentum of an object.

The more you understand and appreciate what momentum does, the more confidence you can develop by knowing that, once you have started in the right direction, you develop more force as you keep moving. Knowing that this is happening in the invisible realm of mind helps you know that you are changing. It is important to know this because, when things change at the thought level, there may not be a corresponding feeling that goes along with the change in thought. Since you are working with changing thought, action, behavior and consequences, you must be patient with yourself. Each of those steps takes time to accomplish. Knowing that you're in process of changing is the key. Your thinking will change and then your behavior will change so that the consequences of your behavior will change.

*Ephesians 3:20 Now unto him that is able to do **exceeding abundantly above** all that we ask or think, according to the power that worketh in us ...*

The Law of Abundance is the drawing power of your active mind and your subconscious mind that creates, over time, abundance. Just as surely as you are reading this, you are at some particular point in life. The point in life where you are has been determined by what is in your mind and subconscious. You have abundantly more than you have ever had in life—not necessarily more things but more words, thoughts and potential for doing things on a larger scale simply because you have more knowledge. You thought, acted, spoke, heard and thought some more. Then you created a habit force and, over time, that intense process produced the situation in which you are now—in need of recovery. That is overstating the obvious and for a very good reason.

By understanding this basic principle and universal law, that, over time, thought produces reality, you will come to realize some basic facts. If you do not like your present reality, change it by creating visualizations of positive abundance in

147

your life. You gain these visualizations through applying the right scientific principles and taking the disciplined way.

Being *disciplined* means that you will not deviate from your pathway toward success. Draw this energy from your thoughts of future success into a visible goal in your imagination and vision. Make it as real as you dare. Add as much detail as you can. Build on it each day. Use your creative talents to bring it into focus. It will, no doubt, take time. But you must either accept your reality as it is or you must change it. Success or abundance does not apply only to money. There is success in communication skills, spirituality, relationships and so on. When creating the abundance of financial gain, remember: we are not the sum total of our possessions. Seek first the higher planes of mental and spiritual life and material things will follow.

You have been on the low road towards destruction. Through the abundance of your thinking, the high road awaits you. It is difficult to change your thought patterns and habit force overnight. Until now your mind has been filled with negative thought patterns. Begin to think, on a daily basis, that you are not limited, inferior and inadequate but that you are unlimited, superior and more than adequate. You are becoming qualified to take on any task with courage and success.

You must begin to realize that within you are all the potentialities for health, wealth, happiness and success. The kingdom of your mind can become a wonderful place in which to live, and you can begin to create the kind of mind you want when you let go of all the internal and external negative influences. But only *you* can decide that you want a new life. Don't forget: there will be abundance one day, and it will be a direct result of what you think. Abundance will come. That is the law. What abundance do you want manifested in your life, in one year, two, five or ten years?

*Psalms 37:11 But the meek shall inherit the earth; and shall delight themselves in the **abundance** of peace.*

*Matthew 25:29 For unto every one that hath shall be given, and he shall have **abundance:** but from him that hath not shall be taken away even that which he hath.*

The Law of Magnetism is one of the invisible principles and powers that bring abundance to you.

Let us explore the nature and history of magnetism. The connection between magnetism and electricity was discovered in the early 19th century. *Enough neurons firing over and over and in tandem with other neurons carrying an electrical current can create a magnetic field.* This field is created by the moving electrical charges forming the current. The production of a current can create a change in the magnetic field around us.

As we look at the structure of the atom, we see electrons and protons. Because the electron has both an electric charge and a spin, it can be considered a charge in motion, giving rise to a tiny magnetic field. Without getting too far into the technical and scientific elements of how this magnetic force is created, it serves us well to know that we create positive and negative magnetic forces that surround us. Our bodies have magnetism within their cells and within the atoms that make up our physical bodies. It is a force that can be used for our good.

Electricity, as we have talked about it in explaining how the brain transmits thought, is important, and magnetism is a large part of what is important in terms of drawing power. Part of the power operating in all of us is electric. When the neurons fire, electrical energy is produced and the brain stores up quantities of magnetic substances in the cells of the brain and body. This is a scientific fact.

If you keep your thoughts positive and optimistic, your mental, physical and spiritual magnetism will draw to you what you want. It will happen with or without your cooperation. Magnetism without direction and choice can lead to chaos. With the use of *The Revelation of Power,* you can begin to magnetize peace and serenity or any other worthwhile future you can envision. You have the ability to magnetize what you want into your life. That is the important element of this law: magnetism in you works!

By the power of magnetism, you have drawn to you the circumstances that surround you. If what you have now is not what you want, you need to begin to want and imagine something else to magnetize. There must be a shift in your magnetic polarity from negative to positive in terms of what you want in the future. Focus on the positive for the future and your thoughts will magnetize it for you.

As you learn to use this law and become aware of its power, you will become more convinced through experience that this law is working for you to bring you the things you want in life. Magnetism works whether or not you participate in the process. *The Revelation of Power* is in *you.*

Start now by choosing your goals and using the power of magnetism for good, positive outcomes. The more power you harness and use through the power of your thoughts and actions, the more power you generate to magnetize and bring to you what you want.

You can begin to train your mind, brain and body to use this great universal law of magnetism for the benefit of your own life. It is an element of *The Revelation of Power* that can be directed, built up and channeled. The result is that you begin to exert more positive influence in your life. You can become a magnet through the power of your mind to attract to you the main focus of your thoughts. You can start now to learn how to magnetize the education, cars, houses and persons you need in your life as you change how you think. It works! Whether you work with it or not, you are going to magnetize what is in your mind and draw it to you. What is in your mind?

*Psalms 73:28 But it is good for me to **draw** near to God: I have put my trust in the Lord GOD, that I may declare all thy works.*

*Isaiah 5:18 Woe unto them that **draw** iniquity with cords of vanity, and sin as it were with a cart rope ...*

*Isaiah 12:3 Therefore with joy shall ye **draw** water out of the wells of salvation.*

*Hebrews 10:22 Let us **draw** near with a true heart in full assurance of faith, having our hearts sprinkled from an evil conscience, and our bodies washed with pure water.*

*Hebrews 10:38 Now the just shall live by faith: but if any man **draw** back, my soul shall have no pleasure in him.*

*James 4:8 **Draw** nigh to God, and he will draw nigh to you. Cleanse your hands, ye sinners; and purify your hearts, ye double minded.*

*Jeremiah 31:3 The LORD hath appeared of old unto me, saying, Yea, I have loved thee with an everlasting love: therefore with lovingkindness **have I drawn thee.***

Adventure is not outside man; it is within.
David Grayson

People travel to wonder at the height of the mountains, at the huge waves of the seas, at the long course of the rivers, at the vast compass of the ocean, at the circular motion of the stars, and yet they pass by themselves without wondering.
St. Augustine, Early Christian Priest

Chapter 15

The Law of Magnetic Control informs us that we can control the magnetic force. Choice of the positive over the negative at the level of thoughts allows us to focus the magnetic flow of energy. This positive flow becomes a powerful charge of energy that, over time, allows us to use higher levels of magnetism, which is control.

Magnetism is not just a force operating independently. It is now under our power and direction through the use of controlled thinking. As we learn how to use this power, it becomes another element of *The Revelation of Power*. A change in mental activity means that every thought we have creates a match that comes back to us. We reap what we sow.

Magnetic control acts like a magnetic force we are sending out continuously and it brings back to us what we have sent out. And when we control our thoughts with purpose we produce a control that, in effect, uses the law of sowing and reaping along with the law of multiplication. This is why, when we start small with drugs, alcohol and breaking laws, our behavior grows into a destructive force. If these things go on unchecked, we multiply the results of what we are doing until we are out of control. Then the very force we are supposed to be using for our benefit *controls us*. We become subject to the force and repeat bad behavior with bad results and, after a while, we cannot understand how we keep doing the same things over and over while declaring we will never do those things again. We are now slaves to our own magnetic force, run riot. Either you exercise control over this force or it controls you.

The Law of Attraction is magnetism similar to gravity. Gravity is the force of attraction between the earth and the moon. Attraction or gravity between bodies exists. The focus of magnetism through goals attracts what you desire. Attraction is different from gravity because attraction may also test you in your progress toward the goal you want to achieve. These laws and principles act in concert. They are very similar in the way they affect our lives. Because growth is necessary, you need resistance. The resistance comes in many forms that test your resolve. You cannot "grow" your body or mind without exercise and resistance.

An atom contains several kinds of particles. Its central core, the nucleus, consists of positively charged particles, called protons, and uncharged particles, called neutrons. Surrounding the nucleus and orbiting it are negatively charged particles, called electrons. Each atom has an equal number of protons and electrons. The nucleus occupies only a tiny fraction of an atom's volume but contains almost all of its mass. Although *they are vibrating at tremendous speeds* the power of attraction keeps them in place while in motion.

Fundamentally, this law describes the powerful force of attraction that holds our solar system in place while in motion. Attraction keeps our planets revolving around our central point of focus, the sun. This same force keeps the subordinate systems of atomic and molecular matter circulating around a center. In physics, this law of attraction is defined as the mutual action by which bodies tend to cohere. It means that there is a power of attraction between objects even in the subatomic world. Actually, everything you see as a solid object is really a mass of vibrating atoms that are in constant motion.

This power has been named gravity or magnetism or, for the purpose of explaining this aspect of power within us, the law of attraction. Think for a moment of all that power and potential. All of these subtle bodies of electrons are coordinated around their microcosmic center and we can use their power to draw other thoughts, people, situations and things to ourselves.

The law of attraction has tremendous power when it is harnessed and used properly. This is a potent universal law; this attraction or law of synthesis is the beginning of mutual attraction. The law of attraction can help explain why coincidences seem to occur at unexplained times. What seems like coincidence is this coming together of powerful ideas or a convergence in time by the use of this powerful force within us. You do not believe in magnetism and attraction? Step off a high building and see how fast you are attracted to the earth.

Laws and principles help you build on solid, unseen, eternal foundations. These laws can be counted upon to serve you as you expose them to your thought power. Remember: they will respond to how you use them.

*John 12:32 And I, if I be lifted up from the earth, will **draw** all men unto me.*

The Law of Expectation is the act of expecting with eager anticipation. It is similar to vision and imagination in that expectation looks into the future.

However, the energy and emotions that can stimulate thought move toward but not beyond what we can imagine. Expectation is anticipation, not an event. We assume, expect or believe and that informs and helps create our experience. Let me say this again: Because the act of expecting with eager anticipation is similar to vision and imagination, expectation is directed toward the future.

Take courage. Your confident expectation and contemplation of a new future, even if it starts just with your intention to expect something different in your life, will pay off when you decide you already have *The Revelation of Power* and you are going to use it.

By changing our expectations, we change our experience in every aspect of life. Instead of having eyes that visualize defeat and depression, we can have eyes that shine with expectation. What you expect is often what you get. When the human mind holds a fixed set of ideas, it creates a force powerful enough to make an expectation into a living reality.

Sometimes the results go way beyond our wildest expectation. As addicted persons, we develop a form of insanity. We do the wrong things repeatedly and expect positive results but the only result is that we end up in jails or institutions and look into the face of death repeatedly.

Expectation is in the future tense. The law of expectation is experienced in the now but happens over time. We think of expectation in terms of an event and a time yet to come, even days or years to come in the future. The time ahead through our expectation is a look into the future with hopes about the probability of a particular outcome.

Expectation gives us a more favorable chance of succeeding by using reasonable possibilities that we will have a chance to obtain what our prior set of expectations have envisioned. It is the womb of time combined with positive expectations that can activate hope and belief so that, over time, you produce a more desired result.

Continued use of the law of expectation changes into a well-grounded, reasonable hope and this presumptive belief becomes a new reliance and trust in the power of expectation. Over time, this power to change your future circumstances becomes a confident mainstay of support in your growing arsenal of tools for positive change.

Eventually, you can begin to trust with some confidence and assurance that many of your expectations are beginning to become reality. And this repeated process gives some measure of security and a glimmer of hope where there was none. No matter what the circumstances, the power and law of expectation can give you the optimism and enthusiasm you need to be successful. This is not wishful thinking or self-deception but an anchor of hope, knowing that there is no cause for despair because you can expect a favorable outcome despite present conditions. Problems are there to be solved.

Learning expectation requires time. Therefore, we must be willing to wait intentionally. Sometimes, we must watch and hold ourselves ready and continue to keep in mind a view of our expected end. Patience is absolutely necessary if expectations are to materialize.

A note of caution: we have been a people of low expectations about ourselves. These low expectations are generated by any number of views based on a poor self-image. Therefore, we must stand guard against and be vigilant of being apprehensive when we begin to use this law so that we do not begin again to dread the future.

It is easy to fall back into old patterns of expecting the worst and setting up negative expections, so that any setback confirms our previous hopeless, pessimistic expectations. Expecting the worst sometimes brings a stunning result based on our own expectations.

Practice positive expectations. Become aware of how you are thinking. Change negative thoughts into a state of continual, confident, cheerful anticipation for the good. The law and principle of expectation will serve you and bring dividends that go beyond your dreams. As proof, I offer this: Look at where you are now and ask yourself if this is beyond what you expected?

Again, let me say: take courage. Your confident expectation and contemplation of a new future, even if it starts *only* with your *intention* to expect something different, will pay off when you decide you already have *The Revelation of Power* and you are going to use it.

*Jeremiah 29:11 For I know the thoughts that I think toward you, saith the LORD, thoughts of peace, and not of evil, **to give you an expected end.***

You can't cross the sea merely by standing and staring at the water.
Rabindranath Tagore

My great concern is not whether you have failed, but whether you are content with your failure.
Abraham Lincoln

Never, never, never, never give up.
Winston Churchill:

The ultimate measure of a person is not where they stand in moments of comfort and convenience, but where they stand in times of challenge and controversy.
Martin Luther King, Jr.

*Luke 12:32 **Fear not**, little flock; **for it is your Father's good pleasure to give you the kingdom.***

Chapter 16

The Law of Cycles is an interval of time during which a characteristically repeated event or sequence of events occurs. For example, sunspots increase and decrease in intensity in an 11-year cycle. A single complete achievement of a periodically repeated event, such as a year, constitutes a cycle of the seasons.

Another way to understand this force is to picture a clear pool of water. A rock is dropped into the center of the pool. The waves move out in ever-increasing circles. The expansion of the waves is limited only by the force that the rock creates striking the water. When the limit of the pool is reached, a return wave is created by the reverse action of the wave striking something. In life, there appears to be the cycle of life and death, cycles or seasons of time, spring, fall, winter and summer. There appears to be a time for all things.

Everything has a time to rise, and a time to fall. Whatever rises falls and whatever falls shall rise again—mountains, oceans, deserts, nations; societies all rise and fall, come and go, grow and die. Continually, they appear over time and retreat into some other form. That is the principle of cycles. What goes around comes around—maybe in a different form, maybe multiplied, but it comes back around. If you want to change what keeps coming your way, you must change yourself at the level of what goes out from you. And that starts at the level of the invisible you and moves to the creative, electrical force of your circle of thoughts, which initiates your cycle. Get on your cycle and ride to a new destination.

Ecclesiastes 11:1 **Cast** *thy bread upon the waters: for thou shalt* **find it after many days.**

The Law of Cycles of Return can be related to the continuation of the above law of cycles. This law, called the "cycles of return," deals with the return of the manifestation from the original action. The rock in the pool is the beginning. This law is about the return action. Whatever you deal with will come back again to be dealt with again. When you defeat an enemy like bad behavior, it will come back to try you again. Knowing that this is natural gives you confidence. It is another opportunity to gain strength. The cycle of lifting weights must be repeated time and time again for muscle growth. The same principle applies in the realms of thought and experience.

This law can be compared to the law of sowing and reaping. While sowing and reaping have more to do with specific thoughts, words and actions planted in the mind, the law of cycles of return has to do with the overall waves of positive and negative energy that we send out into the invisible realms because of our thought processes. These waves of energy will return both with like vibrations and with opposite vibrations or waves of energy. They may come through people, events, tests and trials.

Basically, we produce our environment and circumstances over time, especially in a free society despite the mental and social limitations imposed on us by ourselves and or others. This law is the principle of cause and effect. Every cause has its effect; every effect has its cause. Everything happens according to law, which is why each of these laws is so important to you. As you study and learn these laws they allow you to take advantage of *The Revelation of Power.*

Chance and so-called luck are only names for a law not yet explained through the use of words. There are many planes of causality, but nothing escapes the law. It is always at work with chains of cause and effect that govern all of life and are manifested in matter. If a person were to follow each chain in the link of causality, it would be found that the chain has its beginnings and endings in the invisible, non-material realm—the realm of spirit and energy.

Some of these laws discussed in *The Revelation of Power* cannot always be proven; they must be observed with the mind. Some of these laws are understood only on a spiritual level, usually obtained in higher states of meditation. These laws sometimes can be used to determine the cause and effects of any event.

This is why, in group and individual counseling work, the clients are asked to look into their own past to understand why they act in the present as they do. When this law of cycles is used with conscious effort, desired results can be produced in a person's life by steering himself or herself along definite paths of new positive thinking patterns.

When this law is used in an unconscious (not alive to higher principles and laws), haphazard, undisciplined mind, the effects could become potentially disastrous for the individual. Our so-called accidents or *"catching a charge"* could occur without warning to individuals who toil through life without awareness. We are responsible for the very thoughts that we produce and the final result of our own mental activity.

The most harmful mental causes that prevent a person from thinking and acting as the higher self would dictate are a result of a lack of knowledge about the conscious use of universal law. *The Revelation of Power* is, without doubt, one of the most important educational journeys in a person's life. Ignorance can be removed only through the Word of God, knowledge, wisdom and understanding of universal laws. The reality of thoughts that we manifest produces the desired or undesired effects in our lives.

In every thought, action and deed, a person sets in motion unseen causes and effects. These causes will vibrate from the mental plane throughout the entire physical and spiritual structure of body, out into the environment and finally into the ever-present force of universal law. And the universe is ready to carry out your commands. These laws do not discriminate. Eventually, this same vibratory energy returns to its author, riding upon the return swing of the pendulum in cycles of return.

Luke 6:38 **Give, and it shall be given unto you**; *good measure, pressed down, and shaken together, and running over, shall men give into your bosom. For with the same measure that ye mete withal it shall be measured to you again.*

The Law and Principle of Reciprocity is the main law and principle of the universe. It governs the totality of whatever comes out of you. Whatever comes out of you comes back to you, increased or multiplied. You reap what you sow; what you give you get. Whatever you manifest is manifested back to you sooner or later, increased or multiplied.

The principle of reciprocal power reveals that the use of words, vibrations and the power in all of us, when spoken or projected, will create a return in our lives. We live in a universe where there is a reciprocal condition and a relationship whereby energies and vibrations or words that come out of us interchange, interact and return to us. We are rewarded measure for measure and proportionately equal to what we have said and done. Sometimes in that exchange of energies and vibrations called words, there is an increase in "what comes around." This may be due in part to the fact that we are working on a reward (consequences). Actions and words in the beginning bring smaller consequences and we may not be aware of the return but, over time, the return is so great we can be overwhelmed by it.

Expressed words have vibration power that acts in the invisible realm of all things that vibrate. This means that everything you say has a vibrational effect on everything around you.

Reciprocal power is a potent tool that allows us to dispose of negative emotions by talking about our concerns and having someone give us positive feedback. By aligning ourselves with positive energies, talking becomes a cleansing process that opens up our inner selves to the source of all positive life.

As we continue using reciprocal power, we become eager for continued enlightenment and guidance because we can finally see some positive results. In addition, we set up and lay out new areas of investigation by giving our brains something to work on. Just by rearranging our thoughts into the form of a request, we begin to form and shape our future because, as we hear ourselves speak positively and hopefully, we develop a positive expectation. As our brain begins to form new, definite, powerful connections, the release of positive energy begins to thread together new future arrangements. As we project positive energy in the form of reciprocal power, we formulate new ideas that begin to orchestrate a new destiny.

*Psalms 126:5 They that **sow** in tears shall **reap** in joy.*

*Hosea 8:7 For they have **sown** the wind, and they shall **reap** the whirlwind...*

*Hosea 10:12 **Sow** to yourselves in righteousness, **reap** in mercy; break up your fallow ground: for it is time to seek the LORD, till he come and rain righteousness upon you.*

*2 Corinthians 9:6 But this I say, He which **soweth** sparingly shall **reap** also sparingly; and he which **soweth** bountifully shall **reap** also bountifully.*

*Galatians 6:7 Be not deceived; God is not mocked: for whatsoever a man **soweth**, that shall he also **reap**.*

*Galatians 6:8 For he that **soweth** to his flesh shall of the flesh **reap** corruption; but he that **soweth** to the Spirit shall of the Spirit **reap** life everlasting.*

*Galatians 6:9 And let us not be weary in well doing: for in due season **we shall reap**, if we faint not.*

Universal Law

Let me introduce these observations from diverse cultures and different times, taken from various locations around the world. See if you can tell why they are all saying the same thing.

Christianity: "All things whatsoever ye would that men would do to you, do ye even so to them."

Judaism: "What is hateful to you, do not to your fellow man?"

Islam: "No one of you is a believer until he desires for his brother that which he desires for himself."

Brahmanism: "This is the sum of duty: Do not unto others, which would cause you pain if done to you."

Hinduism: "This is the sum of all true righteousness: deal with others as thou wouldst thyself be dealt by. Do nothing to thy neighbor which thou wouldst not have him do to thee after."

Buddhism: "Hurt not others in ways that you yourself would find hurtful."

Confucianism: "Do not unto others what you would not have them do unto you."

Taoism: "Regard your neighbor's gain as your own gain, and your neighbor's loss as your own loss."

Zoroastrianism: "That nature alone is good which refrains from doing unto another whatsoever is not good for itself."

Native American: "Respect for all life is the foundation." The Great Law of Peace

The teachings of Ptahhotep (2388BC), the oldest known book found in Africa: "Don't be mean towards your friends. They are like a watered field and greater than any material riches that you may have, for what belongs to one belongs to another."

Why are all of these sayings alluding to the same thing? One clear reason is that the truth cannot be concealed from the mind that seeks it. Truth is simply that which exists and cannot be changed. Truth is constantly begging to be revealed.

In my opinion, all of the above statements are based on the law of reciprocity, meaning that you reap what you sow, what goes around comes around. What comes out of you comes back to you multiplied. Therefore, to do unto others is to do unto yourself. Maybe not immediately, but, over time, you get what you give. That is why, at the level of reality, it is best to treat someone else the way we want to be treated because what we do is coming back to us.

How did all these different cultures from different times and locations arrive at this point? Because all of these cultures discovered what is real. We live in a field of energy that will give you back what you put into it. In my opinion, all these cultures discovered the basic law of the universe.

Most people would rather die than think; in fact, they do so. Everything is created from moment to moment, always new. Like fireworks, this universe is a celebration and you are the spectator contemplating the eternal Fourth of July of your absolute splendor
Francis Lucille

The more you praise and celebrate your life, the more there is in life to celebrate.
Oprah Winfrey

I'm fulfilled in what I do... I never thought that a lot of money or fine clothes—the finer things of life—would make you happy. My concept of happiness is to be filled in a spiritual sense.
Coretta Scott King

Happiness cannot be traveled to, owned, earned, worn or consumed. Happiness is the spiritual experience of living every minute with love, grace and gratitude.
Denis Waitley

Aim not for what you are, but for what you could be.
Lucas Hellmer

Chapter 17

The Law and Principle of Seasons is a law and a principle that directly affects you. For the purpose of understanding seasons and their effect, we must begin with how seasons affect humans. That point of origin can be a seed or anything that can grow and combine with other elements. The genesis of an idea has its origin in many areas of the mind. When we speak of the mind and the invisible realm, we may be speaking of particles, electrons, neutrons, protons and quarks, which, when combined, become atoms and electrical energy.

Like a seed, an idea has its beginning and from the invisible seed of thought comes a living reality. Over time, the seed produces a yield. The process of growth, from seed to flower, idea to manifestation, happens in its proper season. The principle illustrates that whatever you plant in your mind will grow. And, in due season, it will produce. Over time, there will be a remembrance and celebratory understanding of what you have planted. Or, conversely, there will be a horrific reminder of the negative seed you planted in your mind. If there are weeds—negative thoughts in your mind—they, too will grow and, in their season, will produce a yield. Begin to plant in the garden of your mind what you truly want in life.

There is truly a time and season of planting when everything is just an idea. This is the time for you to create goals and objectives. This is the creative process, where you give form to your intentions in your imagination and vision. The process of making dreams come true begins during the season of planting. The work we need to do in this season is to take things apart, looking closely at our plans, and putting them back together again. This is the season in which you organize information for the purpose of creating a new reality. While this planting season is invisible on its surface, powerful forces are at work within you.

At the appropriate time, the season of ideas will come springing forth in you toward fruition. While the transformation of seed to plant that breaks the ground does not give us a clear picture of what the plant and yield will look like, we can now see the results of the previously unseen creative force. Prior to this emergence, some person simply watered the dirt in which the seeds were planted.

Evidence of the unseen can now clearly be seen. Light and heat from the sun take the plant higher and higher. So it is with seasons. There comes a time when ideas take shape and grow over time into something greater in size than the original seed. However, all the power necessary for growth was in the seed. With continued nourishment, the seed grows. With continued study, reading and the application of positive information, we grow from the seed of thought.

All these things take place in their own season. If, at any point, either the proper nourishment or the proper positive information is stopped, positive growth stops and decay sets in, taking over and ruining the entire positive growth process.

There is a season of fruition or yield, when the intended purpose of the seed is fulfilled into what it was meant to be. Seed and thought must have a yield. If a seed is properly nourished, over time, it will produce a yield, just as thoughts, if properly nourished over time, will produce a life.

There is also a season when nothing is happening. There is no visible growth—only the death of old things. The harvest is over. The yield is collected and the season of winter makes everything appear cold and dead. During this season, once again wonderful things are invisibly taking place. The mighty oak tree has gone through many seasons from acorn to the mighty oak tree with deep roots.

Why is it important to know these laws and principles? Because you can assess which season you are in so that, no matter what you see or feel, you can identify what you are going through as just a season of growth. This allows you to have peace of mind no matter which season you are currently in or have just come out of or are going into.

*Leviticus 26:4 Then I will give you rain in due **season**, and the land shall yield her increase, and the trees of the field shall yield their fruit.*

*Psalms 1:3 And he shall be like a tree planted by the rivers of water, that bringeth forth his fruit in his **season**; his leaf also shall not wither; and whatsoever he doeth shall prosper.*

*Proverbs 15:23 A man hath joy by the answer of his mouth: and a word spoken in due **season**, how good is it!*

*Isaiah 50:4 The Lord GOD hath given me the tongue of the learned, that I should know how to speak a word in **season** to him that is weary...*

The Law of Process helps in the design of objectives and goals we set and hold consistently in our mind. This law operates simultaneously in our conscious mind and subconscious mind. When we have mindfulness and focus and know that we have things to achieve in our life, the invisible, creative realm of the subconscious begins its work.

The subconscious gives form to our intentions, making our dreams come true step by step in the invisible realm. This process works with or without our conscious effort to take apart and put together ideas and information, thus organizing concepts and maximizing the goals we have set in our conscious mind. Holding our focus releases the power of the subconscious. Feeding the subconscious with positive information reinforces the process until what we experience is no longer held in the imagination or just in the subconscious but has become a living reality.

On the conscious level, if we wish to reach a certain goal, we must set a direction (create order), anticipate well and advance in small but sure steps. Any achievement can be managed if we take the necessary, small, well-thought-out steps to get there. Skipping a single step or taking a shortcut often results in failure. But failure is just another way of taking the wrong path. Part of the beauty and unfolding revelation of this law is to know and to treasure the accomplishment of a single step in the constructive direction towards a goal. That realization of the process is what makes the journey of life so exciting.

When the process is working and you have learned to be aware that it is working, wonderful things begin to happen because you realize powerful changes are taking place within you. You learn to become innovative in this evolving, ever-renewing process. You begin to see new options, and the decisions you make become more powerful, allowing you to become a *habit-maker* as well as a *habit-breaker*, thus beginning the mastery of habit force.

*Mark 4:27 And should sleep, and rise night and day, and the seed should spring and grow up, **he knoweth not how**.*

*Ecclesiastes 3:1 To every thing there is a season, and **a time to every purpose under the heaven** ...*

The Principle of Will can be understood by looking into the realm of psychology. In psychology, the term *will* is used to describe the faculty of mind that stimulates motivation of purposeful activity. Also, for your consideration, human will can be determined by externalized interaction of contradictory fundamentals, resulting in action at the spur of the moment. In other words, enough mental or emotional pressure from the outside can alter your will.

This view takes into account that the subconscious, memory and habit force sometimes exercise power over the will especially when the will is not trained to use current, conscious, positive information.

The use of will is closely associated with the power and principle of choice, which we will discuss later. We will discuss the principle of human will separate from the subject of choice because, in my view, sometimes we make choices spontaneously and then employ our will to carry out our choices.

The principle of will is a human faculty by which one deliberately chooses or decides upon a course of action and employs will to achieve that course. It is the act of exercising the will that takes us to our goals. Make no mistake: it is the diligent purposefulness and determination based upon personal choices that employ the will. These choices are already made in our belief systems and subconscious habit force. Learning to take control of the will is part of how you can attain the self-control and self-discipline necessary to overcome the power of addiction.

The implementation of human will can produce a purpose that is so determined that the resulting course of action will be accomplished. Obstacles do not matter; time is not important. Human will has shattered records and forged completely new levels of achievement. When employed properly, the human will is not just a choice but also a power that can push aside all other views and remain focused on a particular outcome.

The fact that the principle of human will can be used as motivation even before any action is taken is a powerful beginning. It can be a determining force for change. Say to yourself, "My change will come," and own the experience. This affirmation can be used in commanding oneself to action. It can be used to indicate future action, expressed with the certainty that something will happen, and to repeat this phrase indicates that your habitual action will bring results.

The power of human will cannot be overestimated. However, let me suggest that will alone is not enough. Human will, especially in the case of those who are addicted, is not enough. All the other laws, principles and positive input are necessary for continued success.

*Isaiah 41:10 Fear thou not; for I am with thee: be not dismayed; for I am thy God: **I will** strengthen thee; yea, **I will** help thee; yea, **I will** uphold thee with the right hand of my righteousness.*

*Isaiah 41:13 For I the LORD thy God **will** hold thy right hand, saying unto thee, Fear not; **I will** help thee.*

*Isaiah 41:14 Fear not, thou worm Jacob, and ye men of Israel; **I will** help thee, saith the LORD, and thy redeemer, the Holy One of Israel.*

*John 15:7 If ye abide in me, and my words abide in you, ye shall ask **what ye will**, and it shall be done unto you.*

*1 Thessalonians 5:18 In every thing give thanks: for this is **the will of God** in Christ Jesus concerning you.*

*Hebrews 10:36 For ye have need of patience, that, after ye have done **the will of God**, ye might receive the promise.*

*1 John 2:17 And the world passeth away, and the lust thereof: but he that doeth **the will of God** abideth for ever.*

Chapter 18

The Law of Will Power is about the strength or power of will to carry out one's decisions, wishes or plans. Will power is used when every part of the intellect, vision and imagination is focused and we deliberately decide upon a course of action.

The simple but undeviating act of exercising will power creates a determination and diligent purposefulness that pushes aside obstacles both invisible and visible. Exercising the will requires self-discipline. Determination is necessary in the use of will power to overcome old emotional ties to negative behavior. To decide on a course of action using will power is to yearn for something and to have a resolve that is so powerful that the force of your will determines your conduct every day, in every aspect of your life when choices matter.

Will power involves placing our focus on the desired goal and understanding that our hopes must be channeled through the powers of thought, thus concentrating all of our reasoning power on a firmness of mind that says: my will cannot be denied. All of these things do happen with or without our consent because the association of ideas in our consciousness will cause us to act in a fashion consistent with our innermost thoughts. If you are not going to use your will power, then you will become a servant of deeper powers of will that are hidden in your subconscious.

You can have a liberated will and use the power of your own boundless will but you must use discretion in what you think and what you do in order to shape your future. Taking control of your will requires a daily inner fight and you must be resolute and determined. Also remember that you must always act from a moral base. Your will can help you brace yourself against the storms of life. It is up to you to override your emotions and negative thinking. It is you who must take charge of your own mind—to insist, to press the issue, not to take no for an answer but to put your foot down daily and resist the nonsense that has been allowed to roam around freely in your mind.

I shall, I will and I am going to use my power to shape my will to accomplish a new future. Remember this and *mean* it. Stop at nothing and go to any lengths to exercise your will in the right direction. Push yourself to the extremes in pursuit of your own peace and serenity. Defy the odds, face the danger, see it through and don't stop. Become single-minded and set your heart on your goals and commit yourself to burn the bridges of the past and step into a new life. Go for it! Take up your new life in earnest. Devote and dedicate yourself to developing a powerful will that will take you where you would like to go.

As you continue to exercise the power of your will, others will notice and will be impressed by your actions and achievements. Know that you can take control of your will. It will raise your expectations for the future. Continual use of your will power will allow you to predict the future in a positive way and see it carried to completion as you accomplish each goal on a daily basis. You will begin to respect yourself but, after a while, you will command and inspire respect from others.

When others see you exercise the power of your will, it will be impressive to them. They will be struck with awe but you will know that it is because you have mastered just one of the universal laws that you now command this admiration from others. After a while, you will develop a reputation and have good standing in everyone's eyes. This takes time but no one is going to give you respect until you respect yourself.

This seems like a rose-colored picture of your future. Well, it can be. You can gain honor and make a positive impression on others. People will begin to take interest in you. Only you can arrest your outlaw mind and let these truths sink in. Only you can drive home the truth to yourself. Only you can penetrate who you are in your essence and use your will power. I cannot emphasize this enough. If you do not take control of your will, something else will!

Laws and principles govern all creation, both seen and unseen. The laws and principles that operate in the outer universe, discovered by scientists, are often called "natural laws." But there are subtler laws that rule the hidden planes and the inner realms of consciousness. Contained within these laws is the true nature that operates the creation of thought to matter. Knowledge of these laws has an effect upon the mind. Our mind is the creator and builder of most of what we see in the world today. The key is to stay in full mindfulness of the power of our will in the application of universal law as it relates to self and to others. When we talk about *will power*, we see that the devil said *five times* what he willed.

*Isaiah 14:13 For thou hast said in thine heart, **I will** ascend into heaven, **I will** exalt my throne above the stars of God: **I will** sit also upon the mount of the congregation, in the sides of the north ...*

*Isaiah 14:14 **I will** ascend above the heights of the clouds; **I will** be like the most High.*

God answered the devil in his covenant with Abraham. He said *five times* that Abraham and the gentiles are also blessed. The blessings of Abraham, under which we live, are an area of the Bible you may want to study. We have powerful privileges and we need to know what they are.

*Genesis 12:1 Now the LORD had said unto Abram, Get thee out of thy country, and from thy kindred, and from thy father's house, unto a land that **I will** shew thee:*

*Genesis 12:2 And **I will** make of thee a great nation, and **I will** bless thee, and make thy name great; and thou shalt be a blessing:*

*Genesis 12:3 And **I will** bless them that bless thee, and curse him that curseth thee: and in thee shall all families of the earth be blessed.*

*Genesis 13:16 And **I will** make thy seed as the dust of the earth: so that if a man can number the dust of the earth, then shall thy seed also be numbered.*

The Principle of Choice is closely associated with human will, but there is a necessity to separate the two. We can make mental choices without exercising our will to get the job done or carry out the task. The art of choosing the right path and walking it is what we are striving for. Cultivation of proper choices allows us to become more self-determined people while going in the right direction. The practice of making the right choice is to exercise the principle of choice, but you must first know that you have the freedom to choose differently. As other areas of our consciousness are freed from error, negative energies and thought patterns, we learn to pick the right course with knowledge and wisdom. This leads us to become more deliberate in our decision-making process, as we learn to make positive choices from a wealth of positive alternatives. Problems are there to be solved through making the right choices. Choice is the goal. Regardless of feelings and emotions, correct choices are to be made.

Once we are sure that what happens to us is a reflection of what we really believe about ourselves, including our choices, we realize that we cannot go beyond what we believe. Everything we say comes back to us in many ways. But our ability to choose opens up whole new worlds of opportunities for us because we can definitely choose to change what we think about ourselves. Changing into a person with a purpose and the ability to choose the positive is a power that *will* change us.

Having a range of positive choices is what we learn along the pathway of recovery from the numerous resources available to us every day. Only we can make the choice to go after positive information that will liberate us. Only we can exercise our will on a daily basis until our actions are rooted in recovery and our choice of any other pathway becomes foreign to us.

*Deuteronomy 7:7 The LORD did not set his love upon you, nor **choose** you, because ye were more in number than any people; for ye were the fewest of all people...*

*Deuteronomy 30:19 I call heaven and earth to record this day against you, that I have set before you life and death, blessing and cursing: therefore **choose** life, that both thou and thy seed may live ...*

The Law of Force is the capacity to do work or cause physical change. The focused use of energy and strength makes use of knowledge and turns energy into active power. Force is power against resistance. That force gives us the power to resist the temptation to return to our old way of living. The exertion of power is the use of physical strength or aggression either to compel oneself to action or to restrain oneself from action.

The use of intellectual power or enthusiasm, especially as conveyed in writing or in speech, is a power or force. A form of moral strength is developed within personal character. The law of force can be seen in the capacity for affecting the mind or behavior of others. There is great force in the intensity and power of a logical argument.

There is the force of many, such as an armed force. There is the power and force to practice daily a new routine until it becomes habit force. To break through resistance, to move objects, to clear obstacles, sometimes full force is necessary. No matter how much is required in order to recover from old habits, it is necessary to summon from within the force necessary to meet every challenge.

The use of force and power suggests that one should be bound to a course of action by physical or moral means or by the operation of a compelling dynamism called force. Splitting atoms releases an atomic force. You are made of atoms, molecules and cells. Now that you know you have force and power inside every cell in your body, use it in a positive way!

*Psalms 147:5 Great is our Lord, and of great **power**: his understanding is infinite.*

*Proverbs 18:21 Death and life are in the **power** of the tongue: and they that love it shall eat the fruit thereof.*

*Ecclesiastes 5:19 Every man also to whom God hath given riches and wealth, and hath given him **power** to eat thereof, and to take his portion, and to rejoice in his labour; this is the gift of God.*

*Isaiah 40:29 He giveth **power** to the faint; and to them that have no might he increaseth strength.*

*Matthew 10:1 And when he had called unto him his twelve disciples, he gave them **power** against unclean spirits, to cast them out, and to heal all manner of sickness and all manner of disease.*

*Luke 10:19 Behold, I give unto you **power** to tread on serpents and scorpions, and over all the power of the enemy: and nothing shall by any means hurt you.*

*John 1:12 But as many as received him, to them gave he **power** to become the sons of God, even to them that believe on his name ...*

*Romans 1:16 For I am not ashamed of the gospel of Christ: for it is the **power** of God unto salvation to every one that believeth; to the Jew first, and also to the Greek.*

*Acts 1:8 But ye shall receive **power**, after that the Holy Ghost is come upon you: and ye shall be witnesses unto me both in Jerusalem, and in all Judaea, and in Samaria, and unto the uttermost part of the earth.*

*2 Timothy 1:7 For God hath not given us the spirit of fear; but of **power,** and of love, and of a sound mind.*

One person with a dream can accomplish more than 100 others without one. If you have a burning desire, you can accomplish anything. The biographies of great men and women are full of stories of how they did seemingly impossible things because they had a dream.
Author unknown

He who cherishes a beautiful vision, a lofty ideal in his heart, will one day realize it. Dream lofty dreams and as you dream so shall you become.
James Allen

Ultimately, the only power to which man should aspire is that which he exercises over himself.
Elie Wiesel

Power never takes a back step—only in the face of more power.

Malcolm X (1925 - 1965), Malcolm X Speaks, 1965

Power concedes nothing without a demand. It never did and it never will.

Frederick Douglas

You survived one hundred thousand other sperm to get here. What do you mean you don't know what to do?

Les Brown

Chapter 19

The Principle of Discipline is the training of mind, body and spirit to produce a specific character or pattern of behavior. This is especially true of the kind of training that produces moral or mental improvement. With practice, discipline gives you greater control over your behavior. You achieve greater self-control by forcing yourself to comply with rules, thus bringing a sense of order to chaos. An orderly life comes from a compliance and obedience to rules and to authority.

By practicing obedience to rules, laws and principles, you expand your whole self to a greater degree than you could accomplish by any other means. Discipline is the surest means to greater freedom and independence. It provides the focus to achieve the skill level and depth of knowledge that translates into more options in life. Commitment involves discipline over a specific period of time. Discipline and commitment provide the bridge between where you are now and where you want to be in the future.

Discipline requires being taught and being teachable. Discipline means you learn how to accept correction until you learn to self-correct and self-judge in order to establish control over your own actions and behavior.

*Job 36:10 He openeth also their ear to **discipline**, and commandeth that they return from iniquity.*

*Matthew 10:24 The **disciple** is not above his master, nor the servant above his lord.*

*Luke 14:27 And whosoever doth not bear his cross, and come after me, cannot be my **disciple.***

The Law or Right to Decree is the power to speak to the future and summon the future from the present.

Every day, we use these powers and laws that we are discussing. Just think for a moment. You have been talking for years, and your conversation has shaped your present circumstances, even if what you talked about was shaping a negative outcome, as in the case of criminal thinking, association and negative goal orientation as in robbing and vandalizing. To get to the point of carrying out negative behavior, you had to talk to yourself and to others to convince yourself and others that this illegal act could be committed.

At some point, your actions may have become automatic through the power of habit force. However, you had to talk your way into the action, completely discounting other, legal ways of accomplishing your goals. The talking led to a feeling of self-assurance. This self-assurance about your proposed action was a false sense of security, based on a negative use of the law of faith. The head trip led to the feeling of anticipated euphoria, control, possession and, of dominance over the particular event.

Sometimes your inner conversation thrived on overcoming any adversity and pressure or the possibility of failure. In other words, you had to use a form of negative faith to prevent distractions and the fear of not obtaining your goal. That kind of negative faith and negative habit force enabled you to render inoperative, all logic and laws of probability that you might get caught. In addition, that kind of negative attitude allowed you to dismiss morality and eliminate fear, enabling you to carry out the plan and dare to take any risk. That is what the power to speak the future can do, even when used in a negative way. Of course, when we are in this

181

negative state of mind, we do not believe that we will have to pay a price. Sometimes we can accept that risk as a part of the bargain necessary to carry out the act. It is only after repeated incarcerations in institutions and near-death experiences that we begin to ask ourselves, "How can I turn this around?"

In order to change where you want to be, you must change the information base from which your ideas, imaginations and visions spring. You have to reverse the process we just discussed. This reversal is absolutely necessary, starting with having a simple talk with yourself. The important thing to remember is that you can begin to talk your way into a new life. It is the law.

Persistence means absolutely refusing to give up on either yourself or your dreams in spite of difficulty. Persistence means having the will to continue in the face of struggle. Persistence really means never giving up. Nothing in the world can take the place of persistence. Talent isn't enough. Nothing is more common than unsuccessful men with talent. Genius will not take the place of persistence. Genius does not constitute success simply because some brilliant person went to the grave, unborn.

Education alone will not do it; the world is full of educated bums. Persistence and determination are the most powerful tools to help you have continued recovery.

- Learned helplessness explains why many people give up
- Once learned, it is easy to justify one's helplessness
- Learned helplessness is the definitive barrier to empowerment

*Proverbs 18:21 Death and life are **in the power of the tongue***: and they that love it shall eat the fruit thereof.*

*Hebrews 1:13 But to which of **the angels** said he at any time, Sit on my right hand, until I make thine enemies thy footstool?*

*Hebrews 1:14 Are they not all ministering spirits, <u>sent forth to minister</u> **for them** <u>who shall be heirs of salvation?</u>*

*Isaiah 45:11 Thus saith the LORD, the Holy One of Israel, and his Maker, Ask me of things to come concerning my sons, and concerning the work of my hands **command ye me**.*

The Principle of Faith operates very much like the Law of Expectation except that faith operates on a firm basis of belief despite present circumstances. Faith is a confident belief in an idea. Faith trusts, with certainty, that the thing desired will eventually be manifested in reality. Faith is not founded on logical proof or material evidence. The act of using the principle of faith is an act of believing that requires a suspension of disbelief because every other means of obtaining a look into the future fails.

The principle of faith operates without our active participation. Where you are in life right now is a result of a set of belief systems that you held previously. Any number of things you believed would happen as you acted in real time. You made the decisions. Regardless of all input from upbringing, social programming, words in music or information from school, you made the choices and acted. Well, you acted using the principle of faith. Whatever direction you took was based on the energy of your belief system. When the principle of inner faith reached out into the active forces and principles of life that always operate around us, it did not focus on whether the information was right or wrong. Faith acted! Scientifically, under the laws and principles of faith, counterbalanced with the laws and principles of the universe, faith acted and that is how you got to where you are. To understand this as a principle is power. Used properly in a positive fashion, it is power to change.

The principle of faith can add assurance and conviction to your life. This principle translates into strong feelings, which can override negative emotions and the power of a negative past. The persuasive force and confidence that come with using the principle of faith, combined with the principle of growth, create a powerful combination. When life experience bears the fruit of your firm belief and assurance, you begin to do the right things in life. Now you know that you will receive, through the principle of faith, the things and results you desire. Faith becomes an unshakeable, fixed belief that you can recover and be a success in life.

In my opinion, the material of faith is thought and energy. Thoughts and energy are, or can be, the future because what we consistently think about has the tendency to become reality. What I envision or imagine may be just a series of thoughts strung together with future hopes. But, with enough effort and action, those thoughts of faith become reality.

*Matthew 6:30 Wherefore, if God so clothe the grass of the field, which to day is, and to morrow is cast into the oven, shall he not much more clothe you, O ye of **little faith?***

*Matthew 9:29 Then touched he their eyes, saying, According to **your faith** be it unto you.*

*Mark 4:40 And he said unto them, Why are ye so fearful? how is it that ye have **no faith?***

*Acts 6:8 And Stephen, **full of faith** and power, did great wonders and miracles among the people.*

*Romans 4:5 But to him that worketh not, but **believeth** on him that justifieth the ungodly, his faith is counted for righteousness.*

*Romans 5:1 Therefore being **justified by faith**, we have peace with God through our Lord Jesus Christ:*

*Romans 5:2 By whom also we have **access by faith** into this grace wherein we stand, and rejoice in hope of the glory of God.*

*Romans 10:17 So then **faith cometh** by hearing, and hearing by the word of God.*

*Hebrews 11:6 But **without faith** it is impossible to please him: for he that cometh to God must believe that he is, and that he is a rewarder of them that diligently seek him.*

A Story about Faith

What I am about to tell you is true. It is powerful and mysterious but absolutely true. I placed this story and event in this chapter because it has to do with answered prayer and how it developed my complete faith in what God is doing in me.

Before working at San Francisco County jails 3 and 7, I worked at the San Quentin prison in California as a counselor. The population of San Quentin was over 6,000 inmates and a staff of some 1,500 guards, officers and medical support personnel.

After a great deal of prayer, planning and talking, my wife and I moved to Pine Bluff, Arkansas mainly because of housing prices.

I began work at the Tucker Prison in Tucker, Arkansas as an alcohol and drug counselor. That is where this story begins.

Being in the ministry, I wanted to make sure I was on the right pathway and doing the Lord's will. So I began to pray on almost a daily basis, asking God if I was where He wanted me to be. The move from California had been difficult and the numerous struggles involved in the relocation made me wonder if I was in the right place.

At the time of this story, I counseled and taught in a nine-month therapeutic community program within the prison at Tucker. As one of several staff members, I was sometimes selected to sit on a classification board. This board consisted of all the prison department heads. Each department had particular personnel needs that required inmates to be placed in those departments. The warden, the assistant warden and their secretary were there to listen to and work with the needs of the heads of each department, such as the farm, personal, training schools, work crews, maintenance, medical, kitchen, etc.

Every week, our clinical supervisor, Mr. Cameron, who was also the head of our department at that time, sat on this board. Once in a while, he had other duties and he chooses someone else from among our staff members to sit on this board in his place. On one particular day, as I was leaving my office, I was selected at random to sit on this board. My job was to place pre-selected clients for our program into the morning or afternoon group of classes that our program was set up to handle.

Remember that my question to God was, "Am I in the right place and am I following His will?" Well, I have a brother and sister who are twins. At the time of this story, they lived in New Haven, Connecticut, where I was born. An inmate came into the classification boardroom. His first and last names were the same as the first names of my brother and sister. My sister's first name is really unusual and my brother's first name is Frazier. (For reasons of confidentiality, I cannot use the client's full name.)

When I began to think of all the random circumstances that brought us together at that moment in time, I was amazed. I thought, "What a coincidence this is!" Was this God giving me a sign? Was this my answer? When I told my brother and sister about that incident, they did not believe me. They thought I was joking and exaggerating or just trying to fool them. When I came home to Connecticut for a visit, I brought the classification roster with me for that date and showed it to them. We thought, "Boy!" What a random one-time event that was!"

Surprisingly enough, this was not the event that makes this story so fantastic and powerful. It was just a small glimpse into the power of God. He further proved to me, beyond any doubt, that He has the power to intervene in the affairs of man and that everything is under His control.

For most people, the coincidence of first names would have been a convincing enough message that yes, I was in the right place at the right time. However, I was not convinced that this was God's answer. So I had enough courage to ask God for an additional indication that I was where I needed to be.

On the weekends, I also worked a part-time job in Little Rock. Little Rock is not quite 50 miles from Pine Bluff. My hours of work at the time of this incident were from four in the afternoon until twelve midnight.

I had recently had a car accident. I was not injured but I had to get another car. I was blessed to get a small, new gas-efficient car. While traveling to Little Rock two weeks after I had been blessed with this brand-new car, I was driving up the hill that overlooks the capitol city of Little Rock as I was traveling north on Arkansas Interstate 530.

I saw a small pickup truck just ahead and noticed a small rock fall off the truck. The rock hit the pavement a couple of times and headed in my direction. Before I could react, the rock hit my windshield just above the hood and below the windshield wiper blade. Days later, a crack developed and it eventually snaked across the windshield. I was so disgusted at having this happen so soon after getting the car that I left the windshield just as it was, cracked.

Perhaps a year went by and, as usual, I was on my way to work in Little Rock on the weekend. As was my habit, I was listening to a Pine Bluff radio station that plays gospel music. At some point, the Pine Bluff station fades out, depending on the weather conditions. Sometimes it fades out not long after I leave Pine Bluff but sometimes I can listen to it all the way to Little Rock. Most of the time, it fades out somewhere between Pine Bluff and my arrival at Little Rock. So I have a Little Rock gospel station already tuned in so that all I have to do is punch a preset button. During the ride, I always wind up turning up the volume to catch the last sounds of the station from Pine Bluff before the sound, fades out. So, when I punch in the Little Rock Station, having forgotten that I turned up the volume, the sound bursts into the car suddenly and remains loud until I turn it down.

On this particular day—a day I will never forget as long as I live—the Pine Bluff station faded out and I reached over to punch in the Little Rock station. Well, as soon as I pushed the button, right on the J—I mean right on the very J of my first name—the radio announcer's voice interrupted every thought in my mind as it boomed into my car from the Little Rock station, saying, "**James Lamb, of Pine Bluff Arkansas.**"

The announcer went on to say, "…will be speaking at our prayer breakfast next Saturday morning." Yes, I heard the entire announcement of my name in addition to the other things that were being said, but my mind was fixed on, "**James Lamb, of Pine Bluff Arkansas,**" booming through the car and reverberating throughout my entire being.

Next, I was just in awe, as I thought of all the variables involved in the timing of that announcement: The time I left the house; the necessary changes in speed that enabled me to get to that exact point on the highway at that precise moment to hear the announcement; what the announcer said; where and when the station was about to fade out; the rhythm of the announcer's voice; and the urge to change the station —all coinciding at that precise moment.

And, as I became aware of where I was on the highway, I was even more amazed and moved at the deepest levels of my being. I was in the very same place where, one year before, I had the windshield hit and cracked by that small rock. Now add all the other variables of the traffic that you can imagine. Add all that to the equation and you tell me what the odds were of something like that happening.

I was also startled by something that permeated my entire being. It was not fear. And I could not tell you what that feeling was except to say that, for a split second, I was overwhelmed by a presence of immense power. It was as if, for a split second, I knew, at a level I couldn't possibly explain: that God has *everything* under control. Nothing in the entire universe is random.

I have not asked God again if I am in the right place. Right on the J of my first name, and I mean right on the very J! Now you tell me how that happened. Was this just a coincidence? I think not. And you would not think so either if it had happened to you. I do not doubt God. I now have complete faith. I know I am where I am supposed to be because He orders my steps and all things are working for my good.

*Psalms 37:23 The steps of a good man are **ordered by the LORD:** and he delighteth in his way.*

*Romans 8:28 And we know that **all things** work together for good to them that love God, to them who are the called according to his purpose.*

Revelation 1:8 I am Alpha and Omega, the beginning and the ending, saith the Lord, **which is, and which was, and which is to come**, *the Almighty.*

God has been aware throughout all eternity where I would be at that precise moment.

Chapter 20

The Law of Action holds that no matter what we believe, feel or know, no matter what our potential gifts or talents may be, only action brings them to life. I can sit next to a full table of food and believe that if I eat that food it will help me. All the mental resolve in the world to believe does absolutely no good unless I am driven to take some action. I can know beyond a shadow of a doubt that I can eat the food and it will be nourishing and healthy for me, but until I actually take some action and eat the food, it will do me no good. I could die of want at a table of plenty.

You can dream for an eternity of the many wonderful achievements and splendid accomplishments possible in life, but, unless you are driven to take some physical action, everything is just a collection of thoughts and pictures in your mind. Those of us who think we understand the power of words and actions such as commitment, courage and love, one day discover that, after continued movement in the direction of those words, the action of those words takes us to a point where we begin to know.

When we act with intensity, eventually, our actions become understanding. For those who dare to aspire and grow mentally and spiritually in a positive direction, there is a definite point where action becomes absolutely necessary to achieve their goals. Energy is the driving force behind change.

The Revelation of Power is truly best utilized in applying different metaphors, words and symbols to our inner energy, and that formula will produce different results. The full impact of using power to change is not cognitive; it is in the experience. Then we begin to understand, on a very profound personal level, how to use power. For example, past pain, regardless of its cause, is energy located somewhere within us. That pain (energy) can be used if we attach a new metaphor to it. Passion and commitment are different word symbols that, with a trained mind, can transform the energy that produced pain into passion and commitment to change whatever is needed to change. That is power that can produce positive action. Thus the title of this book: *The Revelation of Power.*

*2 Chronicles 20:15 And he said, Hearken ye, all Judah, and ye inhabitants of Jerusalem, and thou king Jehoshaphat, Thus saith the LORD unto you, Be not afraid nor dismayed by reason of this great multitude; for **the battle is not yours**, but God's.*

*Psalms 18:39 **For thou hast girded me with strength unto the battle**: thou hast subdued under me those that rose up against me.*

*Exodus 14:14 The LORD shall **fight for you**, and ye shall hold your peace.*

*Deuteronomy 3:22 Ye shall not fear them: for the LORD your God he **shall fight for you.***

*Deuteronomy 20:4 For the LORD your God is he that goeth with you, to **fight for you** against your enemies, to save you.*

*2 Chronicles 20:17 Ye shall **not need to fight** in this battle: set yourselves, stand ye still, and see the salvation of the LORD with you, O Judah and Jerusalem: fear not, nor be dismayed; to morrow go out against them: for the LORD will be with you.*

*Jeremiah 1:19 And they shall fight against thee; but they shall not prevail against thee; **for I am with thee, saith the LORD, to deliver thee.***

*1 Timothy 6:12 **Fight** the good **fight of faith**, lay hold on eternal life, whereunto thou art also called, and hast professed a good profession before many witnesses.*

The Law of Equilibrium and Balance allows you to remain steady. In using these universal principles and laws, you want to remember that balance is most important. A well-balanced approach is necessary for wholesome growth. When your balance is based on a strong connection to your deeper spiritual self, there is a steadiness that directs the flow of your life. While the flow may take you way up or way down, your connection to your deeper spiritual self provides a stability that overcomes the extremes. Your educational efforts must be balanced with a variety of subjects to avoid sounding like a know-it-all. You can become preachy and moralize about others, forgetting to use the art of balancing what others do as an example to you, thus increasing your overall base of information for continued self-correction. Proper balance stabilizes you and, in effect, gives you a stable base from which to keep things in perspective.

This principle takes into account that more than one reality can be held as true in our minds. Everything is not just right or wrong, black or white, either/or. This ability allows you to compromise with others. This understanding also helps you to realize that you are pulled in two different directions at the same time.

If you are in recovery, you have an urge for self-destruction, which you have created yourself. But there is also an urge for self-preservation, which you are presently working on. To be aware of these two forces gives you the knowledge that you can *choose* to live and not die. The principle of balance is a universal law that supersedes all of man's laws, creating stability for everything that is manifested in the universe.

In short, there appear in life to be two equal but opposite forces in life. So, when you begin to create good results as a result of using *The Revelation of Power*, there is an equal force that pushes against your efforts to change. Just knowing this allows you to concentrate greater power to accomplish your goals, knowing there will be resistance. Remaining in balance between the two forces will allow you to have a settled mind, knowing and resting in the fact that these feelings of conflict are normal. And the resisting or opposing force becomes your ally because, in order to move forward and remain balanced, you must grow in courage, power, faith and character, giving you an overall sense of accomplishment.

As this process is repeated, your confidence level continues to grow and you become more self-assured but you are able to keep all this power, thinking and action in balance. This is what is meant by wisdom. Wisdom allows you to leave room for other viewpoints without feeling that you must defend your own point of view if it is based in true knowledge. Low self-esteem is just as non-productive as a puffed-up sense of self-esteem. Both extremes prevent equilibrium and balance.

Like the curve of the infinity sign,∞ even though you may stray far from your center of balance, your life will return to the center.

Balance is reliability, steadiness and equilibrium in your life. It involves giving suitable importance to each part of your life, being grounded and being connected to your deeper self. No matter what direction in which you may wander, balance, based on a strong connection to your deeper self, will always return you to your center.

Balance is necessary in all aspects of your existence. You need balance between your physical activity and rest; and you need balance in your mental, emotional and spiritual activities. You need times of concentrated thinking and times of daydreaming and meditation. You need times of deep feeling and times of simply being. Your overall life also needs balance. You will have times of great challenge balanced by times of mundane repetition.

You become unbalanced when you are paying too much attention to one part of your life and to the exclusion of all the other parts. You would be out of balance, for instance, if you were always to focus on your job responsibilities to the exclusion of your health and personal relationships. You may all too often stay late at the office, eat junk food at your desk and spend all your waking efforts on improving your job performance. In the short run, you may benefit professionally. In the long run, however, your health will decline and you may lose your families and friends because you are out of balance. Another manifestation of imbalance is addiction.

You are out of balance when you are ungrounded. If you are ungrounded, you are inconsistent and uneven. You cannot maintain your focus. You can ground yourself by sitting on the grass, walking on the ground, meditating, gardening or simply gazing at the beauty of nature. When you are grounded, you have stability, like a tree rooted deeply in the earth.

Perhaps most importantly, you are unbalanced when you are disconnected from your deeper, invisible self. Balance begins inside, with your awareness and relationship to your deeper, unseen self. You can increase your connection to your deeper invisible and infinitely powerful new self in countless ways, including meditation, prayer, expressing your creativity, enjoying quiet contemplation and being grateful. The more you come to know the nature of your deeper self, the more you will manifest the quality of balance in your life.

The focus of your balance should be on peace. From the centered position of peace you can easily recognize any thought or emotion that attempts to push you out of balance. With repeated practice, you learn instinctively to quickly interrupt any negative thought or feeling so that you can remain at peace.

Peace must be guarded at all costs. It is the balancing point from which you do not want to be moved. Many times after you have moved into another area of negative thought or emotion, if you are not brought back to a place of balance by a group, friend or some positive input from yourself or other means, you can drift further along the lines of negative thoughts or emotions. If you are not brought back into balance or peace, bad results may follow. Peace and balance are the keys. Peace is the balancing point. Remember that without peace there is no balance.

*Isaiah 40:12 Who hath measured the waters in the hollow of his hand, and meted out heaven with the span, and comprehended the dust of the earth in a measure, and weighed the mountains in **scales**, and the hills in a **balance?***

*Job 31:6 Let me be weighed in an even **balance,** that God may know mine integrity.*

*Proverbs 11:1 A false balance is abomination to the LORD: but a **just weight** is his delight.*

The Principle of Harmony or Common Ground is a principle that can be used for solving problems. It is an area where two or more people can gather together to blend differences. For any addicted person, obtaining their drug of choice by any means necessary is a common approach to all problems, and any obstacles that stand in the way of reaching that goal are dismissed. That kind of personal, selfish approach to life and problems will block out proper feelings, thoughts and any positive regard for anyone else.

The addict will hurt anyone who gets in the way of the primary goal of obtaining the drug. When the addicted person is in treatment and there is no drug available, the addicted person must still be deal with him/herself. If the approach to situations and others has been selfish at the core, then the person still will act selfishly in most situations. That selfish core will cause the addicted person to want his or her way all the time, and he or she will use every possible argument and all of his or her intelligence, built up during a life time, to accomplish what he or she wants.

The addict perceives the counselor and the program as wrong. By way of personal action thought and deed, determined at all costs to prove that he or she is right. Innumerable hours of treatment are lost because of addicts who argue with counselors or refuse to obey group rules as they attempt to make themselves right and both the counselor and the "system" wrong. All attention to detail is lost because the focus is outward rather than inward. This same ability to focus on every detail other than him or her self becomes the argument, and the argument then becomes the activity in place of true therapy, which must include acceptance of rules and authority. No matter how many times this is stressed, the major resistance to harmony and common ground in a treatment setting is the tension between the addicted person, the staff and the rules.

To develop the skills to solve problems in conjunction with another person or situation requires new mental and emotional skills. The principle of common ground gives you the ability to do this. You can leave your self will, which has been out of control, and merge your thoughts and abilities with others' to find a common ground of peace and harmony. This is not easy because you have been out of control for a long time and your closely held denial will not let you see how you really are. You cannot reach common ground with the truth until you are honest with yourself. Being honest with yourself requires daily introspection and acceptance of the horrid facts of life that you find inside yourself.

Another way to express harmony and common ground is through gratitude toward yourself and others. Appreciating other people brings you peace. As a result of your actions of creating harmony, you can bring peace to other people. Spend some time focusing on your attitude. Observe your feelings as they make themselves known to you. Are you feeling drained, irritable or simply frustrated because of some problem? Imagine how you might be able to change your feelings by using an attitude of patience, harmony, common ground and openheartedness toward yourself and others. Then try gratitude.

Gratitude brings us to the place of giving and receiving or common ground and harmony. Gratitude acknowledges our receiving of abundance and, in and of itself, becomes an act of giving back to the universe. Abundance then becomes a natural byproduct of gratitude, harmony and common ground.

How is that possible? How does abundance suddenly appear? Quite simply: it was always there in the universe, waiting for you to call upon it!

Through our addictions and criminal behavior, based on a self-centered lifestyle, we were unable to see the peace that was waiting for us. Gratitude is the act of becoming consciously aware of all that is there for us in life, and then acknowledging the gift. This aligns us with the universal principle that giving is the same as receiving and that what you give you get back. In graciously receiving the gifts that life provides us, we give back the gift of gratitude. Show and express your gratitude and you will see that your life is a beautiful string of miracles!

If you refuse to look at what you have done and who you are you will remain in denial and a continual state of resistance to change even though you might say, impulsively and quickly, "I want to change."

*Acts 1:14 These all continued with **one accord** in prayer and supplication, with the women, and Mary the mother of Jesus, and with his brethren.*

*Acts 2:1 And when the day of Pentecost was fully come, they were **all with one accord** in one place.*

*Acts 2:46 And they, continuing daily with **one accord** in the temple, and breaking bread from house to house, did eat their meat with gladness and **singleness of heart**...*

He who has learned to disagree without being disagreeable has discovered the most valuable secret of a diplomat.
Robert Estabrook

When you are arguing with a fool, make sure he isn't doing the same thing.
Unknown author

You must take personal responsibility. You cannot change the circumstances, the seasons, or the wind, but you can change yourself. That is something you have charge of.
Jim Rohn

One of the greatest moments in anybody's developing experience is when he no longer tries to hide from himself but determines to get acquainted with himself as he really is.
Norman Vincent Peale

Chapter 21

The Principle of Flexibility is the ability to bend repeatedly without being injured or damaged. It is the capability of withstanding stress without injury and the ability to undergo change without permanently being bent out of shape. With this ability, you can be bent and turned into a new mental and emotional shape. The principle of flexibility gives you the ability to be stretched by circumstances and to execute a quick recovery to your original position or to any other beneficial position.

The ability to return to an original position after being exposed to other information or positions is important for a firm, principled foundation. It is also the ability to be bent into another position, thus changing the shape of your ideas up to and including being changed completely. The principle of being flexible can allow you to be buoyant after you have been depressed. Flexibility allows you to be stretched beyond the bounds of inner security into misfortune and sickness, only to rebound to your original position of inner security and peace.

This law involves a pragmatic acceptance of the present moment. We accept others and ourselves the current circumstances rather than rigidly resisting the present moment. The flexibility principle requires an alert and expansive state of awareness. Flexibility embraces and makes constructive use of the moment. Stumbling blocks become stepping-stones and problems become opportunities. Everything serves our highest noble intentions if we make good use of everything that comes our way.

When this law and all other laws and principles are combined with balance, we understand that it is the peace and balance that allows us to accept situations as they are. And, if you do not like your present conditions or situation, then you change them.

If you are unable to employ the knowledge and wisdom necessary to make a choice and take proper action, then the law of chaos sweeps you away. You are constantly at risk for bad results as you flail about, using and being used by laws and principles that govern your life without your being in control. There are some things you can change and some you cannot no matter how much you try. What *can* be changed are your thoughts, feelings and reactions to what happens to you.

The Principle of Forgiveness means seeing everything through love. The opposite of forgiveness is resentment, which aggravates hatred, ill feelings and self-destruction. To forgive and to let go of old anger allows the law of grace to intercede and dispense with the negative vibrations and inner energies that contaminate our essence. To forgive is to excuse the faults of others and to pardon them in our minds and actions. It also means to give up the associated anger that comes with harboring resentments toward others. No longer do we require nor do our actions reflect that a person must pay for past arguments, usually at our own hand. This means that we refrain from imposing punishment on an offender or demanding satisfaction for every offense.

The principle of forgiveness means that we should begin to operate from a foundation of newfound gentleness and tenderness toward others and ourselves because we are all guilty of being less than compassionate with others and condemning ourselves for past deeds. This also means that we should practice a new level of acceptance of ourselves, thus leaving room for mistakes. And we should exercise a newfound ability to be patient with others and ourselves.

This principle of forgiveness does not mean that we should be soft or that we should have some kind of knee-jerk, liberal response to every situation. It means that we want to be helpful and have a kindly disposition. It means learning how to act in social situations, which turns people and events to our benefit.

These qualities should become a part of how we interact with others as a form of brotherly love and a feeling of friendship in which we are responsive to others and care for them with concern. When we are founded on a principle of forgiveness, we can look past a person to see their behavior, which can be corrected through the human kindness of empathy and understanding. And, for those still trapped in the power of a negative habit force, we now have the tool of forgiveness to use for the benefit of such people. It is the development of decent feelings of forgiveness that leads us to being unselfish and becoming more hospitable and tolerant toward others.

Psalms 25:18 Look upon mine affliction and my pain; and **forgive all my sins.**

Psalms 86:5 For thou, Lord, art good, and **ready to forgive;** *and plenteous in mercy unto all them that call upon thee.*

Matthew 6:14 For if ye **forgive men** *their trespasses, your heavenly Father will also* **forgive you***:*

Matthew 6:15 But if ye **forgive not** *men their trespasses, neither will your Father* **forgive your** *trespasses.*

Luke 17:3 Take heed to yourselves: If thy brother trespass against thee, rebuke him; and if he repent, **forgive him***.*

Luke 17:4 And if he trespass against thee seven times in a day, and seven times in a day turn again to thee, saying, I repent; **thou shalt forgive him***.*

1 John 1:9 If we confess our sins, he is faithful and just to **forgive us our sins**, *and to cleanse us from all unrighteousness.*

The Principle of Meditation allows us to experience the invisible reality of thoughts and emotions and to channel the positive energy that is in and around all of us into a productive mental and physical course of action. Meditation is the practice and method of realizing, or reflectively considering, an invisible truth in order to arrive, on an intuitive level, at a personal understanding of principles and truth. You need to find your sacred place within yourself to commune with God.

Genesis 24:63 And Isaac went out to meditate in the field at the eventide: and he lifted up his eyes, and saw, and, behold, the camels were coming.

Before we explore the area of meditation, I want to say this: I would like anyone who can to tell me what Isaac was going out into the field at eventide to meditate on. Don't avoid the question. Do the research and find the answer.

Most who think about the subject of meditation or talk about it from the Biblical position use this scripture and others like it.

*Joshua 1:8 This book of the law shall not depart out of thy mouth; but thou shalt **meditate therein** day and night, that thou mayest observe to do according to all that is written therein: for then thou shalt make thy way prosperous, and then thou shalt have good success.*

*Psalms 1:2 But his delight is in the law of the LORD; and in **his law** doth he meditate day and night.*

*Psalms 119:15 I will **meditate in thy precepts,** and have respect unto thy ways.*

For quite some time in the Christian Church, there has been conversation about meditating on and in the Word of God. However, very little has been written or talked about in Christian circles and Churches about the *type* of meditation that was considered, that is, Eastern meditation.

Let me introduce some scriptures that support mediation that is reflective, internal and points to silence and searching.

Psalms 4:4 Stand in awe, and sin not: **commune with your own heart upon your bed, and be still.**

Psalms 19:14 Let the words of my mouth, and the **meditation of my heart,** *be acceptable in thy sight, O LORD, my strength, and my redeemer.*

Psalms 49:3 My mouth shall speak of wisdom; and the **meditation of my heart** *shall be of understanding.*

Psalms 104:33 I will sing **unto the LORD** *as long as I live: I will sing praise* **to my God** *while I have my being.*

Psalms 104:34 My meditation **of him** *shall be sweet: I will be glad in the LORD.*

Psalms 63:6 When I remember thee upon my bed, and **meditate on thee** *in the night watches.*

Psalms 77:12 **I will meditate also of all thy work,** *and talk of thy doings.*

Psalms 143:5 I remember the days of old; **I meditate on all thy works;** *I muse on the work of thy hands.*

Some Hebrew definitions for the word meditate covers a wide range of words such as talk, speak, complain, pray, commune, muse, ponder, sing, turn over in your mind, contemplate, reflect, study, mull over.

Some methods of meditation require focusing your attention on one thing at a time. One method is to place your negative feelings and emotions in a cloud or bubble and let them float away. In this day and age, people who experience and attain peace of mind through the use of meditation number in the millions. When negative thoughts and negative emotions are eliminated or when we concentrate on positive thoughts, resulting in positive feelings, what is left? The answer is peace of mind.

*Isaiah 32:17 And the work of righteousness shall be **peace;** and the effect of righteousness **quietness and assurance for ever.***

In meditation, concepts and thoughts are viewed as distractions, and the human spirit is led to a quietness that can be called a place of being that is clear and uncomplicated. Meditation, as I have experienced the practice, leads to the contemplation and the awareness of a more profound meaning of life. The resulting enlightenment, experienced over time, stimulates a desire to establish order and peace in your life. Fundamentally, as I experience this new reality with the continued use of meditation techniques, I achieve a physiological state of deep relaxation, combined with a wakeful and highly alert state of mind.

The long-term effect of meditation is both thoughtfulness and alertness, arising from an inner tranquil place. Meditation is deep reflection and the contemplation of something beautiful. It is the realm of unlimited potential. Meditation is introspection and self-examination of what is real in us. Sometimes, what we become aware of may be disturbing, like looking into the fear and pain of our lives. However, continued contemplation reveals that these are only thoughts, feelings and simple energy.

The perception of fear and your own feelings of insecurity in the face of life and death are only emotions and energy to which we attach words and metaphors. Quiet deliberation in a structured daily practice of meditation allows us to move into areas of newfound peace and serenity, which is also just energy to which we attach words and metaphors. Metaphors are words that we use to describe something, sometimes invisible and inside us all.

Meditation over a period of time gives us another way of perceiving and relating to reality. With time, there comes a greater enthusiasm about everyday life. There is a sense of well-being that can be experienced but cannot be explained adequately with words. Our inner selves are somehow directly exposed to a higher consciousness in us that is there all the time, and, as we remove our negative thought patterns and explosive emotions, we experience the beauty of stillness.

We reach in to find this place where thoughts do not rule us. It is in this place where we find quiet and beauty beyond description. As we find this inner place daily, our outer lives slowly begin to conform to this inner energy of peace. This is a road of discovery and insight that comes as we change our perceptions, feelings and behavior in a gradual way and bring them into accord with our new understanding.

Many non-religious people use meditation as a method of stress reduction. Scientific fact informs us that meditation is known to reduce levels of cortisol, a hormone released in response to stress. The practice of daily meditation has been shown to enhance recuperation and improve the body's resistance to disease. You move from confusion to order.

Meditation is becoming more common in places like schools, hospitals, government buildings, prisons and corporate offices. Physicians are beginning to accept meditation and to recommend it to their patients because scientific studies are beginning to show that meditation works, especially to alleviate stressful conditions. You move from weighted down to lighthearted.

In meditation there is a sense that you are somehow allied with some universal, all-powerful, all-guiding influence in life. There is a sense that all mental and emotional barriers and boundaries are transcended and you feel at one with the universe. The process of meditation sparks levels of hope and comfort. You move from fear to courage.

As you learn to be totally aware of everything around you, you begin to enjoy a sense of oneness with everything, and awareness of the present moment reduces the pain of the past and fear of the future. With proper mental and emotional maintenance, this feeling has a lasting affect that stays with you throughout the day. After continued practice, there is a feeling that is exhilarating and intoxicating. The resulting feelings of ecstasy and delight transport us into a comfort zone of inspiring hope. Continued practice of meditation allows us to summon forth states of mind that radiate power and peace.

With time, the daily practice of meditation literally gives us a newfound ability to discover reality. This is because what is eternally real cannot be seen, so we must enter the realm of the invisible. You move from aimlessness to an internal commitment.

2 Corinthians 4:18 While we look not at the things which are seen, but at the things which are not seen: for the things which are seen are temporal; but the things which are not seen are eternal ...

1. Meditation is a process of becoming familiar with one's own real structure as a human being.

2. Focus attention on one thing, usually either the sensation of breath, leaving and entering your body, or a mantra.

3. Anything else that comes into your mind during meditation is seen as a distraction to be disregarded.

4. These practices can give rise to very deep states of calmness and stability of attention.

5. They are known as the concentration, or *one-pointed*, type of meditation.

6. Mindfulness is the other major classification of meditation practices known as *insight meditation*.

7. First, you practice mindfulness and utilizing one-pointed attention to cultivate calmness and stability. But then you move beyond that by introducing a wider scope to your observations as well as an element of inquiry. You move from chaos to order.

8. When thoughts or feelings come up in your mind, you don't ignore or suppress them, nor do you analyze or judge their content.

9. You simply note any thoughts as they occur as best you can and observe them intentionally but non-judgmentally, moment by moment, as events in the field of your awareness.

10. This inclusive noting of thoughts that come and go in your mind can lead you to feel less caught up in them and give you a deeper perspective on your reaction to everyday stress and pressures.

11. By observing your thoughts and emotions as if you have taken a step back from them, you can see much more clearly what is actually on your mind.

12. You can see your thoughts arise and recede, one after another. You can note the content of your own thoughts and the feelings associated with them as well as your reactions to them. You might become aware of hidden agendas, attachments, likes and dislikes and inaccuracies in your ideas.

13. You gain insight into what drives you, how you see the world, who you think you are—insight into your fears and aspirations, too. Become free—not reactive.

14. The key to mindfulness is not so much what you choose to focus on but the quality of the awareness that you bring to each moment.

15. It is very important that your meditation be nonjudgmental—more of a silent witnessing, a dispassionate observing than a running commentary on your inner experience. Observing without judging, moment by moment, helps you see what is on your mind without editing or censoring it, without intellectualizing it or getting lost in your own incessant thinking.

16. The goal of mindfulness is for you to be more aware, more in touch with life and with whatever is happening in your own body and mind at the time it is happening—that is, in the present moment.

17. If you are experiencing a distressing thought, you must resist the impulse to try to escape the unpleasantness. Instead, you must attempt to see it clearly as it is and accept it because it is already present in this moment.

18. Acceptance, of course, does not mean passivity or resignation. On the contrary, by fully accepting what each moment offers, you open yourself to experiencing life much more completely and make it more likely that you will be able to respond effectively to any situation that presents itself.

Follow the daily routine of meditation and each day when you are finished, you will notice how peaceful, centered and balanced you feel physically, emotionally and mentally. It takes about two weeks of continual daily meditation of at least fifteen minutes per day to *feel* the difference and begin to know that you are experiencing an inward change.

Chapter 22

The Principle of the Awakening Self is the awakening of the creative areas of awareness and consciousness. Because such awakening brings with it higher forms of perception and power, one must be careful. Be warned: self-centered misuse of the greater perception and power of the awakening self brings with it consequences based on reciprocity. What goes around comes around or you reap what you sow. These phrases and many like them in this book have been purposely repeated.

An awakening of the true self brings with it the need for moral responsibility. When this time comes in your life, in the midst of all your fears, you will find there is a voice that has been trying to speak to you for years through teachers, preachers, friends, parents, music and the numerous voices of life that you have previously resisted and rebelled against. Stop the struggling and fighting against the light of life and love. Life and peace have been speaking to you through others all your life but you have been resisting there voices.

When the day comes that self is truly awakened, you will finally see the world through new eyes as you realize that it is time to stop waiting for someone else to come and rescue you. You begin to use your newfound wisdom to let go of negative outbursts of energy. When you keep your personal, positive energy, your mind is clearer and more open to sharper insights. This process enables you to enjoy your present moments in life. And, the more you learn to enjoy your present moments, the moments become minutes, hours, days and a new lifetime of bliss.

Begin now and reach for those tools, which are right in front of you, and start to use them. As you apply them continually and with patience, then the awakening will come. It is like waking from a nightmare to find yourself once again in your own bed, safe and secure at home.

Committing yourself to new resolve demands that you begin with yourself and, in the process, a sense of serenity, will come to you. You awaken to the fact you are not perfect and not everyone will always love, appreciate or approve of who or what you are—and that's all right. You begin to learn the importance of loving yourself and, in the process, a sense of newfound confidence is born of self-approval because you have decided to walk toward the light of life and love. You continually take control of your thoughts, creating in your mind and firmly informing your brain what you are determined to do. You inform your brain daily to look for the positive energy, new insights and deep inner perceptions as well as love for yourself and the peace of mind you deserve.

Newfound present experiences of joy and goals worthy of the highest sense of purpose become the driving force of your life. You become more determined as you see this process unfolding before your conscious awareness. Then you realize what has been happening all the time. When you are determined, then and only then will the universe operate for you and give you what you want.

Listen! This is important: Stop justifying and rationalizing your negative behavior. Stop constantly criticizing and blaming other people for the things they did to you. Those people and the things they did to you are no longer a part of your continual thinking and conversation. Think about it. Did all of your anger, fear, morbid suspicions, resentment, worry, suffering, stress and heartbreaks solve any of your problems? Suddenly, you come to the conclusion that you are going to stop putting so much energy into trying to change the people around you. Think about it. Has that kind of thinking and behavior worked for you so far? Has it changed anyone and given you the relationship you want? Of course not! Instead, you are at this moment awakened to the fact that now you will put your energy into doing the inner work on your *own* mind and build a thought pattern that will enable you to use *The Revelation of Power* for your continued awakening to higher realms of power and experience. You will begin to realize that people don't always say what they mean or mean what they say and not everyone will always be there for you when you need someone.

Oh, yes! And by the way, everything is not always about you. In the awakening process, you learn to stand on your own and to take care of yourself. As you learn to take care of yourself, a sense of safety and security is born of self-reliance instead of from selfishness.

You stop supposing and pointing fingers and begin to accept people as they are. You learn to overlook their shortcomings and human frailties, and in the process a sense of peace and contentment is born of your forgiveness. Learn to forgive and stop putting unrealistic expectations on other people because they are every bit as human as you are.

You realize that the way you view yourself and the world around you is a result of all the messages, social programming and opinions that have been existing in your life for much too long. These messages have forced you into dysfunctional behavior patterns, which have become non-satisfying, circular, obsessive-compulsive orbits of madness. The negative relationship between you and the world around you is a bond that can be broken only by understanding that the difficulty is this: that you have attempted to understand the world *only* through your five senses. Those tools (the five senses), without tapping into another source, will continue to cement us hard and fast to this physical world. The five human senses are not adapted to the real inner world of problems, so, no matter how hard we try, we are unable to succeed in changing people, places and things. This stubborn approach of relying totally on our five senses tends to evolve into disastrous personal and negative interpersonal situations. The kind of valid information that you need cannot be found through the five senses because the senses give you only a partial picture of reality.

When you learn to open up to new worlds of differing ideas, concepts and different points of view based on universal principles, your life will change. You will begin to evaluate and to redesign who you are and what you really stand for according to universal principles.

You will learn that there is a vast difference between wanting and needing, and you will begin to discard your negative values as you outgrow them. In this process of awakening, you can finally begin to trust your own experience, born of your newfound knowledge. New patterns of logic, thought, speech, action, emotional response and perception will begin to emerge and you will begin to grow. Hopefully, you will begin to grow in the right direction because your life depends on that.

When you learn that, by truly giving freely, that you are in a right position to receive freely, you will take advantage of that knowledge to give of yourself. You discover that there is power and strength in creating and contributing to life. You stop maneuvering through life merely as a *consumer,* looking for your next fix. You begin to learn that principles like honesty and integrity are not the outdated ideals of a bygone era but the mortar that holds together the foundation upon which you must stand in order to build a new life. You learn that you don't know everything and that the more you grow and learn, the more there is to learn. You learn to differentiate between guilt and responsibility and the importance of setting boundaries. There comes a point where you can say no to someone and say it in love, with care and concern. Submission to and cooperation with victimization and oppression become things of the past. You understand that they are really forms and signs of mental illness.

As you begin learn about love because of the true love you have found inside, you find out who you are really meant to be. Other important kinds of love are revealed to you in dramatic fashion. True romantic love and family love are now possible without getting them confused. You learn how to love and respect another person. You now know how much to give. And, most importantly, you now know when to stop giving and when to walk away if the relationship is unhealthy. You learn not to project your past selfish needs or your negative feelings onto a relationship. You learn that you will not be more beautiful, more intelligent, more lovable or important simply because of the man or woman on your arm. Nor will you become more of a person because there is a child who bears your name.

You learn to look at relationships as they really are and not as you wish they might be. You stop trying to control people, situations and outcomes. You learn that, just as people grow and change, so it is with love. And you learn that you don't have the right to demand love on your terms, just to make yourself happy. It is only your mental habits and memories of how you *think* things ought to be that you from shaping your life into a more harmonious experience. You begin to shed the silly models of pride and egotism that get in the way of your happiness. You eventually learn that it was your negative mind and ego-filled self that had to prove itself right at the expense of your happiness. Now, you eagerly plunge into daily practice of the laws and principles of *The Revelation of Power*. Because you practice awakening daily, you learn to handle these seeming impediments and obstacles to your happiness. You realize and *now understand* it is all just energy and vibrations, waiting for your creative powers to be unleashed upon them to bring you the good vibrations and experiences of happiness that you deserve in life.

You come to the realization that you deserve to treat yourself with love, kindness, sensitivity and respect, and you won't settle for less. You learn that your body really is your temple; in fact, it is the place where you exist in the now. You begin to care for it and treat it with respect. You should begin eating a balanced diet, drinking more water and taking more time to exercise. You soon learn that fatigue diminishes the spirit and can create doubt and fear so you should take more time to rest. Daily meditation will give you newfound energy and enthusiasm about life. And, just as food fuels the body, laughter fuels our soul, so you take more time to laugh and to play in wholesome ways.

Awakening to higher levels of peace and understanding allows you to accept whatever is happening. It does not mean that you have to like what is happening. It does not mean that you have to stop trying to change what is happening. It also means that you stop allowing yourself to get so angry, so afraid, so resentful, so worried and so unhappy about what is happening. You are no longer addicted to these reflexive actions. You understand that you control your inner emotional experience and that, the more you practice, the more serenity there is in the present for you to experience and to acquire additional peace.

You are going to find and learn that, for the most part in life, you get what you believe you deserve, and that much of life is truly a self-fulfilling prophecy. You learn that anything worth achieving is worth working hard for and that merely wishing for something to happen is different from actually working toward making it happen. More importantly, you learn that, in order to achieve success, you need direction, discipline and perseverance. You also learn that no one can do it all alone and that *it's OK* to risk asking for help.

You learn that the only thing you must truly dread is fear itself. Fear keeps us from being joyful, happy and radiant. Fear makes us thankless, complaining and defeated. Fear creates anxiety, doubts, worry and suspicion. Fear causes us to act with indecision, timidity, hesitancy and social shyness. Fear causes you to think about potential problems and difficulties you might encounter tomorrow. Well, you will naturally become fearful unless you stay awakened to the principles of positive faith.

If you are worrying about tomorrow or future problems, you cannot be enjoying your present moments. But, through awakening to your higher powers, you have learned to step right into and through your fears because you know that, whatever happens, you can handle it. To give in to fear is to give away the right to live life on your terms. You learn to fight for your life and not to squander it by living under a cloud of impending doom.

You learn that life isn't always fair, you don't always get what you think you deserve and sometimes bad things happen to unsuspecting, good people. On these occasions, you learn not to personalize things. You learn that no one is punishing you or failing to answer your concerns. It is just life happening. Accepting this and despite this, you feel a sense of mission about your life. As you continue to awaken, this sense of mission and purpose is acted out with a newfound determination and zeal that ordinary people only marvel at.

You learn to deal with the true enemy: your own negative, reactive self. You learn that negative feelings such as anger, envy and resentment must be understood and redirected or they will suffocate the life out of you and poison the universe that surrounds you. You learn to admit when you are wrong and begin building bridges instead of walls. Now that you are experiencing a state of awakening to the beauty of life, you understand that whenever you direct your mind into the habit of noticing and appreciating all the beautiful things you have around you, there is no end to the things that bring you happiness and joy. Having awakened, you now have chosen to think and behave in more self-enhancing and self-fulfilling ways. You have decided you are no longer going to be weak or manipulated by your own emotions.

Now you know that worrying about approval or disapproval from others, especially when it is out of proportion to common sense, is a waste of time and emotional energy. Awaken to the fact that the past is over and no one is going to give you the future unless you give it to yourself. Awaken to working for yourself in the present moment *and be grateful for what you have.* Awaken to the fact that some things in life that you will do are required and not necessarily pleasant. Awaken to the reality that you are in fact in charge of your thinking and consequently your attitude.

Learn to be thankful for and to take comfort in many of the simple things you take for granted—things that millions of people upon the earth can only dream about. What is required to participate in this awakening and more fully in the discovery of your own health and well-being is to simply listen carefully and trust the messages of love from within.

Then you can appreciate the things you have so often taken for granted: just the taste of a good meal as you look out the window and really see what is out there; the song of a bird; the beauty of the sky and the newfound beauty inside you. Slowly, you begin to take responsibility for yourself and to make yourself a promise never to betray yourself and never to ever settle for less than your heart's desire. Finally, awaken with courage in your heart and with faith by your side. Take a stand, take a deep breath and begin to design the life you want to live as best you can.

*John 3:3 Jesus answered and said unto him, Verily, verily, I say unto thee, Except a man be **born again**, he cannot see the kingdom of God.*

*John 3:7 Marvel not that I said unto thee, Ye must be **born again**.*

The Law of the Present Moment deals with the fact that time does not really exist. What we refer to as past and future have no reality except in our own mental constructs. The idea of time is a convention of thought and language, a social and universal agreement so that everything that exists does not happen at once. In truth, we have only this moment, the present. When we cultivate making the most of the moment, we also learn how to make the most of the future. When we hold on to regret for an occurrence in the past, we keep the regret alive in the present by reliving that occurrence over and over in our mind. When we feel anxiety about the future, it is because we keep the anxiety alive with the pictures of events in the past that we imagine will happen again in the future. Time is the abstract concept that gives our mind appropriate ways of understanding our finite existence. When we practice remembering that the here and now is all we have, our appreciation of the present moments improves.

Taking time to examine the past for evidence of how our present is affected is part of the cleansing work that needs to be done so that we do not remain locked in the negative habit force from the past. We can visit the past through our mind, but if the experiences are negative, there is no need to continue living based on past thoughts.

Habit force is an incessant attendant. It can be your foremost helper or your worst affliction. Positive habit force can urge you on to a positive goal; negative habit force can drag you down to a frightful end. But you can control habit force. In fact, if you do not take control of it, it will control you. Habit force can be a wonderful servant. With repetition, it can be taught what to do and how to guide you automatically. Great men have learned to harness the power of habit force. Others, whose end is less than desirable, have also used habit force to their own detriment.

Although it may be good and beneficial to look to the past for answers to our present problems, it is not wise to live our present lives locked in a negative past that keeps us thinking and behaving in negative ways through the power of habit. The continual viewing of the past keeps you from using your higher self productively in the present. Unless you have beneficial memories to draw upon, your look into the past should inform and teach, and nothing more.

To help you understand the power of the present moment more fully, it is necessary to say some things about looking into the future. Looking into the future is also a wise thing to do when we are planning positive action, setting realistic goals or making time-managed excursions into the future. You need to be encouraged to use your imagination and vision correctly. Spending time daily in a disciplined way is important. While it is intelligent and insightful to shape and plan for the future, it is not reasonable to spend an inordinate amount of time living in the future. Making a habit of living in the future in your mind is to lose the power of using the present moment to shape the future. Balance is needed so that, as we prepare for the future, our awareness of where we are concentrating our thought power takes into account how precious the present moment is.

*2 Corinthians 6:2 (For he saith, I have heard thee in a time accepted, and in the day of salvation have I succoured thee: behold, **now** is the accepted time; behold, **now is the day** of salvation.)*

Chapter 23

The Law of Manifestation says that actions, sounds, vibrations and mental energy will manifest themselves as a result of the total output of your life. The total of what you produce is released into the invisible energy force that is around you and the returning reality will be manifested over time. If and when you begin to respect and love yourself and others, more of the energy of love, joy and peace begins to be manifested in your life, and then that positive energy is projected onto your surroundings. Thought is a force of electricity with gravity and power. Its manifestation is the result of a continual working of the dynamics of universal law and principle. Somewhere within you is the spark of the mighty consciousness that you see manifested everywhere outside of yourself. Life is everywhere you look, and that magical, mystical, indescribable essence is both in and around you.

Whatever the powerful mind conceives, excluding any opposing thought and holding that constant, pure thought and believing it with intensity, it will instantly begin to come to pass on a subatomic level. You are in a constant flow of reality and constant state of manifestation. Your life is an unfolding discovery and revelation of your deepest thoughts. When you trace your life back into your past, where you are today is a result of your continual thinking and action toward the manifestation and exposure of your inner self. The real representation of who you are is all around you. The expression of your essence is staring you in the face. If you are unhappy with the final product, then you must change the production and projection of your inner being. That is, you must change your thoughts. You must confront the reality that you have created so that you can see plainly that the evidence of your manifested self— is you. And no one can change you. Neither money nor even relocation to another place can change you because wherever you take yourself, you will still meet you. Only *you* can change you.

Look around you and do not be afraid to unmask who and what you really have manifested in your life. Don't be terrified to look at yourself honestly. Have no secrets, don't hold yourself back. Just open your mind. Don't pull any punches, don't make any excuses and don't blame anyone else. Let your life stand in the spotlight of honesty. Whatever has been done, let it stand in full view of the honest reality and manifestation. Truth will speak for itself if you are willing to listen to the sound of that inner voice as you confront the life that you have manifested. If you do nothing, what is looming on the horizon? What will rear its head and show its face in your future manifestations and presentations? Whatever you do will begin with your inner thoughts to emanate from you and come into the bright light of manifestation.

Psalms 85:10 **Mercy and truth** *are met together;* **righteousness and peace** *have kissed each other.*

1 Corinthians 12:7 But the **manifestation** *of the Spirit is given to every man to profit withal.*

2 Corinthians 4:2 But have renounced the hidden things of dishonesty, not walking in craftiness, nor handling the word of God deceitfully; but by **manifestation** *of the truth commending ourselves to every man's conscience in the sight of God.*

Luke 8:17 For nothing is secret, that shall not be made **manifest***; neither any thing hid, that shall not be known and come abroad.*

*John 14:21 He that hath my commandments, and keepeth them, he it is that loveth me: and he that loveth me shall be loved of my Father, and I will love him, and will **manifest** myself to him.*

*Revelation 15:4 Who shall not fear thee, O Lord, and glorify thy name? for thou only art holy: for all nations shall come and worship before thee; for thy judgments are made **manifest**.*

The universal laws and principles are always at work around you and in you, waiting for you to use them in the right way. In fact, the universe of laws and principles pursues a continuing love association with you that is real and exclusive so that your individual gifts and talents can be manifested in the right way. The universe of laws and principles has been inviting you, through all the countless people who have tried to help you over the course of your life, to become involved with these higher powers. Instead, you have been fighting against this truth and thinking that your way will work. You know you have heard the voice of life and positive change before. The voice is always speaking through friends, books, circumstances and opportunities.

Through your reading, studying and application of the knowledge contained in *The Revelation of Power*, the universal laws and the principles that will change you invite and desire you to go to work. Be warned: these laws and principles will lead you into a dilemma of belief versus unbelief. If your commitment requires faith and hope in a new future and the action sufficient to get you there, regardless of what you have to do to get there, *do* it.

Only you can and must make the major adjustments in your life to join the universe in a dance of life. Only you can join in what is going on around you all the time and in what is happening for your good. Only you can let yourself join in this dance of life. Only you can come to this place, and you must come to it alone. Others may be on their own paths, but it is only you who can get to know the power of your higher consciousness by experiencing it as you obey the laws and principles of the universe. Then and only then will you *know* that the work of the universe for your good can be accomplished through you.

Work hard! Get a dictionary! Get up early and learn how not to grumble and complain. In all things be prepared to use the law and principle of *harmony or common ground* to bring peace and balance into your life. Expect an excellent performance from yourself and let it become a natural one of your *cycles.* Now is the time to use the principle of *will power* and *choice.*

Set your will in motion toward a worthy goal and make the necessary choices that will get you there. Follow others who expect extraordinary performances from themselves. Don't be afraid to be an exceptional disciple. Use the principle of *discipline* as a power to change you. Being a leader is something you should expect from yourself, and you will find that you are rewarded many times, but it is just as crucial to be a great pupil. We can't all be trailblazers all the time. Sometimes your best way to learn and grow is by being a follower. If you are going to do it, do it with the grace and style worthy of someone who has learned to be humble and to submit to the greater principled issue at hand.

Be persistent about working hard. Being successful is not about a sprint to the finish line. It is more like long-distance running and the endurance you need to run in a marathon. *Never give up* on developing yourself because the principle and law of *cycles of return* will continue to shape a new, powerful you. Always give more than you promised within the stated timetable. The repeated, high-level success that people who work hard get starts with knowing and embracing the wisdom that hard work will help you achieve your goals and dreams and that there just is no substitute for hard work.

Be curious about new things and be eager to learn. Don't be afraid to study and ask questions. And read—constantly! Whenever you are—at the doctor's office or the dentist's office—there are interesting things to read. Carry a book with you if you have to wait or travel and have time to read. Make good use of your time. Educate yourself and stay abreast of current events.

Repeated success is not about memorizing facts. It's about being able to take information and create, build or apply it in new and important ways. Never stop the learning process. Do not be afraid to use the laws and principles of *expansion and growth* to grow in the right direction. If the opportunity presents itself, go back to school. Go to the library and get a library card. The self-help section in any bookstore is full of wisdom, and the accumulated knowledge of countless people who have learned to be successful is in there. Learn from them. Listen to self-help tapes.

Develop a taste for programs on television that are informative and educational. Successful people want to learn everything there is to know about everything that is interesting and important in life. They want to know more!

Don't be afraid to network with people who can help you accomplish your goals. Begin to use the powers that reside in the laws and principles of *equilibrium and balance*. You can begin to move with confidence in new circles of people and to make new contacts. Don't be afraid to get to know lots of different kinds of people. When they see that you are serious, they often stand ready to help you get ahead and achieve your goals. Many people won't help, but many more *will* help you. For those people who aren't willing to help you, be ready to use the principle of forgiveness. Don't burn bridges.

Take the time to cultivate the skill of listening to positive friends, neighbors and co-workers.

There are all kinds of people in the world. Make yourself adaptable and principled by using *flexibility*. Successful people have special people who, in addition to being friends, are always ready to help whenever they can. You have talents that can be developed over time. Just know this and press forward into unlimited possibilities for the future.

To make your goals reachable, they must be definite. Put the law of *attraction* to use. And, in order for the pathway to open for you, your mind/brain must know exactly what it is you want. The more precisely your computer mind/brain understands what you are trying to accomplish, the harder it will work to bring to your attention the steps necessary to accomplish your goals. Proper use of the principles of *action* will activate the laws of *magnetism* and draw to you the ideas, methods and people for your benefit.

Try never to form a goal based on unclear or vague terms. Give specific instructions to your vision and imagination and remember that, with your newfound understanding, these are powerful tools in your own mind. You have begun and can continue to learn about how to control your mind/brain for a positive outcome. Your mind/brain can help you accomplish almost anything if it knows precisely what you are aiming for.

Thriving and prosperous people work on themselves and never quit! They consciously use the law of *process* to improve daily. You now know about and are able to use principles and laws of *force* and *faith* to break through any resistance to attaining your goals. This combination continually works for your benefit. The *overnight wonders,* who fail to remember and use any controlled process, become presumptuous, so their success quickly disappears. You know that, over time, *magnetic control* will work for you because you have used it enough to know that it works. So, now you know that you never have to give up striving and reaching for a new, prosperous life. Go ahead! What are you waiting for? Work on your personality; develop your leadership skills. You may find that you have hidden management skills and the ability to add every other detail of a successful life. When a relationship goes sour, know that you can learn from it and expect to do better next time. If an important relationship is running low on respect and love, then take time to renew it. No longer do you have to consent to flaws in your life. *Get busy and fix them!*

You can be triumphant and a person who will not accept defeat because you are extraordinarily creative and powerful. Use the powerful laws and principles of *expectation* to expect good things no matter what. You have the *right to decree,* so begin to speak your new future into existence. It will work for you. And remember: the laws of the universe do not change. But, as you change to move in concert with these powerful laws, they become part of the power that actively changes you and brings you what you want.

Go around looking for opportunities and asking yourself, "Why not?" With your newfound *Revelation of Power*, you will see new combinations, new possibilities, new opportunities and challenges where others see problems or limitations. There will come a time when you may wake up in the middle of the night, yelling, "I've got it!" Humble yourself so that you are prepared to ask for advice and to try things out. Consult experts and amateurs, always looking for a better, faster, cheaper solution. Successful people are creative! The law of *reciprocity* is always at work. You reap what you sow.

Applying the principles of *The Revelation of Power*, you will eventually become a self-reliant person, willing to take responsibility for your actions. If you really want to be incredibly successful, don't worry about blame, and don't waste any time by complaining about what other people do.

Just get busy with perfecting your own skills. Make the necessary decisions and move on.

Learn how to relax and keep your perspective within the limits of your present skills and abilities, knowing they too will grow. Even in times of stress or turmoil, keep the principle of *balance* in mind. Know the value of timing through the *cycles of return*. Develop a sense of humor, and exercise patience daily with yourself and others. Whatever you do, don't panic or make impulsive decisions. Remember to use daily *meditation* and quiet time to your advantage. Most of life is preparation. Take time to breathe easy, ask the right questions, and make sound decisions, even in a crisis. Live in the logic of the now—not in the emotion of the moment. Involve yourself and use the laws and principles of *reciprocal conversation* and *meditation.*

No one can muster the enthusiasm, hard work and courage to reach a goal he or she doesn't really care about. This is where passion is needed as a motivational force. A reachable goal is one you really, really, REALLY want! It's something that will change your life, enhance your health or wealth and make you proud. Now that you have the knowledge of tremendous power, use the *present moment* and the laws of *abundance* and *manifestation* and begin to prove to yourself that they work. Using these powers gets your juices flowing, gets you up in the morning and keeps you going all day long. Because doing the right thing is the right thing to do, it has now become of paramount importance to you. Set goals that are really worth achieving through the knowledge of the powerful principles of *The Revelation of Power.*

Emotions are important when controlled by a skilled mind. Remember the law: emotions are a part of the law of *vibration* and are powerful in the implementation of *The Revelation of Power.* They are some of the most powerful explosive forces inside us. Used properly, the law of *force* is influential and commanding. With the power of a sound, healthy mind, emotions allow us as human beings to perform the most heroic acts and, unfortunately, the most barbaric of acts as well. But now you have the power to choose. You can add to the beauty of life instead of continuing to destroy yourself and others. Enthusiasm, hard work and courage can change your life.

The continued perfection of your mental and emotional skills will allow you to be extremely successful at living in the *present moment*. You will begin to know that *now* is the only time you can control. And, as you continue to control your present moments, day by day you build the future, one present moment at a time. Take full advantage of each day. And remember: the law of *seasons* dictates that whatever you have planted in all areas of your creative ability will yield a harvest. Don't waste time. Experience your *self-awakening* by beginning to use *The Revelation of Power* to your advantage!

It is hard for an empty bag to stand upright.
Benjamin Franklin

There is real magic in enthusiasm. It spells the difference between mediocrity and accomplishment.
Norman Vincent Peale

The only thing that stands between a man and what he wants from life is often merely the will to try it and the faith to believe that it is possible.
Richard M. DeVos

To get what you want, stop doing what isn't working.
Dennis Weaver

Winners take time to relish their work, knowing that scaling the mountain is what makes the view from the top so exhilarating.
Denis Waitley

Change

I have worked in San Quentin, San Francisco county jails and the Arkansas Department of Correction. It is my hope that this message is filled with enough information and urgency to provoke serious thoughts of change in those of you who have created prisons and bondages in and around your mind.

Across this world and nation, countless men and women, young and old alike and many just like you, are vegetating in juvenile halls and in delinquent youth facilities, jails and prisons. More and more prisons are being constructed to provide accommodations for you, yours and future generations when they grow to adulthood. The question for you is: can you become motivated enough, dedicated enough and tired enough of your present life to challenge the negative expectations that many people have of you?

For those of you who are fortunate enough to be regaining your freedom, you need to prepare an agenda to survive outside the walls of incarceration. The true incarceration is in your thinking, action, behavior and habits. If you do not make a strong effort to change these things, the magnetic power of your thoughts and behavior will bring you back, again and again, to the same situation.

But for those of you who are facing a lot of time, I suggest that you strive to educate and discipline your mind. If you have access to a library, read every relevant book that you can get your hands on to improve yourself. Get together with someone or a group of other inmates who want to change. Start your own self-help group. Be bold enough to educate yourselves about history, the Bible, math, English, spirituality, meditation, and your culture. There are self-help writers around the country and the world who would be glad to respond to a letter asking to help you and your group. I am sure they would even donate books to your prison library.

It's time to flip the script. Or you/we can complain 24x7 about the problems of poverty, drugs, violence, racism and other injustices, the prison system and society in general. But, unless you/we choose to initiate a personal change, a group change, you/we will remain puppets and mental, physical slaves of unjust conditions. Unless you/we change, we will be incapable of changing the circumstances around us. There is no other way. Are you scared? Would you rather get mad than study and develop? Would you rather curse the darkness or light a candle?

I saw and heard an inmate get angry at a sign above the picture of a prison under construction. The sign read, "If we build them, they will come." He got mad because he felt it was a vindictive statement that presupposed that the incarcerated somehow *wanted* to be put in prison. Well, if you do not change and just continue to get mad, what do you think will happen? Of course, you have a choice! You have the final say in the matter. So, what do you say? Your actions will tell what you are really saying.

If you are in prison or some other confined situation, the interactions between prison authorities and you, the imprisoned, can vary from person to person. All prison guards do not behave in the same way; neither does every prisoner display the same behavior as other prisoners. But a relationship of any kind that is based on an inmate's defiant behavior and the guards' attempts to intimidate or frighten the prisoner will eventually give rise to open hostility.

In prison, the basis of the so-called association between guards and prisoners is that guards issue institutional orders and prisoners either must act in accordance with the rules of the institution or suffer the consequences of disobedience. These consequences include prisoners being placed in solitary confinement in *The Hole, the Max,* or in *Lockdown,* which is also known as receiving *hole* time. In some extreme situations, prisoners are forced to comply through physical subjugation.

In the matter of the evil master and slave concept, there are commonalities between a guard and bad habits as master and a prisoner as a slave to bad behavior.

The similarity between the guard's role (obey rules) and the master's role (obey rules) can be found in the guard's absolute power to control the prisoner. This control is carried out by enforcing rules on the prisoner; closely watching the prisoner to ensure compliance with those rules; punishing, abusing and, if need be, physically confining the prisoner through banishment to solitary confinement or through necessary physical restraint. When given the chance to obey the rules of society through parents, judges, God, the Bible, prior incarcerations and run-ins with the law, the prisoner to bad habits and defiant behavior continues to be out of control so he or she is placed in a confined situation where he or she is forced to obey.

Prisoners to bad habits or prisoners in prison or those addicted to drugs and alcohol have developed their habits through years of practice. Those who disobey rules do it at home, in school and at work. They start with disobeying parents, then teachers, preachers, judges and then even God's rules. The seeds of disobedience have grown into a rebellious nature and actions that defy logic and common sense. Eventually, what such a person learns is, "I must rebel at all levels, even in prison." And, believe me, we have the verbal skills to argue forever with whomever and whatever is right.

On the other hand, the resemblance of the prisoner to the slave is that both are subjected to strict rules. The prisoners of uncontrolled behavior are now confined and controlled like animals, mainly because prisoners were so out of control when they were still living in society. Now prisoners in prison or with the prison of drugs and alcohol in them are often brutalized physically as well as psychologically and deprived of basic human rights only because, when given these rights, people who are prisoners of their own bad habits abuse people, themselves and society.

The tension between the guards and prisoners is the same as the tension between the prisoners and the rules, parents, society, the Bible and God. Believe me, I know because I lived to see all of that and more fulfilled in my own life. It was my own rebellion and my desire to have my own way from the time I was a young man that caused the tension and the consequences that I wanted to, and did, blame on everyone and everything else but me.

Let us take the evil master and slave relationship a step further to point out that many people, of all races and ethnicities, have permitted themselves to be modern-day slaves to appalling and shocking thoughts, actions, behaviors and habits. Indeed, a person does not have to be Black to display a slave's state of mind. Without knowing it, too many of us—whether we are Black, Asian, Chicano or White —perpetuate *the master's evil will*, whoever the evil master is: the devil, bad habits, rebellious thinking and behavior, alcohol and drug addiction or criminal thinking and behavior. Through our own rebellion and self-destructive behavior we are reaping the consequences of bad personal management. For those individuals who are in defiance and denial, here are some identifiable signs of self-perpetuation of slave conduct, be it in prison or in society.

Slave Thinking Disorders

1. A slave's way of thinking requires that he/she will neglect to educate him/herself, which in turn creates mental slavery.

2. A slave's state of mind will promote cheating and other crimes against his or her own community and

other people instead of helping to break the chains of poverty by earning an honest living.

3. A slave's frame of mind will continue self-hatred through committing violence in his or her own community, on people of his or her own ethnicity. This violence includes murder, which amounts to genocide.

4. A slave will deal, buy and/or use drugs that will make him/her and others function as slaves, addicted to drugs, to misery and to defeat.

5. A present-day slave will promote the wicked ways of his own slavery to disrespect and abuse women, passing that behavior on to his children.

6. A contemporary slave will abandon his/her children—leaving them for someone else to raise—just as the old masters abandoned Black children by selling them off to other slave owners, not caring about their fate.

7. A current slave-minded person will foolishly commit crimes that cause him/her to end up behind bars, incarcerated and in mental, spiritual, drug and physical bondage.

If you are in prison or jail or have prisons and bondages in your mind, then you need to take a serious look at your lifestyle. Take a look at this inventory and then examine it again. Look within yourself for any similarities to the behaviors I have just listed and find a way to work on eliminating your modern-day slave traits. If you cannot admit to any of the seven signs, you are in denial. But all is not lost. The first step toward defeating a slave's way of thinking begins with your recognition that it exists in you.

There are two ways to view your bondage, habits or incarceration: either your present situation will convince you to straighten up your life, or you will continue to believe that you did not create your own problems and that you are not responsible. Or today will be the beginning of a wasteful future, sometimes even behind bars. Even worse, you could just wind up on death row. So, in the final analysis, you can either complain or *do* something about your situation.

If you are truly preparing yourself for a different lifestyle, then be prepared to address the state of emergency regarding drug addiction, alcoholism and social upheaval that you left behind. The so-called *wars* on crime that claim success by pointing to wholesale arrests and incarcerations do not correctly address the problems in our communities. These measures fail to deter or to rehabilitate the criminal mentality. Meanwhile, for a generation of disgruntled youth and adults, living the antisocial lifestyle and going to prison have morphed into a plague that may bring down entire communities, cities and ultimately a nation.

Placing blame is beside the point. We must focus on an effective solution. The approach that is necessary for resolving a spreading social epidemic begins with understanding that you can play a role in the healing process. Let your misery become your ministry to others who suffer like as you once did. Join an organization that is committed to helping those who suffer as you did. Become proactive. Learn all you can learn and help others. You can use your power to decree right here:

I Acknowledge here and now on this month _____, day _____, and year_____, to put aside my differences with the community at large, no matter what those differences are, be they ideological, political, religious, philosophical, racial, economical, geographical, criminal, material, personal and collective retaliation, or any social reliance on violence against the community through alcoholism, drug addiction, criminal thinking or criminal behavior. This document is an oath of responsibility for those who are committed to the peace and restoration of our communities.

I give my word to take accountability for my crimes and the pain that I have inflicted upon the general public, my victims, my family and myself.

I give my word that I will no longer take part in female and child abuse.

I will make a pledge to myself that I will do my time without loud-mouthed whining, manipulating or blaming others.

I promise that when I am released I will no longer engage in illegal profiteering,

I promise myself that I will eliminate any self-destructive behavior and personal vices like illicit drug usage, drug dealing, and abuse of alcohol, inhalants and anything that would intoxicate the mind, impair my judgment and jeopardize the peace of the community.

I will reach out and help others by being a daily example of being a man of his word.

I promise to teach my children by example and to cherish my wife by consistently healthy living and to honor my parents by being the man they desired me to be.

I promise to put faith in God first, the needs of my family second and concern for my fellow man third.

I recognize that, to carry out this word of honor, it is possible only through the power and assistance of Almighty God.

Chapter 24

Fear and Anger

It has taken over ten years of preparation, study and additions to the original book, *The Power to Change*, to write *The Revelation of Power*. Many of the additions were made as a result of comments either from people who read the first book or from those who use *The Power to Change* as a teaching tool in a prison setting.

The two subjects that will be addressed in this chapter have been added as the result of talking to clients and teachers who placed a high value on two subjects: fear and anger.

In my opinion, it is fear that keeps those in recovery from striving forward in the face of opposition. Fear replaces faith and anger replaces peace. If you are in recovery, you face various fears: fear of a new lifestyle; fear of your own feelings; fear of going back to school; fear of people who are sober; fear of socializing and not being *high* when you walk into a social situation; fear of talking to women while you are sober. Fear, fear and more fear! Just think about it. What has held you back?

As small children, we hear about monsters under our beds, the bogeyman in the closet and other things that secretly move around in the night. These kinds of fears are located deep in the subconscious; as a result they are holding us prisoner against our will. Most humans fear the unknown, whether it is the absence of light, fear of death, starting a new job, or anything else they have not experienced before.

It is the fear and anger in our own minds that keep us from being free. To overcome your anger, you must take control of the fear that is the very source of that anger inside yourself. Fear is an emotion or *energy in motion*, as I like to refer to it. If you fail to triumph over the fear, anger will continue to manifest (law of manifestation). In my opinion, anger is a secondary response to an inward, unidentified fear.

The reason someone is outwardly angry is that, inwardly, they are fearful. Fear is one of the most terrible and intense emotions we can experience. Fear is such a paralyzing and terrible emotion that we respond with anger at having been subjected to it. A person who continually lives in fear will manifest it through being continually angry. Some of the outgrowths of fear are anger, depression, self-pity, hysterical activity and all forms of escapist behavior, including drinking alcohol, drug usage and fantasizing.

When we fail to understand this connection between fear and anger, it causes many people to live in a frustrating cycle of trying to deal with the outward symptoms of anger without ever identifying its root cause. It is like trying to get weeds out of your garden by merely pulling the tops off the weeds. Because the roots are left untouched, the weeds in the garden of your mind will grow back quickly. If you are trying to teach people who are persistently angry, you need to help them look beneath their surface self to discover what constant fears they may have at the root of their being. In spite of many people's diligent and persistent attempts to deal with their personal anger, they will never find continuing relief until they get to the real root of the problem, which is the fear that is triggering the anger.

Fear manifests itself in many forms. The most common manifestation is anger. Whenever you are angry, you are angry because you are afraid. It is impossible to be angry without finding its cause in fear. Example: Think of the last time you were angry. If you trace it back, you will find that the source will always be fear. The source cannot be anything other than fear. I repeat: Whenever you are angry, you are angry because you are afraid.

In my own life, I had a problem with women. I would invite them into my life with charm and the approach of a kind lover. Then, at some point, I would leave them, either moving on to someone else or just dropping them.

While I was going through group therapy, some of the group members began to ask me why I kept hurting and leaving women. They continued taking me back, past excuses and denials, to a point where I was discussing what happened the first time I had fallen in love. I was around 15 and I fell head over heels in love for the first time with this young girl who was also about 15. For some reason, I put her on a pedestal and would not pursue a sexual relationship with her. With others, sex was ok, but, for some reason, not with her. She tried to tell me in her own way that she wanted a sexual relationship with me but I could not see it.

One night, I went to a party and, at some point, one of the guys was talking about his sexual exploits. He was a little older than I was, maybe 17 or 18 at the time. As he went through his description of what he did to this girl and how she responded, etc., he and everyone else was laughing, envying him and begging for more details. I was enjoying it myself until I found out he was talking about the girl I was in love with.

Suddenly, the whole room went out of focus. The floor of the room tilted slightly as I realized that I was staggering backwards. I could still hear the laughter and the music, all the sounds of a party in full swing but something inside me changed dramatically. The sounds of the party seemed far off. I heard this sound like a roaring wind inside myself. It was my own breathing. I felt reduced and shrunken inside and, slowly and silently, I slinked away to the bathroom. I felt like I could not catch my breath. My lungs were working but I felt like I was going to faint. I felt as if I had swallowed a big rock. My throat was dry and tears poured from my eyes and ran down my face. The big rock felt like it was in my stomach and chest. I felt like I had to throw it up but I could not get this rock out of my stomach and chest. I found a phone and called her from the party. I cried, I begged, I pleaded—but I lost her. That was when I began drinking at age 15.

In group therapy, the questioning continued. "What happened after that?" they asked. I responded by telling them that I went out and got another girlfriend. She was nice, young, pretty, etc. I had a sexual relationship with her and then just left her. I continued to do the same thing—love 'em and leave 'em—because *I was afraid of being hurt again.*

I was asked how I felt when I had been hurt. I was asked to provide details. While describing what I felt, I realized two things occurred almost simultaneously. First, I realized that I never wanted to feel like that again and, second, that I never wanted to hurt anyone else like that again. I also realized that because, I had been hurt and because I was afraid that I would be hurt again, I was the one who did the hurting. I understood why I abused women mentally and emotionally even to the point of walking all over my first wife, a woman who really loved me. Fear had become a part of my dysfunctional lifestyle, my personal psychology and entrenched in my habit force. I made a vow to myself right then that I would never cheat on any woman to whom I was committed. I made and kept that promise to myself because I no longer wanted to bring that kind of pain into the lives of others.

Believe me, the law of reciprocity brought pain into my life on several occasions since then. Perhaps it was a result of the many women I had hurt. So I really do believe that you reap what you sow and sometimes *in spades*. I am a witness to that fact.

Of course, by now, I have seen this process repeated in group therapy many times. When a person is abused, he often winds up abusing others. In the group setting, we find that many, who were young people and were sexually abused when very young, either wind up doing the very same thing to others or become subject to some other manifestation of fear and anger.

Therefore, it follows that some of the other manifestations of fear—impatience, frustration, cruelty, self-hatred, jealousy, envy, prejudice and tiredness—have their root in fear. Fear is not always bad. We have been equipped with the emotion of fear in order to protect us from real danger. Healthy fear plays a very direct and important role in our daily life. Fear comes to us in many forms, but it could very well be described as an unpleasant feeling of a threat or danger, whether real or imagined. The true function of fear is to make us alert and ready for action when we anticipate a real threat, not an imaginary one.

The fear that destroys, however, is our personal fear of the unreal, that is, our tendency to let our minds dwell on fantasies or upon what we think will happen in the future. Our emotions, being without intelligence, cannot tell the difference between fact and fantasy, and they react just as if what we are thinking about were real. (If I talk to you long enough about a lemon and describe it well enough, you will salivate even if no lemon is present.)

Fear—what is it and why is it so important for the person in recovery to know about it? Well, Fear is *False Evidence Appearing Real*. Fear is an emotion that responds to threatening situations that have not happened. And the only way to get through fear is to know what it is and to face it.

And, yes, I am repeating some of our previously stated fears here on purpose.

Our greatest fear is living a clean and sober life. I say it is fear because it takes courage to live a lifestyle that is without any drugs at all. The first instinct in an addict is to use. Not to use creates fear—fear of any situation; fear of walking into a roomful of sober people; fear of talking to women without being high; fear of meeting new people who are not addicts; fear of feeling inadequate. It is the fear we experience when we feel we will not have enough to feel secure and happy in our new lives. There are thousands of manifestations of fear. The list goes on and we know those fears are very real.

Deuteronomy 31:6 Be strong and of a good courage, fear not, nor be afraid of them: for the LORD thy God, he it is that doth go with thee; he will not fail thee, nor forsake thee.

Isaiah 41:10 Fear thou not; for I am with thee: be not dismayed; for I am thy God: I will strengthen thee; yea, I will help thee; yea, I will uphold thee with the right hand of my righteousness.

Luke 12:32 Fear not, little flock; for it is your Father's good pleasure to give you the kingdom.

Attempting to flee those fears by using drugs and alcohol has brought us back to jails, institutions and near death experiences time and time again, and fear is the our greatest enemy. However, in spite of fear, we simply cannot logically justify allowing fear to stop us from doing something that we really believe in or wish to do. We did not let fear stop us from crime. Why should fear now keep us from enjoying a productive, positive life?

Fear is a normal emotion, and people who seem to be fearless simply act correctly in the face of fear. Fear does not stop them from moving forward. Fear does not stop them from doing what is right. Can fear be healthy? Certainly, when it keeps you alert in situations that can be very dangerous to yourself or others! Fear of going back to an old, negative, self-destructive lifestyle can be a very healthy fear.

Identify the particular fear that is causing your conflict and personal suffering. Fear is generally a very uncomfortable feeling—a form of personal suffering. When our emotions go beyond our ability to reason logically, then we are in a vulnerable position. We do not like to be afraid, but still, our fear can keep us from harm. So, yes, we need to be aware of danger and be alert, but, once we are alert, we cannot do much more than whatever we think is best in that particular situation.

If we let our fear take over completely, we can become immobilized and completely helpless. Similarly, many of us are afraid of irrational things, meaning things that do not really pose any threat to us. The kind of fear that is based not on a real threat, but on what our minds have manufactured as a threat is, in reality, a phantom, something that isn't there. For example, fear of spiders, small enclosed spaces or open spaces. We fear exams, making mistakes, rejection, criticism and even not being loved.

Life can become really difficult simply because illogical projections and delusions are taking over our normal, rational mind and insignificant things can begin to determine our whole life. In that case, we can start to talk about having a phobia. These are some basic fears that we all experience to a greater or lesser extent—the fear of loneliness, the fear of dying, the fear of being out of control, the fear of being abandoned, the fear of being poor and destitute, the fear of disease, the fear of growing old and the fear for personal safety.

*Isaiah 44:8 **Fear ye not**, neither be afraid: have not I told thee from that time, and have declared it? Ye are even my witnesses. Is there a God beside me? Yea, there is no God; I know not any.*

*Luke 8:50 But when Jesus heard it, he answered him, saying, **Fear not**: believe only, and she shall be made whole.*

Let us say that, all of a sudden, without any warning, you get fired from your job. It's definitely not a good experience, and it is a valid cause for concern. But, while losing your job is the external reality, what is the reality that is going on in your mind? For one thing, losing your job is a really unpleasant event. Yet, in your mind, you begin to see yourself going on to lose your home, your family. Then, suddenly, you begin to see yourself out on the streets, without any hope, begging for a living. You have seen the homeless with signs saying, "I will work for food." "Homeless, need help." Imagine that!

There is only one problem, one thing wrong with this picture. In reality, none of this has happened yet. This is the problem with most of us: we fear the future —a future, I remind you, that is not here yet. Our minds race with negative consequences, most of which are pure speculation and, quite frankly, probably will never happen. In this kind of situation, powerful emotions are brought to the forefront of our sensitive state of mind.

As we know, emotions come in all sizes and shapes; from the power of rage to the rush of joy, from the sweetness of gratification to the darkness of depression. Whether positive or negative, those feelings, fears and emotions can make us feel so alive! When we are fiercely angry, the adrenalin flows and our bodies are alert and charged. When we are thrilled with the anticipation of a joyful event, we feel light and optimistic. Because fear, too, is an emotion, there is first an event that activates the fear. Then there is the way we feel about the event, what we say to ourselves, our beliefs and how we think others would respond in our place. All these thoughts move through our mind to a point at which we examine our beliefs and expectations to find out if they are realistic or irrational.

Some people enjoy fear, because, in activities like riding a roller-coaster, living on the edge or performing some death-defying event, we get an adrenaline rush: a physical reaction to make us alert and ready for action. Some people actually get addicted to this natural drug and get into extreme antisocial activities. This can easily lead to needing more dangerous situations more often, so people who are addicted to this type of thrill may tend to take ever-increasing risks of criminal behavior, until the plan fails and they are back in jail or institutions, facing life-and-death situations.

You can completely manage your own life because you do not need to or cannot possibly control what happens to you in your life; you need only to control how you *respond* to what happens to you in your life. Basically, you can find yourself in two types of unpleasant situations: the ones you can change and ones you cannot change. If you can change the situation, you should do something about it instead of getting upset. Not acting in such a situation will only cause you frustration. If you cannot change the situation, you will have to accept it. If you don't, it will lead only to frustration and a negative and unpleasant state of mind, which will only make the situation worse. Remember: learning how to deal with fear and anger is not a one-time event. It will take you one day at a time to achieve this understanding and to train yourself how to change your patterns of thinking.

*Luke 11:3 Give us **day by day our daily bread.***

*Job 28:28 And unto man he said, Behold, **the fear of the Lord, that is wisdom;** and to depart from evil is* *understanding.* (And, I might add evil thoughts, which produce evil actions, behavior and negative consequences.)

This is why I am introducing scriptures throughout this study on fear. The Word of God is our daily bread, and we need it daily to offset the nonsense that goes on in our heads.

Sometimes, our responses to fear and anger turn into verbal or physical aggression. Or we may deny and minimize the incident while at the same time using intimidating body language. However, the final outcome of uncontrolled outbursts of anger and violence stemming from fear usually leads to jail, financial costs, loss of family, guilt, shame and loss of friends. As you look into your past acts with the intent to change your behavior, it will be easier to focus on what is important to change, especially if the outcomes were unpleasant.

One way of getting an unbiased opinion is to talk about your fear, feelings and anger with another person who is not involved with the event that sparked your anger or fear. By talking with others, you may be able to share the responsibility of looking at the anger that provoked a negative response from you to see if you can come to a different conclusion about how you could have handled the situation. Even if you have only one person who can listen to you, it will help to get the situation out in the open, where it can be looked at from a different perspective.

Positive, free-flowing emotions usually expand our energy and feelings of being capable. When we are happy, for instance, we have feelings of expansiveness and our hearts and minds are open to all that is around us, in all its detail and splendor. We connect with nature more confidently and with greater understanding, we are more spontaneous and we feel more comfortable and balanced as we go through our daily lives. The roots of our relationships grow deeper when we are expanding our energy. With hope, we are learning to live in the newfound power that is within us through experiencing *The Revelation of Power.*

When we experience negative emotions, our energy is sapped. If we are frightened or guilt-ridden, we hinder ourselves. Then we begin blocking others out. Chances are that, when this has happened in the past, we covered up our feelings with some drug. When we are angry our energy may temporarily increase and be expressed as a short outburst. Then, our angry feelings quickly shrink into depression, resentment and feelings of being misunderstood after being locked up again in prison or in our personal mental prison.

*2 Timothy 1:7 For God hath not given us the **spirit of fear;** **but of power, and of love, and of a sound mind.***

With power and love, power from God, love of Him and a growing love for our newborn spiritual self, we build a strong mind on a daily basis. As we do so, we still have to be careful because we must wage a mental battle every day to maintain our received peace.

Although your emotions may change significantly from day to day and experience to experience, you still have an underlying emotional quality that you were born with. Your basic emotional character varies because it is affected by a number of factors. What kind of home did you grow up in? What social forces helped to shape you? Has your education or lack of education shaped you? Any number of environmental events has had a direct bearing on who you are today. Did we come into this world angry? Do we still carry the fear produced by the cutting of the umbilical cord that brought pain into our lives? What about the shock that followed our birth, along with the slap that began our breathing and our first experience of separation, isolation and the insecurity and fear that were our first memories of this new world into which we were born? Before that rude awakening, we had known nothing but the security and warmth of our mother's womb, in which all our needs were met.

Isaiah 44:2 Thus saith the LORD that made thee, and **formed thee from the womb**, *which will help thee; Fear not, O Jacob, my servant; and thou, Jesurun, whom I have chosen.*

Are you a calm person by nature? Are you just happy-go-lucky or always fretting about something? Is your personality aggressive or passive? Are you extroverted or introverted in nature? Whatever your personality traits, you must remember that you can transform any emotion (energy in motion) into something positive. That is one of the basic principles taught in *The Revelation of Power*.

You have *The Revelation of Power* to turn anger into power for positive change. As you grow in this power, it can become exciting to control yourself continually on that level. Positive, personal, emotional attributes that enable people to succeed in life are precious and should be the goal of those who wish to build a refined character. These and many other positive emotions, including self-awareness, empathy, self-confidence and self-control, are essential elements of anyone who is striving to exist at higher levels of conscious awareness.

Isaiah 54:14 In righteousness shalt thou **be established**: *thou shalt be* **far from oppression***; for thou* **shalt not fear**: *and from terror; for* **it shall not come near thee**.

Daniel 10:12 Then said he unto me, **Fear not***, Daniel: for from the first day that thou didst set thine heart to understand, and to chasten thyself before thy God,* **thy words were heard, and I am come for thy words.**

Perhaps the most important factor in setting our basic emotional attitude is the extent to which we have either confidence in or doubts about the universe and our place in it. If you believe that you are at home in the universe, that it operates to support your growth and that all of us are connected to our deeper, wiser, higher consciousness that applies to others and to the entire universe, you will have a positive and expansive emotional quality about your life.

The most basic expansive emotion is contentment. Contentment is the result of your learning how to use and continue to live in the principles of *The Revelation of Power.* Once you understand that problems and frustration are basic facts of life, it can reduce your expectation that life without problems is possible. Instead, you can view each "problem" as an opportunity to grow, expand and become stronger.

In other words, nothing is perfect, so don't expect it to be. Just know that there is a way to deal with the problems of life. One way is to believe that problems are there to be solved. If your personal belief system tells you those things can be or must be perfect, it is very easy for you to feel hurt. At a deep level you need to realize that things can and will go wrong. You should therefore try to avoid negative actions or reactions, because they are very real energy vibrations that come out and increase the reasons for continuing problems.

If you feel fearful and unsafe and view the world as a hurtful and dangerous and cold place, devoid of meaning and filled with pain, you will tend to experience more of the same contracting, negative emotions. The most basic contracting emotion is fear. But listen think: where is that experience happening? That's right! It is happening inside you.

Fear expresses itself as anxiety, shock, concern, rage and confusion Fear is something that your own mind creates, so only your own mind can do something about it! Exaggerated fears can originate from wrong or childhood trauma. If you try to find out what originally caused the problem by looking into your past, the problem may gradually dissolve. Or you may find answers about how to change the present because you know the root of the problem. Admit to your own suffering because of your fears and get help now. Do not let the feeling of fear turn your life into continual misery.

Since fear is based on something that you think may happen in the future, it is clearly a mental process that tries to predict the future. In this sense, fear is a projection of your own mind.

We can be afraid to fall, but once we are falling, we are afraid to hit the ground. Once we hit the ground, we may fear that we are badly injured. Once we know we have a bad injury, we may fear the pain and the consequences of becoming disabled and not being able to work for some time, etc. So one could say that fear is always based on something that has not happened yet, and is therefore a creation of our mind rather than a fact. The formula to change that false mental feeling lies within our own minds—the very place fear started. Everything is energy, and everything can be changed into something else. If you remember these lessons and use them to develop a powerful mind, fear will no longer be the enemy but it will serve as another opportunity to demonstrate *The Revelation of Power.*

None of us carries pure trust or mistrust, so none of us experiences only positive or negative emotions. We are all a mix of emotions, and this is good. In order for our human experience to be complete, we need all the emotions. All of our emotions, expanding and contracting, are necessary for processing and moving through life's most significant experiences. Joy allows us to open our hearts to positive experiences, and grief helps us to admit and accept what we have lost. Guilt allows us to move toward acceptance of what we have done and knowledge of what can be accomplished through positive action. Contentment gives us a connection to our surroundings.

Despite the fact that emotions can bring us pain, they are vitally important to our human function and growth as we learn to transform our energies into positive steps in the right direction. Therefore, to explore this fear in detail and cover all of its aspects is to take it apart mentally. The idea is to allow yourself to examine the worst of your fears, but only in your mind. Don't allow your fears to lie in wait in the shadows of your mind. Pull them out and explore them.

Once you do this, you will see that, no matter how crazy your fears became, they were all projections of your own mind run amok. After you are aware of this fact, then you can feel more at ease in starting to search more deeply into your own mind for the really horrible repressed memories, the kind that make you cringe.

At this point, remember: you are not evil in essence but you have done many things that exhibited really bad behavior. If you start feeling some memory coming to the surface, even when you are not prepared to deal with it, grab it and pull it out and make sure you bring the roots with it. Be in control of it. Be the one who allows it to come to the surface. Don't be afraid to look right at it and to explore all aspects that you were always afraid to do before. You can use this process to recognize patterns in your present behavior that need to be eliminated. Once these repressed memories have lost their power in your habit force, deep in your subconscious, you are on your way to freedom. This process can be repeated until all of your present actions are based on a refined and recreated character, imbued with honor and truth.

*Psalms 51:5 Behold, I was **shapen in iniquity***; *and **in sin** did my mother conceive me.*

We are born in sin. We are not born sinful. We are lost and need to be redeemed. We are shaped by the iniquity that is in the flesh and in the world. We are not born evil. We are simply shaped that way. We are born cursed by eternal death from Adam, but thank God for the last Adam, Jesus.

1 Corinthians 15:45 And so it is written, **The first man Adam** *was made a living soul;* **the last Adam** *was made a quickening spirit.*

Romans 5:14 Nevertheless **death reigned from Adam to Moses,** *even over them that had not sinned after the similitude of Adam's transgression, who is the figure of him that was to come.*

1 Corinthians 15:22 For as in Adam all die, **even so in Christ shall all be made alive.**

In addition to being necessary components of our process, emotions are important messengers that can provide us with a great deal of information about ourselves. They are energy signals that communicate among our physical, mental and spiritual aspects. When, for instance, we are locked in a strong negative emotion, we are receiving the clear message that we are somehow out of balance. Although we tend to cling to positive, expansive emotions and avoid negative ones, it is important that we allow ourselves to experience all of our emotions. How can we challenge ourselves to embrace the negative and practice using its power to transform us into someone of character if we are afraid or stopped by fear or anger?

The more we learn about our emotions and develop trust in our growth process, the more we will be able to move through them and find their value. They serve not only to illuminate our bright side but to give us insight into our future as well. Sometimes, rather than moving through negative emotions or changing them and using them as part of our growth process, we become stuck within them and they become part of our self-definition.

For example, we all know people who have gone through a divorce. Although some move on with their lives, others remain permanently locked in the emotion of bitterness, even going so far as to commit acts of property and personal destruction. Negative emotions are meant to give us information and help us move through experiences. We do not want them to become locked within us. We want to use them for the processes they provide and the lessons they teach and then let them go.

Fear comes from our feelings of separation and disconnection, caused in turn by our basic lack of trust. We experience fear when we do not trust the world or our place in it. Fear is by far the most basic of the constricting emotions, and includes alarm, panic, terror, anxiety, intimidation, apprehension, worry and suspicion.

Matthew 10:31 **Fear ye not** *therefore, ye are of more value than many sparrows.*

Isaiah 41:13 For I the LORD thy God will hold thy right hand, saying unto thee, **Fear not; I will help thee***.*

Your new life of recovery is a struggle to conquer your personal fear. Fear can be conquered only when you are about to fail or when you actually fail. It is only when you are about to fail at something or when you do fail that you have the chance to confront fear. Only then are you offered an opportunity to succeed. It is impossible to succeed when you are already a success. You can succeed only when you are about to be a failure or when you are already a failure and are working through obstacles to become a success. Success offers few opportunities for you to experience fear; failure showers you with them. Let me ask you a question. Can you see fear? No. It is in the invisible realm of your thoughts and emotions.

When we are afraid, we experience a false sense of helplessness. Actually, we are never helpless if we are willing to ask for help. Fear is the decision to relinquish our powers and give in to the invisible ghost of fear. The relinquishment is always a conscious act, although it occurs so quickly that we may miss it on a conscious level, especially if we are used to being afraid or are not aware of our own mental processes that lead to fear.

We may, for example, shy away from intimate relationships because we believe that people are not to be trusted. What may actually be happening is that we have an underlying fear of abandonment, a fear that if we allow people to get close to us, then they may hurt us deeply by leaving. In order to release this fear effectively, it helps to understand that beneath our fear of relationships may be a general fear of abandonment, and beneath our fear of abandonment we have a general sense of distrust of other people. If we can change our perspective and learn to trust our personal, guided path in the universe and our new faithful selves, we can take some of the power out of our fear of relationships primarily through our newly elevated and more confident sense of self.

Think of a fear that you feel intensely and ask yourself, "How does this fear play out in my life?" Many of us, for example, fear having no money. Because we are fearful of becoming penniless, we restrict our giving to others. This creates a cycle of limitation—our fear of not having enough and our failure to share creates situations in our lives that reflect back to us our fear of not having enough. If we have such an indication, it is telling us that this is an area where we can do productive inner work. That work consists of knowing that whatever you give comes back to you, multiplied. That is the way the universe is set up. Did you ever wonder why television ministers preach about giving money and then they receive it from across the country? Although some reading this may not believe it, but money comes to the minster because many know this scripture to be true: "Whatsoever a man reaps that shall he also sow."

*Romans 8:15 For ye have not received the **spirit of bondage again to fear;** but ye have received the Spirit of adoption, whereby we cry, Abba, **Father.***

*1 John 4:18 There is **no fear in love;** but **perfect love casteth out fear:** because fear hath torment. He that feareth is not made perfect in love.*

*Revelation 1:17 And when I saw him, I fell at his feet as dead. And he laid his right hand upon me, saying unto me, **Fear not;** I am the first and the last...*

*Revelation 19:5 And a voice came out of the throne, saying, Praise our God, all ye his servants, and **ye that fear him,** both small and great.*

Our life of experiencing the love of God through Jesus Christ is to learn how to perfect our love. We experience anxiety and fear in our minds and quickly cast it out through the Love of God. We experience it but do not let it live and grow in us. Therefore, the torment that comes with continually focusing on fear is cast out. Love and trust God and He will keep us in peace by faith because our minds are fixed on Him.

*Romans 5:1 Therefore being justified **by faith, we have peace** with God through our Lord Jesus Christ ...*

*Isaiah 26:3 Thou wilt keep him in **perfect peace,** whose **mind is stayed on thee:** because **he trusteth in thee.***

The following daily exercise might be helpful in understanding and allowing a healthy expression of the energy of anger. (Words, emotions and feelings are vibrations and energy.)

1. Think of a past situation that has made you angrier than you would normally be.

2. Feel the power of the angry energy that is produced by thinking about that incident and transform that energy into something positive.

3. Recognize that you are at a point where you can make use of *The Revelation of Power* that lies within you.

4. Fearlessly examine the source of your anger and be courageous enough to look at it carefully to determine if it is hiding some deeper feelings from the past.

5. Declare with power and force that you have the power of choice about how, or even if, you will express your anger. (This is most important.) Become clear about what action will best protect, support and further your well-being and future goals.

6. Using the energy of that anger, commit to your best path of action and follow that path to its positive conclusion.

7. Notice how it feels to transform your anger into its highest and best use through *The Revelation of Power*.

What we put out is energy and vibrations. What we get back is the same energy and vibrations. One way to begin the shift in the vibrations you send out is by thinking, acting and behaving more generously towards others. When we act with generosity, whether with money, time or service to others, we start a positive vibration cycle that is unrestricted by fear. The world will mirror back, in energy and vibrations, our generosity and our belief in abundance with experiences that provide abundance all around us. One of the sayings I have heard in meetings and therapy is that you have to give away what you want to keep.

When I am teaching a group, I often say that you can get the best out of me. I will study, meditate, pray and whatever else I have to do to help you. I have found that I am still selfish, but now in a good way. I will give away my best. I may not get it back from you but I will receive back from the universe what I have given you—my best.

Perhaps the most difficult and devastating fear in today's world is free-floating anxiety, or fear that is unattached to any particular event or situation. Free-floating anxiety attacks are one of the main reasons we take tranquilizers and mood enhancers. It is also the primary reason we seek artificial positive emotions (sexual excesses, drug and alcohol abuse, shopping, and adventure filled with unrestrained behavior, etc).

Free-floating panic attacks are endemic in our society today, possibly because we are so disconnected from our deeper spiritual selves. Although prescriptions for antidepressants and escape experiences may help us temporarily to function with our exploding, free-floating anxiety attacks, they do not remove its root cause. Free-floating anxiety and panic attacks, in some cases are clear signs that we do not know or trust our process for dealing with life.

There are some positives to exploring fear. Fears provide us with opportunities to build trust. Embracing and transforming our fears and working on our basic sense of trust, we become stronger and more empowered in the way we operate in our personal world and the world in general. You can actually function on a much higher plane of creativity and clarity. As you become more consciously aware of your gifted self and perceive your interconnectedness with the living universe, your insight and intuition rise to new levels. Fear, which is just a word to identify some form of energy that is interpreted by our brain, can be transformed into something much more powerful: trust. This does not mean that you may not be hurt or afraid at some point, but you are now capable of taking a positive risk.

Fear and anger have illusionary elements to them, because they are often misplaced. We may believe that we are angry about a particular situation, when in fact years and layers of hurt and disappointment underlie the current anger and are really the driving force behind it. That is a tremendous amount of stored power that you can use creatively. I have often used this transforming energy to move forward. I have frequently said to myself, "I will not be stopped by fear but will be motivated by it." It is now a part of my action tools that help me move forward in the face of any challenge.

Years and multiple layers of pain and abuse are often so hidden in our past that they have become an instinctive part of us that produces outbursts in our current life. If we look deeper, we find that these feelings may include disappointment, unworthiness, guilt, and fear of rejection or the need for acceptance. If we can trace our anger to its root cause, that anger and its *relatives*— irritation, frustration, resentment and bitterness—can provide us with a great deal of information about ourselves and the power to move forward in a newfound, positive direction.

Addiction is a brain disease that affects the biological and sociological aspects of human behavior. Addiction is definitely not solely a moral failure. The drugs and alcohol used by an addict take over the brain's natural ways of distributing dopamine and endorphins down the pleasure pathways and lock the person into trying to compete with the craving of the brain.

Drug and alcohol abuse and addiction are more detrimental when they begin in adolescence. The brain is still undergoing dramatic maturation, physically and functionally. The younger a person starts abusing drugs or alcohol, the greater the chances that he or she will eventually go on to become addicted. However, addiction is treatable. The sooner the addicted person obtains help the better. Statistics have shown that the longer one stays in treatment the better the chances are that treatment will be successful.

Addicts are often portrayed as following one of two paths, either being weak-willed and succumbing to their addiction or having some form of spiritual experience that turns their life around. These extremes make it difficult to understand the complexity of addiction. The truth is that addiction alters the brain in ways that can make recovery much more difficult than *just stopping*. Recovery can be a disorganized, imperfect process, and long-term abstinence can take years to accomplish. Setbacks are common, yet many addicts ultimately do recover.

You have *The Revelation of Power* now, inside you. Go forward now to conquer your fears and take positive risks. You are a present and a gift to the world because you are exceptional and a one-of-a-kind creation. Many answers to other people's problems lie within you. Use these answers as you continue to conquer your own problem areas. Take things slowly. Just one day at a time, lived to its fullest, can lead to the life you really want. You now understand that you have the power to handle anything that comes into or against your life.

Take time to count your many blessings instead of your present troubles. Your new attitude will come; your new, revived emotional state will become real. Thinking about what you are grateful and thankful for keeps things on a positive note. This does not mean that you are ignoring the problems facing you. It means that you will be approaching life from a place of power and strength and not from the position of a victim, blaming everybody and everything else for your problems. You have the talent and the knowledge to rise from the ashes of your former life. Take time to explore the knowledge around you.

Be courageous and operate from a position of positive power when making decisions about your own life. Do not let anyone limit you or your thinking. Dream big and make it happen. If you do not wholeheartedly choose the path you will take, something or someone else will choose it for you. From this moment on, if you do not create the endurance to map your own future, you will have to endure the future you get. You can, you will and you must move forward on a positive path if you are to achieve for yourself the life of your dreams. There are many dreams for you, just waiting for you to discover them.

Realize that it is never too late to turn toward a life of beautiful dreams. Remember: nothing wastes more energy than worrying about the problem you are carrying. Worrying makes the problem grow and become heavier and heavier. Never forget that, just beneath the surface of bad choices, you are a very special person. This book proves that someone, somewhere, who suffered just like you, cares about you.

Your wealth can be stolen, but the precious riches buried deep in your soul cannot
Minnie Riperton

If you're walking down the right path and you're willing to keep walking, eventually you'll make it.
Barack Obama

No one can give you wisdom. You must discover it for yourself, on the journey through life, which no one can take for you.
Sun Bear

Chapter 25

Counseling Theories

In *The Revelation of Power* you have information leading you to the source of power using a Biblical approach to therapy and recovery. You have access to the personal comforting power of God.

John 14:16 And I will pray the Father, and he shall give you another Comforter, that he may abide with you for ever;

John 14:17 Even the Spirit of truth; whom the world cannot receive, because it seeth him not, neither knoweth him: but ye know him; for he dwelleth with you, and shall be in you.

John 14:26 But the Comforter, which is the Holy Ghost, whom the Father will send in my name, he shall teach you all things, and bring all things to your remembrance, whatsoever I have said unto you.

The Holy Spirit brings the unconscious motivations into conscious awareness; it is He who promotes insight and resolves conflict.

John 14:27 Peace I leave with you, my peace I give unto you: not as the world giveth, give I unto you. Let not your heart be troubled, neither let it be afraid.

The purpose of including many of the counseling theories here is to show how embracing, understanding and using the information contained in *The Revelation of Power* can enhance and empower whichever theory you use. Every one of these theories deals in whole or in part with thoughts, beliefs, emotions, and behaviors—past present or future. By understanding the laws and principles of *The Revelation of Power*, you can more clearly see the relationship between the clients and whatever thoughts or actions are produced by the clients. This book gives greater understanding to the clients, allowing them to understand that they have the power to re-create themselves with the help of God.

When clients understand their personal psychology and the relationship between their words and their actions in this universe of energy, this understanding will help them to make the kinds of decisions that will benefit them.

As a counselor, universal laws and principles of growth and expansion along with expectation and abundance are teaching points that can be brought together within each theory. Many associations not previously thought of by your clients are yet-to-be-revealed connections that await the client's creative touch.

The twelve step process is a structured method of achieving the awakening of the spiritual man by following each step. If the client follows the steps, in fellowship with others in the program, he or she will learn about the experience, strength, and hope that other clients have acquired. This new knowledge will reinforce the process of continuing to follow the 12 steps. With each step, the client can become more fully alive with power as he or she understands what *The Revelation of Power* has to offer in relationship with the 12 steps.

What we really are, minus our bodies, is spirit, with thoughts, feelings, beliefs and emotions, both past and present. We are energy and energy can be changed. The theories, the 12 steps and *The Revelation of Power* are all trying to get you to look inside and make decisions that only *you* can make to create change.

Christian, Bible-based rehabilitation seeks to help clients work through psychological and social issues using both long-established therapeutic methods and a viewpoint based on being a Christian. The teachings of Jesus in the New Testament as well as the teachings from the Old Testament are used. Using the entire Bible, Christian therapists guide their clients' *emotional* and spiritual *growth* in spiritual unity through the study of scripture and spiritual services.

Psychoanalysis is a body of ideas, developed by Austrian physician Sigmund Freud and his followers, which is devoted to the study of human psychological functioning and *behavior*. It has three applications: 1) a method of investigating the *mind*; 2) a systematized set of theories about human *behavior;* and 3) a method of treating psychological or *emotional* illness.

Psychodynamic therapy, also known as *insight-oriented* therapy, evolved from Freudian psychoanalysis. Like adherents of psychoanalysis, psychodynamic therapists believe that bringing the unconscious into conscious awareness promotes insight and resolves conflict. Psychodynamic therapy also focuses on the relationship between the therapist and the client as a way to learn about how the client relates to everyone in his or her life.

The humanistic method takes a positive view of human nature and emphasizes the distinctiveness of the individual personality. Therapists in this tradition, who are interested in exploring the nature of human resourcefulness, love and self-actualization, help clients understand their potential through positive change and *inner,* self-directed *growth*. Humanistic therapy is also an overarching expression for Gestalt therapy and client-centered therapy.

Client-centered therapy was developed by Carl Rogers in the 1940s. The client-centered method is based on the empowering idea that the client—not the therapist—holds the answers to the client's problems. The client-centered therapist's job, then, is to listen carefully and strive to understand the client, so that the client can tap into his or her natural ability to *grow* and improve. Client-centered therapy helps the client live *in the moment* and focus on personality change, rather than on the origins of his or her personality structure. The therapist encourages the patient to express his or her *feelings* and does not suggest how the person might wish to change. Instead, by listening and then mirroring back what the patient reveals, the therapist helps the patient explore and understand his or her *feelings* about themselves. The patient is then able to decide what kind of changes he or she would like to make in order to achieve personal growth.

Behaviorism originated with the work of John B. Watson, an American psychologist. Watson claimed that psychology was not concerned with the mind or with human consciousness. Instead, psychology should be concerned only with behavior. In this way, men could be studied objectively, like rats and apes.

Watson's experiments were based on the work of Ivan Pavlov, who had studied animals' responses to classical conditioning. In Pavlov's best-known experiment, he rang a bell as he fed some dogs several meals. Each time the dogs heard the bell they knew that a meal was coming, and they would begin to salivate. Then Pavlov rang the bell without bringing food, but the dogs still salivated. They had been "conditioned" to salivate at the sound of a bell. Pavlov believed, as Watson was later to emphasize, that humans react to stimuli in the same way.

Behaviorism is closely associated with the name of Skinner, who made his reputation by testing Watson's theories in the laboratory. Skinner's studies led him to reject Watson's almost exclusive emphasis on reflexes and conditioning. People respond to their environment, he argued, but they also operate on the environment to produce certain consequences.

Skinner developed the theory of "operant conditioning," the idea that we behave the way we do because this kind of behavior has had certain consequences in the past. B.F. Skinner theorized, quite correctly, that the best way of keeping someone under control is through intermittent reinforcement.

Behaviorism, also called the learning perspective (where any physical *action* is a *behavior*), is a philosophy of psychology based on the proposition that all things that organisms do—including *acting, thinking and feeling*—can and should be regarded as *behaviors*. Behaviorism holds the position that all theories should have observational correlates but that there are no philosophical differences between publicly observable processes (such as *actions*) and privately observable processes (such as *thinking and feeling*) Behaviorism is the sum total of all actions namely *verbal, mental, physical and sensory.*

Cognitive behavioral therapy stresses the role of *thinking* in how we feel and what we do. It is based on the belief that *thoughts,* rather than people or events, cause our negative feelings. The therapist assists the patient in identifying, testing the reality of and correcting dysfunctional *beliefs* underlying his or her *thinking.* The therapist then helps the client modify those thoughts and the behaviors that flow from them.

Rational Emotive Behavior Therapy (REBT), previously called rational therapy and rational emotive therapy, is a comprehensive, active-directive, philosophically and empirically based psychotherapy that focuses on resolving *emotional and behavioral* problems and disturbances and enabling people to lead happier and more fulfilling lives. REBT was created and developed by the American psychotherapist and psychologist Albert Ellis, who was inspired by many of the teachings of Asian, Greek, Roman and modern philosophers. REBT is one of the first and foremost forms of cognitive behavior therapy (CBT) and was first expounded by Ellis in the mid-1950s. One of the fundamental premises of REBT is that, in most cases, people do not get upset merely by adversities but also because of how they construct their view of reality through their evaluative *beliefs* and philosophies about these adversities.

The cognitive restructuring theory holds that your own unrealistic *beliefs* are directly responsible for generating dysfunctional *emotions* and their resultant *behaviors,* like *stress, depression, anxiety* and social *withdrawal,* and that we humans can be rid of such *emotions* and their effects by dismantling the *beliefs* that give them life. This is accomplished by leading the subject to gain *awareness* of detrimental *thought habits,* learn to challenge those negative *thoughts* and substitute life-enhancing *thoughts* and *beliefs.*

The rationale used in cognitive restructuring attempts to strengthen the client's *belief* that 1) self-talk can influence performance and 2) in particular, self-defeating *thoughts* or negative self-statements can cause *emotional* distress and interfere with performance, a process that then repeats in a cycle.

Gestalt therapy is an existential and experiential psychotherapy that focuses on the individual's experience in the *present moment,* the therapist-client relationship, the environmental and social contexts in which these things take place and the self-regulating adjustments people make as a result of the overall situation. Gestalt therapy emphasizes *personal responsibility*. Gestalt therapy was developed by Fritz Perls and Paul Goodman in the '40s and '50s.

What is the power that makes the 12 Steps work?

The 12 Steps work because they are made up of principles and truths based on universal, unchangeable laws. They can be put into action and they will allow you to see how to deal with real-life situations. When you understand the basic truths and underlying laws that operate in the universe, you can better determine your future. These rules and standards are necessary in a system of thought to give you a mental framework and structure. These rules are applicable in most situations and purposes in your own life and, if followed, produce better consequences. As you absorb and use the 12 Steps, you form a mental construct that gives you a basis for proper and effective living.

The 12 Steps also work because of Biblical principles. Yes, God (*G*ood *O*rderly *D*irection) has a course of action to change you. God's Word reveals to us five steps of conversion. The 12 Steps use the same principles of change.

Now that you know what to expect, begin to prepare yourself. Get ready now! The only way to get to where you want to be is to do what it takes to get there. Do it one day at a time, do it fast, do it slow, but do it right. Do whatever it is that needs to be done. Do it in the daylight and do it by the moonlight, but get it done. If you do decide to give up on whatever you have been doing, moving in the direction of where you want to be, you will never change anything in your life.

1. His Word convicts us of our wrongdoing (sins).

2. We then confess our sins and actively get involved with God through His Word.

3. By accepting Jesus the Christ of God as our savior, we begin the conversion process. We become born again by the Holy Spirit. By acting on God's Word and correcting our thoughts and actions, we begin the conversion process. All of these are acts of repentance, turning us around in our hearts and minds and changing the direction in which we are going. In the conversion, or seed maturation process, we learn how to walk, talk, act and please God by faith.

4. As you change day by day, you experience a newfound confidence through the principle of reciprocity, and your acts of faith bring a new character along with confidence and mental tools for living through the Word of God.

5. You continue the process until the excitement of discovery takes over and the thrill of a new life becomes a better high than any chemical that you can use. The result of following these steps is the desire to continue making changes. You begin to understand that the goodness of God leads us to continue to change our ways in accordance with the Word of God. (Repentance).

Remember these five steps and, as you go through the 12 Steps, you will see them again.

- Conviction
- Confession
- Conversion
- Confidence
- Continuance

The Revelation of Power is designed to lead a person to an awakening of the true self and allow him or her to continually live in higher conscious awareness. In addition, a person is given insight into how all of these elements produce results through looking at universal principles and laws.

The Revelation of Power is a progressive revelation of the creative force and power within each of us. Hard work, study, meditation and prayer will release our fullest understanding and experience. This book will show you how the understanding comes from living in true power as it unfolds its secrets, using meditation as the medium of *seeing*.

The Revelation of Power helps you develop a mindset that allows you to work within the framework of all the counseling theories either simultaneously or in each individual area, depending on the needs of the client. All these areas of the mind—thinking, vision and imagination (thoughts of the future), knowledge (the present), memory and conscience (the past) and the heart (thinking)—are explored in this book. In addition, the subconscious, habit force and the self are covered in *The Revelation of Power*.

Each counseling session is designed to bring the person into a fuller understanding of his or her true self by following the course laid out in the therapy. You can take the client through any number of laws and principles, showing him or her how he or she relates to each theory.

The Revelation of Power helps you gain insight into each counseling theory by understanding where to look inside yourself and how to apply universal laws and principles to each theory and therapy to enhance the counseling experience of the client. Look over the list of laws and principles and see how they play a role in each theory. There will be many areas of application that I have not thought of and written about in this book as it relates to clients, counselors and outcomes. As you grow in knowledge and gain a better understanding of the relevance of theory to laws and principles, I am sure you will develop new tools of insight and methods for yourself and your clients.

I consider *The Revelation of Power* to be a powerful guide in teaching you how to handle your client's troublesome situations by helping them in exercising deliberate, learned, conscious control to improve the outcome of any situation. It is in helping them recognize their own personal weaknesses while looking inside themselves and working to overcome those personal faults that help each client to improve on many different levels.

Adventure is not outside man; it is within.
David Grayson

Man's power of choice enables him to think like an angel or a devil, a king or a slave. Whatever he chooses, mind will create and manifest.
Frederick Bailes

Luke 6:45 A good man out of the good treasure of his heart bringeth forth that which is good; and an evil man out of the evil treasure of his heart bringeth forth that which is evil: for of the abundance of the heart his mouth speaketh.

Chapter 26

The Revelation of Power/Ideas for Lessons

For those of you who are in a position to teach *The Revelation of Power,* I hope that the following ideas for lessons will help. You, too, must change as you study and continue teaching. This is perhaps the most profound thing that can happen for you and to you. If you continue to develop your life, you will begin to see new areas from *The Revelation of Power* that used to be hidden from your conscious awareness. As you become aware of your personal mental and life changes, you will improve as you teach, and you will teach with more passion.

Those of you who have read *The Power to Change* already have better laid-out lesson plans. You will notice that both books contain a lot of the same material. This was not done by accident. *The Power to Change* was written without a focus on salvation and the revelation of the love of God through Jesus Christ. Feel free to add your own knowledge and experience to the process of teaching. This book was written with that focus.

To begin teaching, you will need motivation to progress effectively through the lessons in the study. If you do not have or cannot develop a state of mind that can be described as a need, strong desire or something you desperately want, you will not be activated or energized to the point that your behavior will change through the use of these lessons. You must have a direction in which to move forward and a persistence of behavior to effect change in your cognitive and personality development. There must be an agreement between your beliefs and your actions. What you do will tell you what you *actually* believe, not what you *say* you believe. Motivation means that you expect personal success and rewards and that you place a true, high value on attaining your goals.

Remember: as a teacher, you are also going to be studying yourself for the purpose of exercising the degree of true power that rewards your efforts.

Psychologists study the mind, which includes both the conscious and unconscious states of the mind. Neither of these states of mind can be seen. The word psychology or the scientific study of behavior and the mind is a combination of two terms, study (-ology) and psyche (soul, psukhe, Ka and Chi).

I included many words from many languages because they all allude to the same invisible essence of the personality. The Latin psyche and the Greek psukhe mean breath, life and soul. Ka is Egyptian and refers to the invisible person that lives past the body. Chi is the life force that is spoken of by the Chinese. All these words attempt to describe the invisible you inside the body you live in. Therefore, psychology is a study of the invisible self.

You, the teacher, will be working with some of the most defensive, combative, resistant areas of thinking that keep a person locked mentally and unable to develop properly. When you, the teacher, realize that you are working with the following types of mindset described in the following pages, you will understand that the person you are working with is thinking only about what he or she wants. And he or she is thinking, "Just because I want it, whatever it is, it should be mine despite any moral, social or ethical restraints." This is a self-centered attitude that leads to making excuses and justifying any behavior because of the desire to have or to do something.

Those you teach are thinking that another way of avoiding responsibility is to blame anyone else other than themselves for their problems. The following is how your students are functioning psychologically: whenever they can blame anyone else for their situation, they cannot change it because, in their minds, it is not their fault. The part of them that is invisible and operates on information they give it will not allow them to change anything because they keep saying to themselves that it is someone else's fault. This means that they continue redefining the problem for the sole purpose of shifting the focus of any issue away from themselves. But the self is the only one who can implement and sustain true change.

Without admitting their personal errors there is no possibility for change. They cannot change what they do not admit. For all intents and purposes, their problem does not exist and therefore cannot be changed. Lying is a commonly used tactic, to confuse, distort and take the focus off their behavior. Many times they will minimize their behavior by talking about it in such a way as to make it seem insignificant. They are used to getting angry in order to get their way or playing the victim in order to gain sympathy and make others vulnerable to their manipulation.

Another defense manipulation includes being almost combative in every conversation. Each sentence becomes a contest that they have to win. They cannot let anyone else win; they must either win or become deceptive in their thinking, action and behavior until they win. By seeing only what they want to see and not listening to what you have to say, they wait until you finish your point, only to resume their attack with an obvious attitude of defiance, hostility and consummately defending their position. They continue to function with a complete disregard for the truth of the matter.

Of course, there are other levels of deception, such as a shamelessly uncaring attitude about what people say about what they do. They muster up a brazen attitude about everything and never think of anyone's good except their own. They are simply unwilling to put forth any effort and are defiant to the point that they have a complete disdain for authority and refuse to accept any opinion but their own.

These are the errors in thinking, action and behavior that keep them locked in a self-destructive lifestyle. Studying the principles put forth in this book will enable you to help develop a different set of character qualities in those you are teaching.

Should you decide to read, study and teach *The Revelation of Power,* great things await your ability to teach and reach others. The new counseling qualities that you will be demonstrating through your teaching are based on being alert and aware of what is happening outside and inside your own mind. You must also keep your eyes and ears open to new ideas in your approach to teaching and counseling. By being careful to recognize and to take heed to the verbal warning signs in those you counsel, you will become a more experienced and effective counselor and teacher. Teaching others requires that you study. In a sense, you are programming yourself when you hear yourself teach.

Remember: criminals and addicted personalities are well schooled in manipulative language and in their desire to find ways to control and exert power over others. Their greatest thrill in life is doing what is forbidden and getting away with it. This need for power, control and dominance will show up in many areas of their lives. Be mindful that, sometimes, when they appear to be showing interest in a responsible way, they may actually be looking for ways to trap you and exercise power and control over you, the teacher.

Some of the character disorder features in those you will be teaching:

- They define themselves as separate individuals, distinct and different.

- They have a thorough opposition to any authority. *Proverbs 15:12 A scorner loveth not one that reproveth him: neither will he go unto the wise.*

- Maturation and developmental steps always involve resistance to authority. *Proverbs 15:32 He that refuseth instruction despiseth his own soul ...*

- Mistreated children develop into adults who continue on to develop character disorders focused on exaggerated rebelliousness and anti-authoritarian, aggressive acting out. *Proverbs 20:17 Bread of deceit is sweet to a man; but afterwards his mouth shall be filled with gravel.*

- They are always at odds with the rules. *Proverbs 17:11 An evil man seeketh only rebellion: therefore a cruel messenger shall be sent against him.*

- They are most likely to end up committing criminal acts and being sent to jail or prison. *Romans 1:28 And even as they did not like to retain God in their knowledge, God gave them over to a reprobate mind, to do those things which are not convenient ...*

- They have very little tolerance for frustration.

- Their frustration results from barriers that other people put in the way of their satisfactions, wants or desires. *Proverbs 18:7 A fool's mouth is his destruction, and his lips are the snare of his soul.*

- They try to project a cool, calm, laid-back, superficially charming manner.

- They are quick to react aggressively toward anyone who gets in their way and tries to stop them from doing what they want to do.

- They hate being told that they can't do a particular thing. They feel that they *must* rebel, especially when the person telling them to do something is an authority figure

- They let a person know immediately if that person is behaving in ways that make them feel too anxious, tense or uncomfortable.

The clear message is aggression: "Back off and don't get in my way—or else!"

Proverbs 1:22 How long, ye simple ones, will ye love simplicity? and the scorners delight in their scorning, and fools hate knowledge?

Proverbs 4: 19 The way of the wicked is as darkness: they know not at what they stumble.

Their major defense mechanisms:

- The suppression or repression of the conscience and memory *1 Timothy 4:1-2 Now the Spirit speaketh expressly, that in the latter times some shall depart from the faith, giving heed to seducing spirits, and doctrines of devils; Speaking lies in hypocrisy; having their **conscience** seared with a hot iron...*

- Constant attempts to overthrow authority. *Isaiah 30:1 Woe to the **rebellious** children, saith the LORD, that take counsel, but not of me; and that cover with a covering, but not of my spirit, that they may add sin to sin...*

- Not concerned with past or future consequences of any action. *Proverbs 19:5 A false witness shall not be unpunished, and he that speaketh lies shall not escape.*

- Their guilt started much further in the past than in most people.

- Anxiety and apprehension about the future. *Deuteronomy 28:66-67 And thy life shall hang in doubt before thee; and thou shalt **fear** day and night, and shalt have none assurance of thy life: In the morning thou shalt say, Would God it were even! and at even thou shalt say, Would God it were morning! for the **fear** of thine heart wherewith thou shalt **fear**, and for the sight of thine eyes which thou shalt see.*

- Live in the here-and-now, and the present moment is most important to them.

- They do not profit from past mistakes or alter their behavior in light of likely future consequences so they are, of course, at very high risk of repeating behavior that society forbids and punishes. *Proverbs 1:29-32 "For that they hated knowledge, and did not choose the fear of the LORD: They would none of my counsel: they despised all my reproof. Therefore shall they eat of the fruit of their own way, and be filled with their own devices. For the turning away of the simple shall slay them, and the prosperity of fools shall destroy them."*

Important Points:

The lessons in this book contain knowledge based on scientific facts, and this information is designed to help students bridge the gap between the information given in seminars, groups, lectures and videos and turn it into a powerful force for change. This new method will enable counselors to turn presentations into actual energy, called inspiration. This method of observation, learning and

276

teaching is designed to touch your heart and to arouse your emotions. These lessons are designed to set your passion on fire and raise to a fevered pitch your desire to be free. The answer is *The Revelation of Power*. The knowledge presented here is to be viewed as inspirational and motivational. It is designed to help you focus your internal power into *The Revelation of Power* and then to help others with your newfound knowledge.

Teaching the concepts of *The Revelation of Power* requires this understanding: *The Revelation of Power* is not intended to be taught word for word. The suggested lessons are presented as important points to stress and a way to break down the complex work into manageable portions. As a teacher of *The Revelation of Power*, you must read the material and put the ideas into your own words, using the lesson breakdown and points of interest as guidelines. You will find that you will seldom teach *The Revelation of Power* the same way each time. This is simply because, as you learn and experience change in your own life, you will also learn more intricate ways to teach the laws and principles explained in this book.

As you gain a deeper understanding of both yourself and your life experience, your presentation will become more and more interesting and profound. You will find articles and other teaching materials that will dovetail with your teaching process. As you come to know the material in this book, you will weave more interesting personal experiences into your method of teaching. *The Revelation of Power* is designed to be modified as you teach. However, try not to deviate from the sound ethical and moral principles contained in *The Revelation of Power*.

*Proverbs 24:6 For by **wise counsel** thou shalt make thy war: and in **multitude of counsellors** there is safety.*

The information, that follows has been extracted from the text of the book, and is designed for you to use as a guidepost. Of course, it is expected that you, the teacher, will refer back to these areas for study and preparation before teaching. As you absorb the information in this book, you will be better able to teach it to others.

We use power to live every day. The purpose of *The Revelation of Power* is to let us understand how to harness this power for our positive use and to understand the principles behind this power, to which we as humans are subject in this present world. No one is excluded from the invisible authority of universal principles.

The stimulation of the mind and emotions to a high level of activity and awareness in a positive direction is the purpose of using *The Revelation of Power*.

The attainment of mastery over yourself through use of *The Revelation of Power* is an essential step in the process of total liberation for victims who wish to end the oppression of addiction and regain self-respect and mental well-being.

The factual evidence presented here will elicit and arouse motivational aspects in your conscious and subconscious mind.

The Revelation of Power is intended to energize and galvanize your thought patterns and provoke change.

Through committing yourself to a life of discipline and learning, along with daily practice, you can have a new existence.

Today, choose to read, study and observe this material and always use these powerful mental and spiritual tools for the good of yourself and others.

The next area is a sample of how I teach *The Revelation of Power* in a step-by-step manner. The information is arranged in steps in which I discuss each area of the person. I start by explaining that each of us has these components. I write these components on a chart, blackboard or give some visual presentation that can be seen by the whole class. In explaining each area, I use the information in this book, supplemented by other material that I may add to make the lesson as clear as possible. I incorporate the nine areas of the self in the very beginning of the lessons to clarify immediately who and what is at fault and who and what needs to change. The first few lessons are about each person's understanding of himself or herself and how each of us operates within the laws and principles of this universe. Then I go into other areas of the book. Once I have discussed the "self" and all of its components, I go through each of the principles explained in this book. I go over between five and seven principles at a time, depending on the number of questions asked during the class and how much unrelated information is discussed.

The Chart:

Thinking-Action-Behavior-WUTWH-(what you thought would happen) & Consequences

Mind

Brain

Vision	*Future:* vision and imagination —look into the future

Imagination

Knowledge	*Present:* knowledge being used is— in the present

Memory

Conscience   *Past:* memory and conscience
                                    —look into the past

Subconscious

Habit Force

The Heart

The principles of self-discipline can be summarized into the following four steps.

1. Set a goal for yourself

As mentioned earlier, goal-setting is very important in achieving self-discipline. In fact, it is the first and most important step. Without any goals, it is very difficult to get anywhere. So, before you start on a project or work, be sure to set a target, a goal.

2. You must have a strong desire to achieve the goal

When you have a goal, make sure that you have the desire to fulfill it. What's the use of setting a goal if you don't even have the interest or determination to accomplish it? For example, you promised yourself that you would go jogging every morning. But, whenever the alarm clock rings at 6 a.m. your first reaction is to turn it off. So, what's the use of setting a goal if you don't make any effort to fulfill it?

3. You must keep at it in spite of failure

How many times have we set a goal for ourselves and have not completed it because of some difficulties we have encountered? You see, failure is part and parcel of growing up. But does it mean that, once you fail at achieving your goal, you abandon it? No! You must carry on, try again and find out why you couldn't achieve the goal in the first place.

Then try again to achieve your goal. You must persevere in spite of any failures.

4. Take things one step at a time

Finally, you must not rush things. If you have set a goal for yourself, plan how you are going to achieve it. Once you have completed the first step of your plan, proceed to the second step. Try not to think too far ahead when you have not yet completed a particular step. Slow and steady is the key here.

You might ask yourself what self-discipline can give you. First, self-discipline can give you a sense of pride that you may never have had before. Believe me, not everyone has self-discipline. And remember: when you accomplish a goal, you will get a sense of achievement. Try to embrace this good feeling as a part of your reward for doing the right thing. Having self-discipline can also boost your confidence and will power for the next challenge. When you have confidence, everything you do will go more smoothly. Most importantly, you can also acquire new skills and knowledge that you can use to help others.

You will find that most people in recovery admire and respect strong individuals who have won great success by manifesting the will power, humility and self-discipline required for continued recovery.

Many people in recovery and in all walks of life, who have, with sheer will power, self discipline and ambition, improved their lives, learned new skills, overcome difficulties and hardships, reduced their weight, and risen higher in their chosen field or advanced on the spiritual path of personal awakening to higher consciousness. Notice that all of these different skills are needed for a total and wholesome change.

Will power and self-discipline are two of the most important and useful inner powers in everyone's life and have always been considered essential tools for success in all areas of life. They can be learned and developed like any other skill. Yet, in spite of this, very few take the necessary steps to develop and strengthen these powers in a systematic way.

The following are tools I use when teaching *The Power to Change* and *The Revelation of Power.* Both of these tools are used in a PowerPoint presentation. The knowledge of self in terms of self-esteem is vitally important in understanding how both books help you understand yourself and where you need to work on your own mental and spiritual areas of creation.

Knowing self is fundamental to assuming power over self

Self-esteem: confidence in your own merit and abilities as an individual

Lack of self-esteem: feelings of doubt about your own worth and abilities

<u>Self-acceptance</u> To begin looking at yourself, you must begin by accepting who you are and what you have done. This does not mean you accept that you are evil or bad. If that were the case and a person was evil in his or her essence, then he or she could not change. But we all know that people can change. We were shaped in iniquity or by wickedness and conceived in sin but we were not born *as* sin.

*Psalms 51:5 Behold, I was **shapen** in iniquity; and **in sin** did my mother conceive me.*

*Matthew 19:26 But Jesus beheld them, and said unto them, With men this is impossible; **but with God all things are possible.***

*Mark 10:27 And Jesus looking upon them saith, With men it is impossible, but not with God: for **with God** all things are possible.*

*John 15:7 If ye abide in me, and my words **abide in you,** ye shall ask what ye will, and it shall be done unto you.*

*Philippians 4:13 **I can do all things** through Christ which strengtheneth me.*

*Hebrews 10:35 Cast not away therefore **your confidence,** which hath great recompence of reward.*

<u>Self-destructiveness</u> You must accept that you have been self-destructive and have done things to harm your mind, your body and people around you. But you can be the opposite of destructive and become constructive. Lack of self-esteem and a low self-image will deprive you of the ability to believe in your own importance and will make you fail to see any value in your own life.

*Isaiah 30:1 Woe to the **rebellious** children, saith the LORD, that take counsel, but not of me; and that cover with a covering, but not of my spirit, that they may add sin to sin ...*

<u>Self-pity</u> The most destructive thing that you can do is to feel sorry for yourself. That emotion-packed thought process of self-pity cuts you off from positive change. If you accept that you are not worthy of better things because you are so bad, you accept being pitiful. That kind of thinking can be used as another excuse to escape responsibility. You begin to feel so sorry for yourself and how life has treated you that you become your best "pity party" guest. You can become so disoriented in your sorrow, misgivings, regret and self-pity that you refuse to be shaken out of your self-preoccupation or changed by any positive advice. You begin to believe that no one will notice you if they can't feel sorry for you.

Self-help Learn to help yourself. If you don't help yourself, who will? Self-help is a way to deal with problems that everyone faces from time to time in their lives—illness, divorce, the death of a loved one, emotional upsets or strains. Many times, talking over these problems with other people who have lived through them can help us cope with today's difficulties and help us learn how to deal with any difficulties we may have in the future. In the past two decades, the self-help movement has mushroomed. AA, the largest self-help group, reports over one million members in the U. S. One estimate places the total number of people in self-help support groups at 20 million.

1 Peter 5:6 ***Humble yourselves*** *therefore under the mighty hand of God, that he may exalt you in due time ...*

James 4:8 ***Draw nigh to God,*** *and he will draw nigh to you. Cleanse your hands, ye sinners; and purify your hearts, ye double minded.*

Hebrews 10:38 Now the just shall live by faith: ***but if any man draw back,*** *my soul shall have no pleasure in him.*

Self-education Libraries and bookstores are packed with knowledge to help you educate your self. All help is self-help.

2 Timothy 2:15 ***Study*** *to shew thyself approved unto God, a workman that needeth not to be ashamed, rightly dividing the word of truth.*

Self-discipline How can you achieve it? Self-discipline is one of the hardest qualities to attain. Self-discipline means that you must have the ability to control yourself. Simply put, you must force yourself to do whatever is necessary for positive change. Self-discipline helps you to discover how to take control of your life by setting goals and taking real steps to achieve them.

Goal-setting is one of the strongest forces for human inspiration and motivation. Set goals and make them come true. Nothing builds faith faster than setting small goals and accomplishing them on your way to your main goal. You will be exposed to new ways of seeing the world and new ways of leading a happier, healthier and more gratifying life—a life in which you know what you want, how to get there, how to set realistic goals and how to work toward achieving them.

Luke 9:23 And he said to them all, If any man will come after me, let him deny himself, and take up his cross daily, and **follow me.**

Self-discovery Start by examining your inner self. What is your true self? Why are you here on this planet? What is your purpose in life? By asking yourself questions, you open yourself up to discover a deeper level of life. The discovery process, through *The Revelation of Power*, leads you step by step, according to your ability to understand matters of principle in life based on your new acceptance and beliefs. At some point, you come to realize the higher viewpoint of life.

Your thoughts, words, feelings and actions towards everyone under all circumstances determine your life's outcome according to the law and principle of reciprocity. At a deeper level, you will come to understand that life is about learning. Overcoming and learning the lessons in the classroom of life is the process of self-development and spiritual growth. When you discover the real essence of who and what you are—consciousness that is filled with energy, power and potential—you will know what freedom truly is.

*Romans 13:11 And that, knowing the time, that now it is high time to **awake out of sleep:** for now is our salvation nearer than when we believed.*

*Ephesians 5:14 Wherefore he saith, **Awake thou that sleepest,** and arise from the dead, and Christ shall give thee light.*

Self-preservation   Self-preservation is part of the human instinct to survive. Fear causes man to seek safety and may cause a release of adrenaline. The fear of pain is also a part of the human defense mechanism that will move a person away from alcohol, drugs and criminal behavior. When a person has suffered enough pain and discomfort, he or she is inclined to stop that pain by going through recovery. You will reach this stage in your development of self when you know you are worthy of life.

*Revelation 3:10 Because thou hast kept the word of my patience, I also **will keep thee** from the hour of temptation, which shall come upon all the world, to try them that dwell upon the earth.*

Self-knowledge Knowing yourself is fundamental to assuming power over your thoughts and behavior.

Important! Please take note when using these charts:

- Using the charts is a way of enhancing the way you teach *The Revelation of Power.*

- Students can follow the step-by-step process of locating negative areas to explore within the framework of *The Revelation of Power* laws and principles.

- The brain and its six creative areas, listed on the first chart can be explained and contrasted with the universal laws and principles that can be listed on the right-hand side of the chart to show clearly the consequences of any action or thought.

- You can explain any type of knowledge or emotion by using these charts or placing information on a chalkboard.

- You can decide to use all or part of each chart, depending on the students' needs. This allows for more creative input from both you and your students.

- By using the charts, you can explore and track the development of criminal thinking and behavior.

- Positive changes and their results can be laid out by using the charts or chalkboard so that, if the laws and principles are used, they are can clearly be followed to their projected outcome.

- Because each action, positive or negative, is tracked on the charts, questions can more easily be answered.

- Copies of the charts can be made for the student's personal work, outside the classroom.

- These charts are useful for a variety of recovery models.

- List your problems and concerns. Then line them up with the appropriate universal principle and get to work!

You create another chart for both classroom work and personal work done by each student. This chart consists of placing each of these vital areas at the top of a notebook, one area per page, then using the chart to track them, one by one:

The Visible Brain

The Invisible Mind

Vision

Imagination

Knowledge

Memory

Conscience

Habits

Emotions

Feelings

Goals

Results

Thinking

Actions

Behaviors

Consequences

Of course, if you, the teacher, have not invited your students to become Christians, by all means please do so.

*Romans 10:17 That if thou shalt **confess** with thy mouth the Lord Jesus, and shalt **believe in thine heart** that God hath raised him from the dead, **thou shalt be saved**.*

*2 Corinthians 5:17 Therefore if any man **be in Christ**, he is a **new creature**: old things are passed away; behold, all things are become new.*

As you locate problem areas in your life, continue to write them in the area on the chart that relates to the part of your life that is negatively affected. Apply and use the following universal laws and principles to see the new possibilities. Then practice using whatever force is necessary to accomplish your new goals.

LAWS & PRINCIPLES

The Law of Consciousness

The Law of Vibration

The Law of Expansion and Growth

The Law of Momentum

The Law of Abundance

The Law of Magnetism

The Law of Magnetic Control

The Law of Attraction

The Law of Expectation

The law of Cycles

The Law of Cycles of Return

The Law and Principle of Reciprocity

The Law and Principle of Seasons

The Law of Process

The Principle of Will

The Law of Will Power

The Principle of Choice

The Law of Force

The Principle of Discipline

The Law or Right to Decree

The Principle of Faith

The Law of Action

The Law of Equilibrium and Balance

The Principle of Harmony or Common Ground

The Principle of Flexibility

The Principle of Forgiveness

The Principle of Meditation

The Principle of the Awakening Self

The Law of the Present Moment

The Law of Manifestation

If you have decided to study this book, it took courage to make that decision. If you continue reading and studying this book, you should find that you have the courage to change and *The Revelation of Power* will help you accomplish that change. Once you bring one habit under control, you will experience the rush of making some progress toward a more complete change of habits.

Habits are really any actions or behavior that you continue to do over and over. Some habits are bad, like smoking tobacco, taking drugs and overindulgence in alcohol. Some habits, like brushing your teeth, combing your hair and fixing yourself up for the day, are good habits.

Take time to make a list of the good habits you would like to acquire. Take time to list those habits that could directly apply to your life and bring you direct benefit over time. Start the day off with some inspirational reading and meditation. Start a book of ideas and keep a journal of your life. Most people do not choose their future; they choose their habits and their habits determine their future.

Select a habit and work on it for a week. Make a change every day and be aware of that change. It is impossible to change everything at once but you will never really change your life until you change it little by little on a daily basis. You will soon start to feel the rush of reward for your efforts.

We all fail. Confront your problems and remember that what you refuse to master today will master you tomorrow. You already know what bad habits can do in your life. Through this material you can confront your habits. You will never correct what you are unwilling to confront.

In the beginning, you will need discipline. Discipline is forcing yourself to do what is necessary and right because it's the right and best thing for your positive progress. There is a difference between discipline and habit. While forcing yourself to do something that is right may be difficult, discipline's purpose is to bring you to a point where you love the results of what you have created through a new habit. New, positive habits are the children of discipline. When you attack a goal or a purpose with discipline until it becomes a habit, you have a renewed sense of purpose that will allow you to maintain your motivation through hard times. Remember: this is a struggle and a fight but certainly a fight that others have won. Why not you?

Real difficulties can be overcome; it is only the imaginary ones that are unconquerable.
Theodore N. Vail

Our greatest battles are those with our own minds.
Jameson Frank

The true measure of a man is not how he behaves in moments of comfort and convenience but how he stands at times of controversy and challenges.
Martin Luther King Jr.

If you learn only methods, you'll be tied to your methods, but if you learn principles you can devise your own methods
Ralph Waldo Emerson

Chapter 27

Back from Vietnam

I would like to conclude this study with a true story: I had been receiving packages containing various canned foodstuffs and other treats as well as cigarettes from my mother at home. All of a sudden, my mom stopped sending cigarettes. You could not get filter cigarettes in 'Nam, much less the brand that I smoked. I wrote to my mom and asked why she had stopped sending me smokes. I still received the packages with lots of goodies that I shared with my close buddies, but no smokes.

To my surprise, my mom began to write me about an experience she had with God. I just could not understand what she was talking about. She was putting everything in terms of how much personal love she experienced and a kind of closeness to God that I just could not comprehend. I really thought my Mom had gone off the deep end.

At home, we had all gone to church as a family, and nothing in my experience growing up related even remotely to what she was saying. It seemed to me that she was speaking out of some kind of trance and was not really involved in real life or daily issues. She had stopped smoking, drinking and cussing. I wrote her that that was fine for her but I needed my smokes. My feeling in the matter was that, with death creeping around me every day, I wanted at least to enjoy what few treats I had access to.

This book began with the story about the angel who saved my life on the battlefield one night. The next day, I was on my way to the rear (rear areas are base camps away from the front lines), for an R&R (rest and relaxation leave). I jumped at the chance and was on a helicopter headed for the rear while they were still cleaning up the bodies from the most recent battle.

I thought I would be back after three days that I would be spending either in Bangkok or Taipei, Taiwan. Little did I know that there were orders waiting for me in the rear area and I was being sent home! When I heard the great news, I jumped straight up in the air and yelled at the top of my lungs. It felt like someone had removed 10.000 pounds from my shoulders. Man! I was going back to the world!

Many of the guys I left on the battlefield that day I would never see again, but I didn't care. I was going home! Thinking back, it seemed as if, just a few moments before, I was stepping off a chartered, air-conditioned civilian jetliner into the oven blast of heat that was Vietnam. Spit-shined jump boots dulled and the polish melted into the boot. I broke into a sweat that drenched my uniform in short order. Everything was different—the smells, the bugs, the snakes, the mosquitoes that were more like horses with wings. At night, in certain areas, you could not sleep on the ground for fear of being bitten by the rats and other varmints as they patrolled, unafraid, through your tent at night.

But now I was going home. Before I knew it, the jet left the ground and gained altitude. Once everyone sensed we were out of the range of enemy fire, the entire length of the plane broke out into a cheer.

I'd left for Vietnam on a Christmas Eve. When I arrived, it was the day after Christmas. I missed Christmas that year. I came home on Thanksgiving. When I got off the plane and walked down the stairs I got down on my hands and knees and kissed the ground in California. War is most certainly hell.

The cab pulled up in front of my home. I was told later that my mother was upstairs and the rest of the family was downstairs in the living room and kitchen. Guess who was first to the cab after he blew the horn. That's right! My mom beat everyone out of the house and into my arms. She cried and screamed with joy. I had never seen her so happy. We stayed up all night, talking.

Of course, she told me over and over about her experience with God. She was "witnessing" to me. I was really curious. I really wanted to see for myself just what she was talking about because it still sounded kind of crazy to me. Plus, my mom kept moving suddenly as if hit by a small electric shock and saying, "Oh, praise the Lord!" or "Thank you, Jesus!" This was really strange to me but obviously either something had happened to her or she had "lost it."

That same week we went to a small storefront church. I walked in and sat down. The music was lively and, as the preacher began to preach, the people were moving like my mom did. They seemed to be moved by something I could not see and definitely did not feel. I looked carefully at this group of both old and young people. One thing that struck me was that they seemed like normal, ordinary people. Some of them seemed to have this "glow." I kept looking at them and assessing the situation. They were moving and praising God and getting happy but their movements seemed at times unrelated to what the preacher was saying. Again, they seemed to be responding to something I could not see.

I went to these services for a few days and did not know what to make of all this. These people were excited about something but I just did not see or feel what all this commotion was about.

At the end of the service, they would pray for you by laying hands on your head. An evangelist, Sister Redmond, was praying for this young girl about the age of 14. Sister Redmond said, "I command you in the name of Jesus to come out of this girl." A voice spoke out of that girl that a human could not produce or reproduce. The voice was not human. It was a deep, animal-like. That voice spoke out of the girl, and the sound filled the small church. Whatever was in that girl spoke and it said, "I will *not* come out!" The girl did not speak—the "thing" spoke out of her. Her lips did not move!

I jumped out of my seat on the pew and the guy next to me jumped. I looked at him; he was still staring straight ahead at the girl. I almost yelled, "Did you hear that?" With open, bulging eyes, staring straight ahead and mouth wide open, he managed to shape his lips to forcefully say, "Yes!" From that moment on, I was totally interested in what could not be seen. The young girl was delivered that night from the demon and went on later in life to become an evangelist herself.

But, the moment I heard that demon speak, I began to seek the Lord in earnest and had an instant and newfound respect for the Bible. At that unforgettable moment in time, everything in the Bible became very real to me.

Since then, I have had many other spiritual experiences. Some are revealed in this book. Others will have to wait for another day and another book. As I share this real-life event in the *Revelation of Power*, I know that these events cut across denominational lines. However, I make no excuses for that fact. Just as in the Bible, when God chooses to reveal Himself, He will often choose just ordinary people to demonstrate His extraordinary love for all of us. These stories are true and, I hope, will open the door of your heart and mind to realize that God is available to you right now!

Bibliography

Anderson, U.S., *The Magic in Your Mind* Copyright 1961 Published by Thomas Nelson & Sons N.Y.

Akbar, Na'im Ph. D., *Breaking the Chains of Psychological Slavery* Copyright 1996 Mind Products & Associates, 324 North Copeland Street, Tallahassee, FL 32304

Begley, Sharon. *Train Your Mind Change Your Brain: How a New Science Reveals our Extraordinary Potential to Transform Our Lives.* Ballantine Books NY 2007

Cade, Maxwell C., and Coxhead, Norna *The Awakened Mind Biofeedback and the Development of Higher States of Awareness* Copyright 1979, Delacorte Press/Eleanor Friede, 1 Dag Hammarskjold Plaza, New York, N.Y. 10017

Casarjian, Robin. Houses of Healing: *A Prisoner's Guide To Inner Power And Freedom.* The Lionheart Foundation, Boston, MA 2007

Caster, Alburey. *An Introduction to Modern Philosophy in Eight Philosophical Problems.* Macmillian Pub. Co. NY. 1943 & 1963

Davis, Paul and Gribbin, John. *The Matter Myth: Dramatic Discoveries that challenge our understanding of Physical Reality.* Simon & Schuster 1992

Foer, Joshua. "Remember This." National Geographic Society magazine Vol. 212. No. 5 pages 32-57 November 2007

Goswami, Amit Ph.D. Reed, Richard E. Goswami, Margie. *The self-Aware Universe: how consciousness creates the material world.* Penguin Putnam Inc. 375 Hudson Street, New York, NY 1993.

Hooper, Judith and Teresi, Dick. *The Three Pound Universe.* Macmillan Pub. Co. NY. 1986

Hunt, Morton *The Universe Within A New Science Explores the Human Mind* Copyright 1982, Simon and Schuster, Simon & Schuster Building, Rockefeller Center, 1230 Avenue of the Americas, New York, New York 10020

Jakes, T.D., *So You Call Yourself A Man?* Copyright 1997, Bethany House Publishers, 11400 Hampshire Ave South, Bloomington, Minnesota 55438

Kimbro, Dennis *Daily Motivations for African-American Success* Copyright 1993, A Fawcett Crest Book, Ballantine Books, New York

LeShan, Lawrence. *How to Meditate: A Guide to Self-Discovery.* Little, Brown and Company NY. 1974

Losier, Michael J. *Law of Attraction: The Science of Arrtacting More of What You Want and Less of What You Don't.* Pub. Michael J. Losier, BC Canada 2006.

McManus, Erwin Raphael. *Uprising A Revolution of the Soul.* Thomas Nelson, Inc. Nashville, Tennessee 2003

McWilliams, Peter & McWilliams, John-Roger. *Life 101: Everything We Wish We Had Learned About Life In School-But Didn't.* Prelude Press, Inc 8159 Santa Monica Boulevard, Los Angeles, California 1991

Meyer, Joyce *Battlefield of the Mind Winning the Battle in Your Mind* Copyright 1979 pub. Harrison House, Inc. PO Box 655, Fenton Missouri 63026

Norvell, Anthony *Norvell's Dynamic Mental Laws for Successful Living* Copyright 1965, Parker Publishing Company, Inc., West Nyack, N.Y.

Restak, Richard, MD., *The Brain.* Bantam Books 1984

Roberts, Oral *Miracle of Seed Faith* Copyright 1970 by Oral Roberts Tulsa, Oklahoma

Sabo, Don. Kupers, Terry A. London, Willie editors. *Prison Masculinities* Temple University Press, Philadelphia 2001

Samenow, Stanton E, Ph.D. *Inside the Criminal Mind.* Random House, Inc. NY 1984

Semmelroth, Carl, Ph. D. *The Anger Habits in Relationships.* Sourcebooks Inc., Ill 2005

Shreeve, James "Beyond the Brain." National Geographic Society magazine Vol. 207 No. 3 pages 5-31 March 2005

Tipler, Frank J. *The Physics of Christianity* The Doubleday Broadway Publishing Group, a division of Random House, Inc. New York 2007

Walsh, Anthony, Ph.D. *Correctional Assessment, Casework, and Counseling.* American Correctional Association, Laurel, MD 1992

Wanberg, Kenneth W. and Milkman, Harvey B. *Criminal Conduct and Substance Abuse Treatment: Strategies for Self-Improvement and Change.* Sage Publications Inc. Thousand Oaks, California 1998

Wholey, Dennis. *The Miracle of Change: The Path to Self Discovery and Spiritual Growth.* Pocket Books NY 1997

Wilde, Stuart. *Affirmations: How to Expand Your Personal Power and Take Back Control of Your Life.* Hay House, Inc. Carlsbad, CA. 1987

Wynn, Mychal. *The Eagles who Thought They were Chickens: Teacher's Guide.* Rising Sun Publishing. 1994

Vanzant, Iyanla *Acts of Faith, Daily Meditations for People of Color* Copyright 1993, A Fireside Book/Simon & Schuster, Rockefeller Center, 1230 Avenue of the Americas, New York, New York 10020

Zaehiner, R. C. *Christianity and Other Religions.* Catholic Publications 1974.

Zukav, Gary. *The Dancing Wu Li Masters: An Overview of the New Physics.* Quill William Morrow, NY. 1979

Reverend James M. Lamb CADC, CCS

Acts 1:8 But ye shall receive power,
after that the Holy Ghost is come upon you:

You are welcome to write me at:
Lamb of God Ministries International Inc.
PO Box 1253
Pine Bluff, Arkansas 71613-1253

CPSIA information can be obtained at www.ICGtesting.com
Printed in the USA
LVOW04s1837230315

431675LV00033B/1618/P

9 780741 459992